John Gray was born in Belfast in 1947. He was educated at Campbell College and later at Magdalen College, Oxford, where he was president of Oxford University Liberal Club. He graduated in Politics, Philosophy and Economics.

He has worked as a journalist in the City of London, at a wide range of unskilled jobs and, from 1973, in libraries. Since 1981 he has been Librarian at Belfast's historic Linen Hall Library.

John Gray was actively involved in the Civil Rights movement in Northern Ireland and was secretary of the People's Democracy and editor of its paper, *Free Citizen*. In 1971-2 he was organiser of the Anti-Internment League in Britain.

Since then he has been active in the trade-union and community fields. He served for a number of years as chairman of the Belfast Education and Library Board Branch of the Northern Ireland Public Service Alliance, and also as a member of the executive of the Public Officers' Division of the union. He has also acted as a delegate to Belfast Trades Council.

A resident of north Belfast, he was chairman of his local community association and the first chairman of North Belfast Historical Society.

John Gray has written two children's books with Belfast settings, *The Day the Monster Came* and *There are Dragons*. His essay, 'Popular Entertainment', appears in *Belfast: The Making of the City* (Belfast 1982) and he is currently joint editor of the *Linen Hall Review*. He is a regular contributor to arts programmes on BBC Radio Ulster, and a number of his dramatised documentaries on Irish historical themes have been broadcast.

He is married and has two children.

William Walker, James Larkin, Alex Boyd
(*Nomad's Weekly*, 17 August 1907)

CITY IN REVOLT

**JAMES LARKIN
& THE BELFAST DOCK STRIKE OF 1907**

JOHN GRAY

THE
BLACKSTAFF
PRESS

*First published in 1985
by The Blackstaff Press
3 Galway Park, Dundonald, Belfast BT16 0AN*

© *John Gray, 1985
All rights reserved*

*Printed in Northern Ireland by
The Universities Press Limited*

*British Library Cataloguing in Publication Data
Gray, John
City in revolt: James Larkin and the Belfast dock
strike of 1907.
1. Belfast (Northern Ireland) — Dockers' and carters'
strike, 1907
I. Title
331.89'28'3871'094167   HD5367.5.L8
ISBN 0 85640 289 3*

Contents

Acknowledgments		vii
Introduction		ix
1	A stranger arrives	1
2	The hidden poor	15
3	Organised labour	26
4	Orange dissent, Nationalist factionalism	44
5	The battle begins	56
6	General strike	70
7	Strangest Twelfth	83
8	Betrayal	98
9	Police mutiny	111
10	The mutiny crushed	121
11	Fight to a finish	137
12	Bullets and bayonets	154
13	Dockers isolated	169
14	A last stand	178
15	Divided we fall	191
16	Conclusion	204
References		216
Bibliography		240
Index		251

Acknowledgments

Any attempt to list all those who have assisted me in this work over the last fourteen years runs the risk of unfair omission. If therefore I now mention only those who have played a particularly significant role, I hope that others will excuse neglect of their contribution, and take comfort in the final appearance of a story which I think all were anxious should be told. Certainly I have been much encouraged by the willingness of many, often of very differing views, to give help to a project the final nature of which they had to take on trust.

Amongst those who gave special assistance was the late William McMullen whose own recollections were later supplemented by access to his invaluable typescript history of the 1907 dispute. I have to thank Francis Devine, of the ITGWU and Irish Labour History Society, for arranging this and suggesting other contacts. Eric Taplin, of Liverpool Polytechnic, allowed me to see the drafts of his history of the National Union of Dock Labourers and provided valuable guidance on British trade-union attitudes to the crisis. Nearer home, Professor and Mrs Dawes provided me with the memoirs of Michael McKeown's son, John. Others who filled in useful detail included the late Betty Sinclair, Joe Cooper, James Wilson, Denis Smith, Frank Wright, the late Aiken McClelland, Andrew and Joan Boyd, Fred Heatley, Bob Purdie, Jimmy Vitty, former Librarian at the Linen Hall Library, and my present colleagues there, John Killen and Gerry Healey. On the illustrative front, Paddy Fox produced a magnificent album of photographs of the dispute taken by Alex Hogg, while Tony Merrick and members of the Northern Ireland Postcard Club supplied strike postcards. Fergus O'Hare offered useful advice on identifications.

Inevitably the core of the work has depended on the resources of libraries and archive repositories and they have, almost without exception, served me beyond the call of duty. As a librarian myself, first at the Central Library, Belfast, and now at the Linen Hall Library, I have benefited greatly from the extensive resources available in both institutions. Also in Belfast and the surrounding area I have received significant assistance from Queen's University

Library, the Public Record Office of Northern Ireland, the Ulster Museum and the Ulster Folk and Transport Museum. Invaluable material on the 1907 dispute is held elsewhere, most notably in the State Paper Office in Dublin and also in the National Library, and the staff in both institutions proved more than helpful, while in Britain I received assistance from Liverpool Central Library, the National Register of Archives, the British Library of Political and Economic Science, the British Library Newspaper Library at Colindale, the Public Record Office and the Labour Party.

It remains true however that much has depended on the distilled wisdom of those who have gone before me. Here I would like to mention the largely unpublished work of J.W. Boyle, and the pioneering contribution of Sam Hanna Bell and David Bleakley who in the 1950s had the wisdom and foresight to record the recollections of 1907 veterans. Of more recent work, I should acknowledge a considerable debt to Austen Morgan's unpublished thesis 'Politics, the Labour Movement and the Working Class in Belfast, 1905–1923' which is notable for its range of sources, but proved particularly illuminating because, like this work, it is concerned with episodes of social upheaval.

There are then those who at various times provided the resolute prompting and encouragement without which this work would not have been completed. In the early stages these included John McGuffin, and Dan Nolan of Anvil Press, while almost throughout my former colleague at the Central Library, Belfast, Hugh Russell, has proved a good friend indeed. Latterly Paddy Devlin has weighed in to good effect, and the Blackstaff Press has displayed a touching faith, which I did not necessarily share, that the book would see the light of day.

Thanks must go to Cathal McCrystal of the ITGWU and my mother for assistance with the typing of many drafts of the text. Family involvement does not end there as my father contributed significantly to delay in publication by subjecting an early version to a particularly devastating critique – hopefully this has now resulted in a better end product. I am indebted too to Paul Campbell for his help at proof stage. I should also express especial thanks to my wife, Mary, for her help and support, a conventional enough tribute which I suspect in many cases, including my own, provides inadequate redress for the involuntary sacrifices of those who have the misfortune to live with aspiring authors.

Introduction

Today the Belfast dock strike of 1907 is almost forgotten, a mere footnote in history, at best a chapter here and there in texts written principally by academics for academics. Yet the now yellowing and crumbling files of contemporary newspapers bear witness to a major crisis, far more significant than a mere industrial dispute. It is the purpose of this book to chronicle the events of that summer and to explore the issues involved.

These were far from parochial – in a British context the strike was the first serious test of the Trades Disputes Act of 1906 and preceded the more general industrial unrest more characteristic of the end of the decade. In an Irish context the dispute provided the initial testing ground for the then unknown English trade-union organiser James Larkin, and opened in dramatic fashion the modern era of unskilled labour organisation in the country.

The scale of events, including the only serious attempt at mutiny in the history of the Royal Irish Constabulary, called into question the attitudes both of the Liberal Government and of the British labour movement to a new and militant labour agitation in a specifically Irish context. The eventual use of overwhelming military force in the dispute revealed many of the features and failings of subsequent interventions of the same kind. In all these respects the 1907 dispute was a key turning point in Irish labour history and foreshadowed the stormy events of the following years leading to the famous 1913–14 Dublin lockout and beyond; indeed the history of those subsequent events can hardly be fully comprehended without knowledge of what occurred in Belfast.

If the story nonetheless centres on Belfast, on the working class of the city, on its poor and dispossessed and on their experience, that is in itself a matter of broader significance, for few today would deny that they and their city lie at the heart of the Irish question. In recent years the Troubles have spawned a new and extensive literature on working-class society in the North, and yet that overdue exploration has suffered from the blank years that went before in which the anonymous foot-soldiers of the 'Ulster crisis' were denied any traditions that were specifically their own.

That is not to condemn the legitimacy of accounts of the undoubtedly dominant themes in Irish political history, the respective triumphs of Unionism in the north and Nationalism in the south. It is, however, to say that such history, carried on to the neglect of other strands in the story, has about it a monolithic certainty, far from the truth.

The rediscovery of the crisis that gripped Belfast in the summer of 1907 certainly demands a significant reassessment of working-class society in the city in the pre-First World War period. The suddenness, the bitterness and the explosive nature of those events provide a very different picture to the conventional and benign image often given of industrial society in the heyday of what was then characterised as 'no mean city'. It was a time when the unskilled workers of the city were no mere expendable extras in the armies of others, but created a crisis on their own terms, and in doing so revealed in full array social tensions normally well concealed beneath the twin shrouds of Unionism and Nationalism. They demonstrated the possibilities of united working-class action and the dramatic threat that any such development immediately presented to a more barren status quo in northern politics. However briefly, their action raised the question whether there was a viable alternative for the working class to the traditional rivalries for which the city was already notorious.

If such assertions have any validity, why then have the events of 1907 received so little attention even from labour historians? Ultimate defeat in 1907 and subsequent and successive catastrophic defeats for organised labour in the city have left little indigenous tradition of specifically working-class history – veterans have either emigrated or died disappointed and forgotten. Until the 1970s the only significant accounts of the strike came from a slightly stronger southern tradition concerned with the heroic vision of Larkin's 'fiery crusade' and the linking of revolutionary developments within the labour movement from 1907 onwards with those of 1916. If that over-simplistic view has subsequently undergone critical reassessment, the process has still not provided any in-depth evaluation of events in Belfast in 1907. These remain a mere appetiser in histories chiefly centred on other battlefields, and while 1907 has served to establish Larkin's credentials, often with over-romanticised accounts of non-sectarian unity, little has been said about the outcome of that dispute. If this has been discussed, it has been dismissed as a matter of eventual defeat at the hands of 'outmoded bigotry', a force as incapable of rational explanation as is the vision of earlier, almost miraculous, achievement. Either way, it is hardly adequate that the experience of the working class in the largest industrial centre in Ireland should be reduced in this way to the realm of the irrational and hence inexplicable.

Recent work has lifted corners of the veil. The availability of census returns for 1901 and 1911 has provided a variety of detailed, although static, profiles of working-class society in the city. Substantial work has been done in identifying significant and enduring currents of discontent within the Protestant section of the working class and in documenting the formal history of the organised labour movement. Nonetheless, such work, whatever its other merits, has either ignored or in large measure sidestepped the crucial events of the social upheaval connected with the 1907 dock strike. That this is so may reflect a tradition, more valid in the context of the British labour movement, of depending on organisational evidence. However, even in a British context, a new generation of social historians has cautioned generally against this over-dependence in writing 'people's history' and has urged that closer attention should be paid to popular activity. It is advice peculiarly relevant for historians in the north of Ireland, for our 'democratic' tradition, if it has existed at all, has been one made on the streets rather than in parliaments, and it is there that the key battles of our past have been lost and won. The dock strike of 1907 was one such testing occasion when many different factors and forces, identifiable in isolation at other times, came together and interacted in a dynamic and particularly revealing fashion, and did so largely outside the confines of existing formal organisation. It is on this basis that the events of that summer are vital to any understanding of social and political forces active within working-class society in Edwardian Belfast.

In these circumstances, it has seemed appropriate to set the narrative account of dramatic events against a broader background. Only in this way is it possible on the one hand to record the elemental strengths and courage of those involved, or the real merits of Larkin's role, and at the same time to highlight the tremendous difficulties faced by the strike movement. Here the episode calls into question major aspects of northern labour ideology, and casts doubt on the possibilities of effective dissent within what was then, and remains, a crucial Orange and Protestant majority tradition. In doing so, it provides a reminder of the overwhelming forces which, in the peculiar conditions of the northern situation, array themselves against any radical upsurge.

However, to give for the first time a full account of the crisis of 1907 will serve well if it does no more than enable those who are at the centre of today's conflicts to know better their own history. They should not assume that familiarity with past events endows clairvoyance for the future. In other places one might hope to arrest the tendency for history which first occurs as tragedy to repeat itself as farce; here perhaps the motive is stronger because, at least for the working class of Belfast, history has tended rather to pile tragedy on tragedy.

1
A stranger arrives

A succession of fast cross-channel steamers moved steadily up Belfast Lough; they came from many points of the compass – from Ardrossan, Ayr and Glasgow, from Barrow, Fleetwood, Heysham and Liverpool.[1] Passengers coming on deck in the grey light of dawn could see, away to their right, the beauties of the Antrim hills. Soon these distant views were obscured by a thick industrial smog, fed by hundreds of factory chimneys already belching smoke in spite of the early hour. As the ships nosed closer into the port of Belfast, no haze could conceal almost five miles of quays[2] or, looming more dimly almost overhead, the gantries of two giant shipyards. It was evident that this was a great industrial city and seaport.

As the gangplanks went down at the cross-channel quays, just short of the Queen's Bridge, in this the third week of January 1907, unusual visitors could be seen disembarking. Within a few days Keir Hardie, Ramsay MacDonald, Arthur Henderson and others – the leaders of the British labour movement – stepped ashore. It was no imminent state of revolution that brought them to Belfast; they merely considered it appropriate that the first annual conference of the Labour Party, successor to the old Labour Representation Committee, should be held in the fastest-growing city in the United Kingdom.

For three days at the Wellington Hall, the delegates debated the current issues affecting the party. Then as now the relationship between the parliamentary party and the rank and file was contentious, while the main sensation was the threat by Keir Hardie to resign on the issue of women's suffrage.[3] Their presence in the city caused hardly a ripple in the lives of the people of Belfast, earning no police reports, and, after their brief stay, they departed from the cross-channel quays, little thinking that within a matter of months the attention of their entire movement would be focused there.

It is to a police report that we owe the information that one other delegate arrived on 20 January,[4] and we can reasonably speculate that he came from Liverpool, courtesy of the Belfast Steamship Company (in the light of later events, an ironic association). He was distinctive in appearance, like a 'big burly docker from Liverpool or London', dressed in 'a fading great coat' and 'big rimmed hat'.[5] When he spoke it was in the 'approved manner of an English slum... of probably some clog wearing English town'.[6] As a rank-and-file delegate to the conference, there was no immediate reason to single him out from many others. He differed from them in that he had other work to do in Belfast.

This obscure delegate was James Larkin, the organiser of the Liverpool-based National Union of Dock Labourers. He had come to Belfast to attend the Labour Party Conference, but also to attempt to organise the dockers in the port. His background fitted him well for the task, and he had already given indications of his ability to provide inspiration and leadership.[7]

Larkin was born in Liverpool in 1876 of Liverpool-Irish stock. His grandfather was just one of many County Armagh tenant farmers driven from the land in the post-famine period. In Liverpool Larkin himself experienced extreme poverty during the slump of the 1890s, and had at one stage stowed away on a ship to Montevideo. Back in Liverpool he had advantages in the bitter struggle with others for work. He was powerfully built and neither drank nor smoked, and when opportunity came his way he soon established a reputation as a hard-working and conscientious employee. By 1903 he had risen to a position of trust, that of foreman dock porter with the firm of T. and J. Harrison at the south end of Liverpool Docks. There he earned the nickname and reputation of 'the rusher' from the men in his charge. He had not joined the NUDL until 1901 and he was to play no active part in the union until 1905.

His neglect of union activity arose from his political views. He had been an active socialist from the early 1890s and had learnt his skills as an orator preaching the new gospel on the streets of Liverpool. He sympathised with the views of the Social Democratic Federation, which tended to consider trade unions merely as part of the capitalist system, and hence hardly a priority for the advanced socialist.

All this was to change in 1905. The star of the NUDL was far from in the ascendant at the time. Although the union was based in Liverpool, it was not recognised in large areas of the port, and in 1905 the inclination of the employers was to attempt to restrict the influence of the union still further. Larkin's employer, T. and J. Harrison, was one of the few firms which had granted recognition, although the union membership of some foremen had lapsed.

In June 1905 the men went on unofficial strike, demanding that these foremen rejoin. Instead Harrisons, taking advantage of the prevailing strength of the employers' position in the port, repudiated its recognition of the union and imported blacklegs. A bitter dispute followed, in which Larkin established himself as a key leader, but by September the men were defeated.

Larkin could not return to his old employment, but his role in the strike had made him a popular figure amongst the dockers. He was appointed temporary organiser of the union at two pounds ten shillings a week, a position that was soon made permanent. It was an appointment that could not have been made without the approval of the autocratic and veteran General Secretary of the union, James Sexton, with whom Larkin, although of a younger generation, shared remarkable similarities of background.[8] There were however differences of perspective – Sexton's priority in what appeared to be unpromising times was to conserve the existing strength of the union by compromise if necessary. Thus his attitude to the Liverpool dispute, in which Larkin had played a prominent role, was that the strike 'might have been avoided with a little more tact – technically the men were right – but there are, in our opinion, times when even technical rights should concede to reason, and this was one of them'. For him the strike proved the 'urgent necessity of more central control [of disputes] than at present exists'.[9]

For the moment Sexton retained an admiration for Larkin, enhanced by the latter's exceedingly effective work in organising Sexton's successful campaign for a seat on Liverpool Corporation in November 1905. Larkin's work for the union was equally satisfactory – in quick succession he managed to organise new branches in Preston, Aberdeen and Govan. No doubt Sexton welcomed the new accessions of dues-paying members, but for Larkin these gains were a means to an end; for him strong union membership was merely the necessary prerequisite for the revolutionary transformation of society. Now, in January 1907, he was still searching for the place and the time in which to put such ideas to the test.

At first sight, Belfast seemed a most unlikely starting point for any such venture. Here it was that in 1898 delegates to the Irish Congress of Trades Unions had applauded the Conservative Lord Mayor, James Henderson, when, in his speech of welcome, he had described the city as an 'elysium for the working classes'.[10] Now the factory inspectorate could confirm that the district was enjoying a period of 'phenomenal prosperity'.[11]

In the city centre was the most evident symbol of Belfast's pride in its achievement, the new City Hall, built at the then phenomenal cost of £360,000, and opened a bare five months earlier.[12] The raw Portland stone of the new building mirrored the often brash assertiveness of the city's leaders, and their conviction that Belfast could outdo all other cities in the United Kingdom. Such confidence was understandable – in the last decade of the old century the population had risen faster than in any other comparable centre, from 256,000 to 349,000, and this from a base of a mere 19,000 inhabitants in 1801.[13]

The key to this extraordinary expansion lay in the triumph of the city's industry, and here was a ready field for those wishing to coin statistical superlatives or to celebrate the gigantic. At Harland and Wolff, the world's largest shipbuilder, the workforce had risen in the space of twenty years from 5,000 to 12,000.[14] The city could also claim the world's largest linen mill and the largest ropeworks.[15] One Belfast industrial pioneer, Edward Harland, had already received that ultimate accolade of Victorian virtue, a chapter in Samuel Smiles' *Men of Invention*,[16] the bible of self-advancement for the skilled artisans of the city. There were other triumphs of achievement for them to admire, too recent for consideration by Smiles. There was Samuel Davidson who, starting with a workforce of seven in 1881, now employed more than 2,000 at his Sirocco Engineering Works,[17] or Thomas Gallaher, whose tobacco factory in York Street employed a similar number, having developed from a one-man business in Londonderry in 1857.[18] It was characteristic of Belfast that its second shipyard, Workman Clark, should enjoy a nickname as the 'wee yard' which was a gross misnomer – although established only in 1879, it now employed 7,000 and was high in the rankings of United Kingdom shipyards.[19]

Many industrialists made fortunes in an environment such as this. Edwardian Belfast boasted at least three millionaires,[20] and the erection of new country houses, indeed the transfer of ownership of estates within thirty miles of the city, indicated the creation of a new, if unostentatious, aristocracy whose fortunes depended on industrial success rather than land.[21]

One section of the working class, the 'groups of closely organised skilled craftsmen' noted by Beatrice Webb during her visit in 1893,[22] had strong grounds for viewing themselves, albeit on a lesser scale, as beneficiaries of the same process. Generally, they were amongst the best paid in their various trades in the whole of the United Kingdom. Thus skilled engineering workers enjoyed the highest rates outside London, and those with comparable skills in the shipyards could rest assured that their rates were better than those enjoyed on the Clyde or Tyne.[23] Even in less favoured trades, notably linen, premium rates applied for male skilled workers. Here one government report noted, with regard to foremen, that 'the high average in Belfast is noticeable'.[24] Perhaps one quarter of the male labour force was made up of these skilled men[25] who enjoyed pay rates on occasion in excess of £3 a week, and very generally in excess of £2.

How indeed did Belfast's industries prosper in spite of these exceptionally high rates? Due credit must be given to factors such as inventiveness, commercial flair and the very availability of a highly-skilled workforce. Certainly savings on the quantity of labour employed played no part in the process – quite the reverse, for of the city's two classic staple industries, linen was one of the most labour-intensive forms of textile manufacture,[26] and shipbuilding was notoriously unamenable to the introduction of labour-saving production line techniques.[27] This in turn gives the clue to one of the key factors in the profitability of local industry, the availability of that very Irish factor, an inexhaustible supply of cheap unskilled labour from the surrounding countryside.

This connection between the low pay of agricultural labourers in neighbouring counties and the rates for unskilled labour in the city was one well understood by the early pioneers of unskilled labour organisation in Ulster. Thus in 1892 we find Richard McGhee, one of the co-founders in Britain of the NUDL, engaged in a widespread campaign to form an Ulster Labourers' Union principally for rural labourers. During this campaign he was involved in a strike at the new Lurgan waterworks scheme where the men were not even receiving the agreed rates of fifteen shillings a week. It was a situation which outraged McGhee, himself a Lurgan man, who could bring his British experience to bear. He noted the 'miserable wages paid to the working men in the North of Ireland' and contrasted them 'with those paid in England and Scotland where they were paid an average of about a pound or 21/- shillings a week.'[28]

By 1905 little had changed; agricultural labourers in Counties Antrim and Down were paid twelve to thirteen shillings a week, and if they achieved any advances there were others in the remoter Ulster hinterland, earning as little as nine shillings a week, all too ready to flood any improved market. These wages compared with the average of fifteen shillings in England and Scotland, a rate which rose much higher in the immediate vicinity of the great cities.[29]

The consequences of this differential for unskilled industrial workers in Belfast were a matter for routine report by government officials. Those involved in the events of 1907 simply noted 'the prevailing Irish wages of 1907 were on a different scale from the wages of Great Britain'.[30] The *Daily Mail* put the matter in more colourful terms – 'The average earnings of unskilled labour in Belfast have up to now been deplorably low... while the hours and conditions would not be tolerated in England.'[31] There were no exceptions to this rule; even in the prestige industries of shipbuilding and engineering the three out of four men who were unskilled earned no more than fifteen to eighteen shillings a week. In the shipyards, these men earned wages three to four shillings less than those on the Tyne and Clyde;[32] in engineering even labourers in Cork were better paid, and in the whole of the United Kingdom only Dublin paid worse.[33] Given the very high rates of skilled pay in Belfast, the contrast between skilled and unskilled rates was truly staggering, a yawning abyss, unequalled anywhere else in the United Kingdom.[34]

The dockers whom Larkin had come to organise were an important group within the ranks of the unskilled and in 1907 there were no less than 3,100 of them,[35] a reminder that the city, apart from its importance as an industrial centre, acted as the main port for much of the north east of Ireland, and for agricultural produce as well as that of industry.[36] In spite of booming trade, the majority of dockers, more than 2,000 'spellsmen', who were casually employed, were amongst the most deprived workers in the city. Taken on daily as needed by stevedores, they could not be sure of work and often earned less than ten shillings a week.[37] Work when found was brutally hard; it was common for one man to shift 170 tons in a day in two-and-a-half-hundredweight sacks, all taken from the ships on narrow planks. Men often finished the day 'with their backs in raw flesh'.[38]

Their unreliable and miserable wages were reduced further by illegal deductions made by the stevedores who often made payment in pubs and expected treatment in kind.[39] Sometimes pay was not forthcoming at all; a spellsman might be called in on one day to assist in gearing up a ship for unloading, and would receive no pay, and yet the following day when unloading actually commenced he could be refused a start. These casual dockers viewed themselves as the 'white niggers' of Belfast, men who had hardly 'a boot on their foot. . . and clothes on their back.'[40]

The lot of the regular dockers, mainly employed on the cross-channel quays where the pattern of trade was more even, was rather better. There were just over 1,000 of them, a diminishing number,[41] and they earned twenty to twenty-five shillings for a working week ranging from sixty-seven to seventy-five hours, depending on the firm.[42]

The carters, soon to play a key role in Larkin's organisational efforts, were an important allied group. There were some 1,500 of them, one third of whom were, like the dockers, employed by the shipping companies.[43] The rest were employed by independent carting firms. They earned from nineteen to twenty-two shillings a week.[44] Again hard physical labour was involved, and fines of up to five shillings a week could be imposed for the inevitable breakages.[45] These conditions were not viewed as exceptional at the time, and there was no widespread awareness of the existence of major social problems arising from them. Belfast's employers were not peculiarly ruthless; they merely did what employers of the day did almost anywhere in taking advantage of a favourable market factor, and they saw no contradiction between this and their often generous donations to philanthropic charities.

Awareness was further dimmed by assumptions about the benign, even divinely ordained, nature of Belfast's industrial structure. James Henderson had expressed a prevailing view when he told appreciative ITUC delegates in 1898 that 'in Belfast they had large steel and iron shipbuilding yards where fathers and sons could be employed. They had also. . . the linen industry, where the wives and daughters found employment.'[46] Stated blandly, this remained an essential ingredient in any panegyric on Belfast's industrial achievement, and was readily adopted by government officials, notably in the 1908 report on *The Cost of Living of the Working Classes*. In this, low wages were not mentioned, and instead the commissioners noted 'this combination' of linen and shipbuilding which ensured that 'family earnings are in many cases high' and accounted for 'the general prosperity of the working classes'.[47] Such conclusions begged the question as to whether women and children worked in the mills to raise family income to a 'high' level, or out of a dire necessity stemming from the extraordinarily low rates of pay for male unskilled labour.

One of the few individuals who examined in depth the implications of unskilled rates of pay was the Independent Orangeman and radical journalist Lindsay Crawford, writing in the Liberal paper the *Ulster Guardian*. Basing his figures on the classic study of poverty in York by Seebohm Rowntree,[48] he determined that twenty-two shillings and five pence per week was the minimum necessary to maintain a man, his wife and three children, without setting anything aside for holidays, doctors' bills and furniture or making provision for old age. He concluded:

> These figures prove that the employer who employs a man at less than 22s.5d. per week is doing one of four things: either (i) denies him the privileges and responsibilities of marriage and family life, or (ii) expects him to send his wife and children to work to supplement his earnings; (iii) compels him and his family to live below the workhouse level of subsistence, or (iv) counts on the workman or his family having an income from some source other than wages, e.g. theft, charity, prostitution or a private fortune.[49]

Most families chose the second course. Some forty-three per cent of women and girls aged over ten worked,[50] a markedly higher level than in most other centres, and child labour by 'half-timers' was a notable feature of the linen industry. Few of the women workers were the wives of skilled men, indeed one of the privileges of attaining that status was the possibility of escaping work in which the less fortunate had to engage.[51]

Here the linen industry was indeed crucial. In 1906 it remained the largest employer in Belfast, but of the 51,000 people employed in Counties Antrim and Down eighty per cent were women and some 4,000 were half-timers.[52] The same government report which had commented on the high wages of male foremen in the industry gave an otherwise bleak picture; for of sixteen forms of textile manufacture carried on in the United Kingdom, linen, along with 'small wares', enjoyed the doubtful distinction of paying the lowest average rates. In the main categories of full-time female employment pay ranged from nine shillings and fourpence to eleven shillings and sixpence per week. Average male wages were higher at sixteen shillings and elevenpence but were once again, for unskilled grades, subject to the consideration that 'in Ireland the wages of labourers are noticeably low'.[53] For all these categories, flourishing and ruthless disciplinary systems, based on fining, reduced take-home pay still further.

Many of the wives and children of dockers and carters worked in the linen industry and their conditions were associated with fear, poverty, and ill health. Miss Martindale, one of the new generation of factory inspectors appointed following the victory of the Liberals in the 1906 General Election, noted that in certain cases investigations were difficult because 'the workers were at first terrified to give me information'.[54] At the same time, the city's Medical Officer of Health linked high infant mortality with the industry, noting in particular the way mothers worked to within a few days of confinement and then returned to work as soon as they were allowed. Even when the women were at work, cases were discovered where infants 'were constantly fed on bread soaked in tea, and in such the women stated that they could not afford to buy milk'.[55] If children survived weaning they were not spared for long; Miss Martindale noted the practice of patching up 'defective children', or of hawking them from factory to factory in the desperate hope of getting them a start.[56]

While the Medical Officer of Health found acute poverty because 'the weekly wage of both parents [was] very often little over £1',[57] the fate of families where there was only one wage-earner was dire indeed. In the city more than one quarter of households were headed by women, and within this group deprivation could be severe.[58] One step short of the workhouse lay the possibility of outwork, and mothers forced to remain at home laboured, with the assistance of their young children, for some sixpence or eightpence a day. Thomas Carnduff, from Sandy Row, recalled his sister-in-law doing precisely this, working until 2 am to earn sixpence.[59]

Sickness and old age were the direct avenues to actual destitution in an era before the creation of effective social insurance. The prospect of later life haunting many was that of 'old and infirm men and women, unable to work longer [as they] trudged wearily up to the gates of the workhouse' in circumstances where 'much as their grown up children were anxious to support them, they themselves were barely able to provide for their own families'.[60] Old age at least could be considered an act of God, but other misfortunes which struck earlier in life were more often directly related to the man-made environment. This was most dramatically evident in the shipyards where 'your first accident was considered a test, the second and third a matter of form'[61] or, as James Connolly put it, 'our shipyards offer up a daily sacrifice of life and limb on the altar of capitalism. The clang of the ambulance bell is one of the most familiar daily sounds on the streets between our shipyards and our hospitals.'[62] More insidious but statistically far more significant perils lurked in the linen mills, engaged in a form of manufacture defined as a 'dangerous' trade,[63] and there is strong circumstantial evidence that diseases specifically related to the industry made a major impact on the overall health of the city.

Belfast's death rate per thousand of the population was not in itself a particular cause for concern, being comparable with that of Manchester,[64] yet for the fifteen-to-twenty age group it was more than double the Manchester rate, and greatly exceeded it at all ages up to thirty-five. The major killer responsible for this discrepancy was pthisis or consumption. In the fifteen-to-twenty age group the death rate from this cause was more than four times that in Manchester and for women more than five times.[65]

As early as 1852, the mill workers had their own expression, 'poucey', for one affected with pthisis.[66] The Royal Commission of 1893 described the symptoms, which particularly afflicted those at the preparing end of the trade, workers condemned to toil 'in a continual cloud of dust' and eventually 'attacked each morning with a paroxysm of disponea and coughing'.[67] During the same enquiry, the Medical Officer of Health estimated that 'the carders' average length of life is only 16.8 years (of work); if a girl gets a card at 18 her life is generally terminated at 30'.[68] At the other end of the process, the weaving of linen required high humidity; in many cases humidity in weaving sheds was maintained at 100 per cent, at which point 'evaporation ceases, simply because there is no room for the body moisture to evaporate into, hence increase of body temperature above normal and consequently more or less physical distress'.[69] By 1907 government regulations were only beginning to have a marked effect on these conditions, and government officials were still unwilling to accept the damning implications of the available evidence. When a viceregal enquiry into the health of Belfast was held in 1908, it failed to come to any firm conclusions on the link between linen manufacture and disease, on the grounds that adequate statistics were not available.[70]

A more immediately dramatic illness, in that it occurred in epidemic form, was typhoid. When in 1896-7 the city was seriously affected, something akin to panic set in, even amongst councillors not normally noted for concern about public health. Their fears, fanned by lack of knowledge about the cause of the illness and its tendency to strike the homes of the well-to-do as hard as those of the poor, led to a wide-ranging corporation enquiry, which was more illuminating on the general issues of housing and public health provision than it was in its pursuit of the presumed 'miasmic' causes of typhoid.[71]

The chairman of the Public Health Committee, who opposed the holding of the enquiry, used it for a public defence of the city's record. This was a commendable one from the point of view of ratepayers in that he was able to assert that the city required a mere nineteen public health staff, compared with fifty-two in Dublin and a hundred and ninety-three in Glasgow.[72] During the enquiry it was admitted that the city had failed to implement the Notification of Diseases Act because, according to one official, 'if they became aware of the diseases they would not have an hospital to treat them'.[73]

Housing was then investigated as a possible source of the epidemic. Here Belfast had a major advantage in that it had developed later than comparable British cities, and hence a far greater proportion of its housing had been erected, at least theoretically, subject to late-Victorian legislation and by-laws. Some of the work of the Corporation Improvements Committee had served if anything to erode the benefits of this fortuitous situation. Thus the committee had permitted new houses to be built on 'an enormous dunghill'[74] and had allowed at least one of its own members, Sir James Haslett, a former Lord Mayor, and MP for West Belfast, to build speculative housing which drained into open cesspools.[75] While the city had fewer dry privies than most other cities, it was only this epidemic which persuaded the Corporation, long after most other centres, to adopt a comprehensive policy of abolishing them.[76] A decade later, doubts remained about the Corporation's commitment to improving standards of public health. In 1906, the medical profession sent a deputation to the City Hall, urging that any new Medical Officer of Health should be 'properly qualified, adequately remunerated, and independent'. The clear implication was that this had not been the case in the past.[77]

One area which remained both a threat to the health of the working classes and an acute denial of opportunity to their children was the state of the city's schools. The Commissioners for Education in their report for 1905-6 argued that 'the overcrowded state of some of the schools in Belfast is so aggravated as seriously to endanger the health of the pupils and teachers',[78] and yet little was done, to the extent that Augustine Birrell, Chief Secretary for Ireland, denounced the situation in 1913, saying 'no city in the Empire was worse supplied with schools'.[79] The consequences educationally were significant, with some 15,000 children unable to find school places at all, and only one in sixty children reaching secondary education, compared with one in eighteen in England.[80]

These then were the conditions which affected large numbers in the city more or less acutely in normal times, but in Edwardian Belfast there was no guarantee of any such stable condition. The city had no miraculous dispensation which protected it from the periodic crises of nineteenth and early-twentieth-century capitalism. Accordingly its history, though conveniently described as 'simply one of progress',[81] is better characterised as one of instability, and very significantly as one of insecurity for the working class. It was a history marked by the collapse of firms and industries in the face of depression or superior competition, and the discovery, only with difficulty, of new avenues for further development.

This was true of the city's formative years in the 1820s when its first factory-based industry, cotton, succumbed to the competition of Manchester,[82] or in the great depression of 1878-9 when 'many mills were employing only half the usual number of hands and commercial disasters threw fresh numbers of workers into the ranks of the unemployed... [and] cases of starvation were reported daily'.[83]

The dawning of the Edwardian era in no way removed the threat. Indeed the increasingly predominant shipbuilding industry was particularly susceptible to it, for this was a form of manufacture in which it was not possible to stockpile the product during depression in the hope of better times to follow.[84] The effects were very clear when the *Belfast Labour Chronicle* in October 1904 reported one demonstration by the unemployed during the severe recession that was to last well into 1905. On this occasion both skilled and unskilled workers were involved.

> Many of those who crowded the Town Hall and its approaches were skilled artisans to whom their workshops are at present closed. Group after group thronged up the steps and along the passages; engineers, joiners, boilermakers, tailors, coach builders and labourers of all sorts and conditions.[85]

Nor was the respite of the boom years of 1906 and 1907 to last long, for in July 1908 the Trades Council was forced to set up a Distress Committee to cope with a situation in which 'for months thousands of workers were walking the streets, and their wives and children were starving'.[86] On this and earlier occasions suffering was compounded by the attitude of the Board of Guardians which took the view 'that out-relief must be curtailed since it demoralised the recipients'.[87]

While prospects for employment were certainly far better in 1906 and 1907, there was in the meantime another more insidious turn of the screw in the form of steadily rising prices, which were not being matched by pay increases. Nationally prices were to rise by four to five per cent in the years 1902-1908,[88] an increase reflected locally by that other barometer of poverty, the number of pawn shops, which was to increase from 100 to 117 between 1900 and 1914.[89]

What then was the basic atmosphere in which the unskilled lived in 1907? It had changed little since Henry McCormac, an early reformer, made an acute analysis of their plight in his *Appeal on behalf of the poor in Belfast,* published in 1830. He wrote:

> There is always a large though fluctuating amount of the labouring population who have little or no employment, and who are consequently subjected to all the extremes of poverty and famine. The mass is not composed of the same individuals; every labourer may once have belonged to it, and most of them either undergo a lapse into this state or live in continual dread of it.[90]

Now in 1907 there was no actual famine but, in Thomas Carnduff's words, 'the labouring classes were bordering on starvation'.[91]

These too were the conditions in the face of which James Larkin hoped to organise, and he would have received a first-hand account of them from Thomas Johnston, an old acquaintance from socialist circles in the Liverpool of the 1890s,[92] with whom he now sought temporary lodgings. Johnston, a future leader of the Irish Labour Party, but in 1907 a Trades Council delegate for the shop assistants, and secretary of Belfast Socialist Society, was a militant in Belfast terms and might well have shared the views of another, anonymous, socialist commentator of the time:

> Great bumptious Belfast, with its slum schools, its rotten municipal system, its ludicrous pride, its bigotry and intoler-

ance, and its hordes of little ragged starved workers. Belfast with its palatial town hall, its tinsel virtues, and its army of little white slaves, and its big poorhouses, and lunatic asylums and prisons.[93]

An attack with some rhetorical licence perhaps, but even if every detail were true it would have made the work of a labour organiser no easier, for it was a world in which you 'had to make sure you kept in the overlookers' good graces. . . or you lost your job and you lost your pay and when you went home poverty stared you in the face'[94] or, as Thomas Carnduff put it, 'to throw myself onto the labour market in Belfast was to commit mental suicide'.[95]

2
The hidden poor

British socialists were aware of a unique difficulty facing the labour and trade union movement in Belfast. As Bruce Glasier reminded the delegates at the 1907 Labour Conference, it was thirteen years since the British TUC had met in the city, an occasion when 'John Burns had to fly for his life from the infuriated Orangemen'.[1]

If this was a slightly fanciful account of one small incident it was difficult to exaggerate the sectarian divisions within the working class of the city. First in 1832, and then at least once in every succeeding decade, the city had been torn by sectarian riots in which the main protagonists, if not always the instigators, had been the Protestant and Catholic sections of the working class. Economic and social tensions provided the sure ground in which political and sectarian rivalries developed, and each period of rioting had further economic, social and territorial consequences. Although the worst riots had occurred in 1886, and with the defeat of Home Rule in 1893 Ulster had receded from more general British political consciousness, further disturbances had occurred more recently, most notably in 1896, 1898 and 1901.[2]

Now in 1907, Bruce Glasier expressed necessary optimism that 'in the face of the Labour Party, sectarian bigotry is decreasing', but Belfast remained a city in which the police required a special handbook to cover local peculiarities,[3] and in good times the army was called upon to assist the civil authority at least once a year.

Thomas Carnduff, then a working-class youth from Protestant Sandy Row, has left an account of the atmosphere of the immediately preceding years when 'police baton charges were quite a common occurrence'. He himself was a member of the Pass Gang from Donegall Pass whose 'particular aversion was Catholics. We ambushed them, jibed them, slaughtered them when opportunity came our way.' Elsewhere in the city, the sectarian clans were widespread. Other Protestant gangs of the period were the Forty Thieves, the Bushrangers, and most formidable of all, the Bogey Clan, but they in turn were rivalled by a gang from the Catholic Falls Road, the

Cronge Clan, named provocatively after one of the more successful Boer generals.[4]

If there was any truth in the theory of diminishing violence in the couple of years prior to 1907, the legacy of previous experience remained a heavy burden. By the mid-nineteenth century segregated residential patterns were established, reinforced by subsequent events in which any tendency by working-class Catholics to disperse from their original areas of settlement was resisted by pogrom and house-wrecking, and remaining Protestants in Catholic areas fled in their turn. By 1886 riot commissioners were able to produce Belfast's first 'tribal' map with firm lines drawn between the Catholic ghettos and the larger surrounding sea of Protestant areas.[5] In 1907 these boundaries remained, with division most evident in the west of the city where the earliest area of Catholic settlement on the edge of the eighteenth-century town had expanded into a main ghetto, running on the Falls Road/Divis Street axis, through to Smithfield and Peter's Hill. This was bounded by strongly Protestant areas – Sandy Row to the south, and the Shankill Road to the north. Elsewhere in the city, smaller Catholic enclaves maintained a beleaguered existence at Ardoyne and the lower end of the New Lodge Road in the north, around the Markets in the south, and at the inappropriately named Short Strand in the east.

Territorial divisions were mirrored by differences of circumstance. By whatever measurement, whether it was quality of housing, employment, education, or incidence of one-parent families, those living in the Catholic ghettos were likely to endure lower standards of living than Protestants elsewhere in the city. Their perceptions were those of a beleaguered minority, less able to achieve residential or occupational mobility than their Protestant counterparts and, in any case, a declining proportion of the city's population.

Perceptions were, however, all important. In the west of the city, the principal cockpit of civil disturbances, the proportions of Catholics and Protestants were more even. If the Catholic areas were the true ghettos, Protestants felt themselves equally threatened and it was in the west that the most deprived Protestant areas were located. Indeed social differences between the Falls and the Shankill were marginal. Within the Catholic Falls area the dual economy of the ghetto provided a leavening of teachers, clergy, business and professional people. By contrast, in the poorest Protestant areas those with skills and higher incomes were already moving to better districts. Elsewhere in the city the smaller Catholic enclaves were inhabited almost exclusively by the unskilled and were acutely socially deprived, compared with surrounding Protestant areas.[6]

While territorial division was almost universal, it was fortunate for Larkin that the one possible exception to the rule was Sailorstown, the homeland of the dockers and the centre of his future activity. One of the first residential areas to push beyond the old town centre, it still bore the marks of its early-nineteenth-century planners, a gridiron of some twenty streets running between Corporation Street and the docks on one side and York Street with the great factories at Gallaher's and York Street Mill on the other. The elegant three-storey terraces of the early nineteenth century were now often in decay but suitable for squalid multi-occupation, or as cheap lodging houses. Sailorstown did not escape the tensions that affected the city elsewhere but, being one of the poorest areas, its population was often a shifting one and, unlike other districts, it had its cosmopolitan element. Cheek by jowl with the docks, it was the first point of settlement for immigrants, whether Russians, Jews, Germans or Italians, the latter group giving its name to Little Italy.[7] The area was not purely residential; factories, warehouses, hotels and boarding houses broke up the tightly-built residential pattern more typical elsewhere. Thus Protestants and Catholics might tend to live in separate streets or even sections of streets, but they still lived in close proximity, a marked advantage if common cause were found.[8]

The frailty of any such possibility was illustrated by the reputation of one public place where Catholics and Protestants did meet: the Custom House steps, Belfast's Speakers Corner, which lay hard by the quays and close to Sailorstown. Here speeches, as in London, could be received with amusement but often led to violence, to such an extent that in the 1890s the authorities considered railing the area off.[9] This type of violence was part of a larger pattern in which territory was contested far beyond residential districts. At football matches spectators came armed with revolvers[10] and even at places of entertainment there was an unwritten understanding that working-class Protestants and Catholics occupied the cheaper seats on different nights. On one occasion the Grand Opera House, then the Palace Theatre of Varieties, had to close when a performer sang 'The Wearing of the Green' to the wrong audience and was rewarded with a fusillade of porter bottles and rivets.[11]

Nor was the workplace immune from these divisions. In 1886 and in 1893 a new and sinister feature of the disturbances had been the expulsion of Catholics from their places of work, notably in the shipyards. Employment statistics make clear the existence of a Protestant artisan elite and reveal that Catholics, amounting to twenty-four per cent of the city's population, were a deprived minority. Only ten per cent of engineers and seven per cent of shipwrights were Catholics: with the rapid expansion of the shipyards the effect of this disadvantage was increasing. Elsewhere Catholics comprised only eight per cent of municipal clerks and officials and thirteen per cent of commercial clerks. By contrast, they were over-represented amongst the poorest occupational groups, providing some thirty-two per cent of general labourers and forty-one per cent of dockers.[12] The social impact of this imbalance in occupational distribution was made even greater because of the exceptionally wide gap between skilled and unskilled wages.

As far back as 1864 the Rev. A. Hume had argued in an influential pamphlet that this was the natural order of things, noting that 'in the departments of skilled labour it is curious to see how the lower kinds of it only are found in the Roman Catholic division'. Those jobs carried out by Catholics included ones requiring 'no apprenticeship' or suitable for a 'smart labouring man', while those 'requiring a high order of intelligence or a more careful process of training lie on the Protestant side'. From this Hume went on to offer a wider analogy, arguing that 'the natural position of the white, like that of the Protestant, is on the higher steps of the social pyramid'.[13]

In the same period, Bernard Hughes, one of the few prominent Catholic businessmen in the city, saw rather more practical reasons for the relative disadvantage of the Catholic community, arguing that 'there are few Catholic employers in town, and the others will not take Catholic apprentices, for the workers will not work with them either as apprentices or journeymen. Every trade has an Orange Lodge; and these people know each other, for they have signs and passwords; so that the Catholic population has no chance at all.'[14] Some thirty years later, Beatrice Webb was to become perhaps the first English labour commentator to note that Belfast's skilled workers were 'contemptuous and indifferent to the Catholic labourers'.[15] Nonetheless, commentary by Catholic spokesmen on discrimination or relative deprivation was infrequent at least until the turn of the century; a reflection perhaps of low expectations in the hostile world of the city's wider economy where they expected Protestant employers to employ Protestants and limited their arguents about Catholic employment to 'railways, banks and other industrial concerns where Catholic capital is invested',[16] or to employment by the City Corporation where the issue of political patronage was involved. However, in 1903 clear evidence of growing concern among Catholics at their exclusion from better-paid occupations came with the establishment of a Catholic technical school at Hardinge Street, specifically designed to prepare Catholics for entry to the skilled trades. The prospectus asked, 'Which is the better?' and compared skilled and unskilled rates of pay. By 1907 the first pupils to leave the school were securing apprenticeships in the shipyards and elsewhere, assisted by cash prizes awarded by the school;[17] though it should be noted that almost all of them were to be driven from their work in the pogroms of 1912. However, in the circumstances of 1907, the progress of the experiment suggests a rising level of expectation among Catholics; it also implies that their own explanation of the reasons for their failure to acquire skilled jobs was more complex than one of mere discrimination and included an awareness of educational and financial disadvantages.

Tempting though it is to view the Protestant artisan elite as instrumental in excluding Catholics, the picture is less clear cut. Skilled workers were in no sense a single organised group, indeed in the shipyards quite the reverse; there they were divided into some twenty specialised occupations with separate work locations, different rates and systems of pay and different working relationships.[18] Within the sprawling, and hence not readily controlled, shipyard environment, the twenty per cent of the workforce who were aged eighteen years and under – ranging from rivet boys to those commencing long apprenticeships – may have had more part in hooliganism or, more seriously, sectarian attacks, than did the skilled men with aspirations to respectability.[19]

There were certainly tensions between skilled workers and labourers but these often arose regardless of religion. For many skilled workers there was resentment at the very idea that the unskilled should organise, although 'it didn't show itself in the sense of advising [labourers] not to join a union. It was rather that they looked upon them as a lesser breed without the law.'[20]

In circumstances where at least some skilled workers were in effect subcontractors responsible for the employment of their own labourers, they might naturally ask of unskilled trade unionism 'What the hell – is it good for him? He is my labourer!' Again, skilled workers were at pains to protect their trades from dilution from whatever quarter; they did so principally by financial restrictions imposed through their own unions. As one labourer recalled, 'with the indemnities and one thing and another that had to be laid down to get a trade, many many families could not afford to put their children to a trade'.[20] In normal times this social barrier between the skilled and unskilled had an importance of its own and was a serious obstacle to united working-class action. Although the shadowy influence of the Orange Order may in certain areas have specifically reinforced this division with a sectarian one, the more general reason for Catholic exclusion, and hence for the preservation not merely of an elite but of a Protestant elite within the working class, lay with the restrictions imposed by skilled trade unions. These particularly disadvantaged the poorest sections of society and hence the Catholic community.

On a wider level, skilled artisans in Belfast, as in other great industrial cities, provided much of the ideological leadership within the working class, and in Belfast they did so in a manner which was fundamentally conservative. Even the small minority who provided the early leadership of the labour movement did not necessarily contest, indeed they often shared, some of these basic attitudes. In one important respect this scheme of belief stemmed from the peculiarities of their own divided city. Skilled workers were overwhelmingly Protestant, and to Protestantism they ascribed the various aspects of their very definite pride in their achievement and linked together such virtues as self-improvement, inventiveness, skill, industriousness or even sobriety and cleanliness. There was a dangerous ambivalence in this self-image. Its various features could be, and were, often stated positively, and did not preclude friendship or working relations with 'reliable' Catholics, but they were propositions readily capable of restatement as a series of negatives, hostile to all Catholics. The process was most evident in the enduring controversy over Home Rule, where arguments about the damage Home Rule might do to Belfast's industries were readily transmuted into denunciations of Catholic sloth and unreliability.[21] At the very least, skilled workers showed singularly little inclination to give any firm lead against sectarianism, especially if faced by such tensions in their own working situations.

Their jingoistic enthusiasm for empire, often shared with their employers, was, on the face of it, a more outward-looking emotion, albeit one which tended strongly to reinforce their social conservatism. This enthusiasm for the flag flown on a worldwide stage was soundly based on evident material benefits at home. Indeed, of all cities, Belfast did well out of the late-Victorian era of imperial expansion which coincided with the city's period of most rapid growth. As the *Belfast News-Letter* put it, 'colonial expansion goes hand in hand with shipping prosperity', and specific examples were not hard to find.[22] One case in point was the return in triumph to the city of Lord Dufferin, Viceroy of India, in 1896 following the conquest of Burma, an occasion when William Pirrie was able to tell an ecstatic audience of orders already received by Harland and Wolff for ships to undertake the new trade.[23] In this way an older tradition of colonial service in the community was given a new biting edge by industrial success. Later, the South African War proved the occasion for celebrating the tonnage of Harland and Wolff ships used as troop transports, a statistic still proudly remembered in 1907.[24]

Other industries too benefited by the connection, and at least one, the Sirocco engineering works, stemmed directly from it. The founder of the firm, Samuel Davidson, devised improved tea-drying machinery while working on estates in India in the 1860s and returned to Belfast to manufacture it. By 1907 this was the basis for a great firm which had not only cornered its original market, but had extended into ventilating plant and was later, with splendid ecumenism, to equip both the British and German battle fleets.[25] Belfast's products pursued the ever-expanding imperial frontiers and celebrated the fact, as in an often-quoted advertisement for the firm of Cantrell and Cochrane which described its lemonade as a 'gift from Mother Empire', and the familiarity of the product 'to the Vice-Regal entourage'[26] may have been a selling point to those glad to drink the imperial dream while working for it at home, as much as to those actually experiencing it abroad.

Enthusiasm for empire was not unique to Belfast. In other shipbuilding towns it was often an important element in the creation of a strong and enduring tradition of socially unifying working-class conservatism. In Belfast this broad canvas of imperial development was capable of a narrower reinterpretation, one which emphasised loyalty to the Protestant community and only then justified actions taken in this cause in terms of imperial rhetoric. In Belfast, therefore, celebration of the empire could be used as part of a divisive armoury – indeed by 1909, under the auspices of a Union Jack Committee, leading Unionists had no hesitation in doing this[27] – although, ironically, nationalists of the period demanded no more than Home Rule within a context of imperial development.

Any new and widespread movement amongst the unskilled might well raise previously unasked questions in these areas of belief, but it would certainly challenge existing relations between masters and men. It was in these relations that the conservatism of the skilled elite was perhaps most pervasive. It is true they had a stern and doughty conception of their own rights within a limited sphere, hence they were trade unionists well capable of strike action on their own behalf, and yet they saw themselves as beneficiaries of a paternalistic and often idealised relationship with the employer. In Belfast, where so much employment was dependent on ships and shipbuilding, the nautical image of 'the captain of industry' was understood in the widest possible sense. The employer was responsible for the success, even safety, of the industrial concern upon the stormy seas of economic fortune and could command allegiance accordingly. William Pirrie, of Harland and Wolff, was perhaps the most prominent of these men and one of the few who spent ostentatiously in Belfast, a man who would think nothing of seating 160 to dinner at Ormiston on the outskirts of the city.[28] He was not thought the worse for it and, where nautical imagery failed, other more pastoral fantasies were acted out to symbolise his relationship with his workforce. One such occasion took place in the summer of 1898 when William Pirrie and his wife were guests of honour at the annual excursion to the Giant's Causeway by the Loyal Order of Ancient Shepherds, this being one of several benevolent societies, with a sizeable shipyard membership, which flourished alongside the trade unions. On returning to York Street Station, 'the party formed themselves into two lines facing one another and, crossing sticks and umbrellas, which did service upon the occasion for crooks, cheered lustily as Mr and Mrs Pirrie passed beneath this improvised pastoral canopy'.[29]

The same spirit was evident in 1907. As we shall see, no employer was more reviled than Thomas Gallaher of Gallaher's Tobacco, and yet, when on 25 June 2,000 employees left Great Victoria Street Station for their annual excursion to Dublin, the cries were 'Success to Gallaher's Limited' and 'Long life to Mr Gallaher'.[30]

Skilled workers themselves played a key role in the employment of the various gradations of unskilled labour. They were on occasion subcontractors themselves, and more generally foremen played the major part in recruitment. In this way they became directly involved in the arena in which the struggle for employment was most intense, and the one in which the vast majority of workers of both religious persuasions came into direct and often divisive competition. As employers, skilled men did little to combat these divisions. Some might themselves actively discriminate, but generally a more insidious process occurred. Foremen in particular had an overriding responsibility for continuity of production and might often view it as safer to allocate various levels of unskilled labour on a sectarian basis.[31] Indeed, amongst the unskilled, sectarian solidarity was often seen as a more effective instrument than the use of labour sanctions in preserving limited advantage in a market where an infinite supply of replacement labour was always available.

The endemic characteristic of the unskilled labour market as an internecine battleground was maintained precisely because the majority of working-class Protestants and Catholics remained trapped within it. Catholics were disproportionately over-represented amongst the unskilled, but a forgotten 'majority' of Protestants, far from any 'labour aristocracy', constituted an absolute majority in every broad category of unskilled labour.[32] The picture was more complex than this and in a way calculated to make non-sectarian co-operation amongst the unskilled more difficult. The broad categories of unskilled labour were subdivided into many different occupations, with differences of pay and conditions, and each of these frontiers was contested. There was a clear tendency, albeit marginal, for Protestants to achieve relative advantage in this more detailed aspect of struggle amongst the poor. Within the docks they manned the cross-channel quays where trade was regular and hence a higher proportion of permanent, as opposed to casual, dockers was employed; by contrast, Catholics dominated the deep-sea docks, with an irregular trade and a far greater dependence on casual labour. Such distinctions extended to women's work where Protestants were no more than a bare majority, some fifty-three per cent, of spinners but seventy-one per cent of the better-paid weavers who worked in more favourable conditions.[33]

The response of the two sections of the community to these

circumstances also differed. Within the Protestant community it was more likely that a family could avoid absolute destitution in hard times because there was a greater chance that others within the extended family – the common pattern in both religious groups – would have secure or even skilled employment and thus be able to provide assistance. Perhaps more important, there was the possibility that relatives or others within the social network could 'speak for' you if you became unemployed. This was the process which saved Thomas Carnduff when he lost his job. His brother, a craneman in the shipyard, 'spoke for me to his foreman and in a week's time I received word that I was to start'.[34] Within the Protestant community there was a greater possibility of upward social mobility and although for the vast majority this was, in practical terms, the proverbial pot of gold at the end of the rainbow, the hope alone enabled many, in spite of adverse material circumstances, to share the triumphalist ideology of those who had succeeded. There was, however, a potential for labour militancy amongst the Protestant unskilled if, as in the years leading up to 1907, far from seeing aspirations fulfilled, their living conditions were threatened. The demoralisation and low expectations more prevalent amongst Catholic labourers did not necessarily provide any more favourable ground for the labour organiser.

Larkin soon had available a uniquely qualified adviser on the problems of organising the unskilled in Belfast. This was Michael McKeown, one of the founding fathers of the NUDL nationally and a significant trade-union pioneer far beyond the Belfast docks. McKeown was born in humble circumstances in Drumintee, County Armagh, and left Ireland with a firm hatred of landlordism. He settled in Birkenhead where he worked in an iron foundry until 'he saw a man empty himself as well as his barrow full of pig iron into a furnace'. McKeown moved to the docks and was a ready recruit for the newly founded NUDL. He won his spurs in the great Liverpool strike of 1889 during which he was Secretary of the Birkenhead Branch.[35] McKeown soon became first Vice-President of the union and its most active organiser nationally.

It was in this capacity that he was sent to organise Ireland in 1891. He reached Belfast in July and soon established a branch with 367 members, but was also active elsewhere. By the end of the year no less than fourteen of the NUDL's thirty-eight branches were located in Ireland and it was as a tribute to this work that the union's 1891 congress was held in Belfast. Strikes soon occurred in Cork, Waterford, Limerick, Drogheda, Sligo and Londonderry, and more seriously in Belfast.

It was in April 1892 that the Belfast NUDL members were locked out and replaced by blacklegs. McKeown reported that 'every artifice that low cunning could devise has been employed to stamp us out' and, in spite of aid to the tune of £240 from union headquarters, the men were defeated by the end of August.[36]

The final episode in this disastrous dispute was surely one full of significance for Larkin who now, fifteen years later, was setting out to reorganise the men. In 1892 it had been the union's misfortune that, in spite of its British base, its origins were still very clearly and inextricably linked with the radicalism and Nationalism of a generation of Irish emigrants. McKeown was one of these men; so also were the union's co-founders, the Ulstermen Richard McGhee, later a Nationalist MP, and Edward McHugh.[37] Among those who helped establish the new union at recruiting meetings in Britain was Michael Davitt of Land League fame.[38] During the 1892 lockout McKeown travelled to Glasgow to speak with Davitt at a meeting. His son later recalled the consequences: 'The local *Belfast Evening Telegraph* had streamer headlines on their Monday evening issue following the Glasgow meeting: "Are the Orangemen of Belfast going to allow themselves to be led by a Fenian?". The shot got home; the union was split and the cross-channel steamer dockers, a majority Orangemen, left the union.'[39]

Larkin soon asked McKeown to take up the reins again where he had left off in defeat, and he was to become Secretary of the reformed NUDL organisation in Belfast. Larkin also, of course, had the assistance of Thomas Johnston to advise him on the state of the existing labour movement, assistance which might prove crucial in any new struggle waged by the unskilled.

3
Organised labour

Belfast in 1907 was the foremost centre of the labour movement in Ireland. Almost a third of the trade unionists in the country lived there and it was also in Belfast that workers had first sought independent labour representation and had proceeded furthest in obtaining it. During the years 1901 to 1907 trade union membership in Ireland had stagnated, increasing only from 67,000 to 70,000,[1] a situation which encouraged interest in the apparently contrasting developments in Belfast. Appropriately, Belfast played a leading role in the Irish Trade Union Congress and helped to mould its policies.

As early as 1889 Belfast Trades Council had actively supported the creation of an Irish Federated Trade and Labour League. This did not necessarily indicate any great breadth of vision, as the collapse of this forerunner of the ITUC was to show. When Dublin Trades Council organised a Sunday sports meeting under Federation auspices, Belfast protested that such actions tended 'to violate those principles which are the true basis of a true Federation of Labour' and demanded that the Dublin executive 'abstain from using the name of the Irish Federated Trade and Labour League for a like purpose'. When no reply was received Belfast withdrew and the short-lived Federation collapsed.[2]

When in 1894 the ITUC was more successfully established, again with Belfast support, the motives of the city's delegates were essentially parochial. They, like other Irish delegates, had resented the expense of attending conferences in Britain at which there was very little time for the discussion of Irish matters. Belfast delegates were, in addition, hostile to the tendency of British labour leaders to raise Irish labour issues directly with the Irish Parliamentary Party. The ITUC did not represent any radical departure in its own right, its work was to be 'analogous and auxiliary to the British Trades Congress',[3] and in the period up to 1907 Nationalism was never an issue. On the contrary, the major development of the period, one encouraged by trade unionists throughout Ireland, was the expansion of the amalgamated or British-based unions.[4]

The ITUC remained the preserve of skilled workers and it was not until 1906 that an unskilled worker was elected to the Parliamentary Committee. This predominance of an artisan elite was reflected in the innate social conservatism of the movement. P.J. Leo, President in 1894, captured well the spirit of the era when he saw the role of the trade unions as 'to promote and cultivate better relations between the employer and the employee'. He told delegates that 'the old, time-worn and barbarous method of strikes will soon become as obsolete as the handloom or flintlock'.[5]

William Walker, the rising star of Belfast labour, was President in 1904 and showed little more awareness of the coming struggle. He told delegates:

> Funds have been spent on strike after strike which has arisen, not always because of the employers' wish not to concede terms, but often against economic conditions which can only be changed by Parliamentary action. Surely it is a wiser and saner policy to spend £1,000 on the return of a member to the House of Commons than to spend ten times that amount on a strike which is often not successful.[6]

This view had not always prevailed in Belfast. Thus in 1892 Samuel Munro, the Secretary of the Trades Council, while admitting that strikes were 'a barbarous method of settling disputes', went on, 'we are also bound to admit (for it is impossible to close our eyes to the fact) that under the present conditions of society they are a necessity, and have also their good side, and often display to us in various forms the true nobility and manhood of the great mass of workers'.

It was not that in the years between 1892 and 1904 the battle on behalf of unskilled workers had been won – far from it. Munro was writing at the latter end of the brief wave of 'new unionism' which had spread from Britain and briefly involved a wide variety of unskilled workers, including Belfast dockers. For a short period it was possible for Munro to assert on behalf of the Trades Council that 'we are proud of having recognised the rights of the unskilled labourer to a share in our work and advantages'. Reverses soon followed: the tobacco workers 'were locked out... and after a prolonged struggle were defeated', and three societies formed for women workers in the mills 'collapsed' so that 'the women workers are now left at the mercy of the employers'. By the end of 1892 the situation was bleaker still, as the Trades Council, in spite of an increase in skilled membership, was 'sorry to find that the unskilled labourers have, with one exception, not only failed to maintain their position, but have lost a great number of members'. As we have seen, the dockers, once in a position to contribute to the tobacco workers' strike fund, were themselves crushed in this phase.[7]

The Trades Council did not altogether abandon efforts to organise the unskilled in the following years, but faced distinct handicaps in doing so. From 1892 a deepening recession made the economic circumstances much less favourable, and because in Britain the 'new unions' were also on the retreat they no longer had the resources to send frequent missions to Ireland. The meeting in 1893 of the British TUC in Belfast provided a new spark to action, and efforts were made once more to organise women workers; but the endeavour met with little success, perhaps because of the gross underestimation by skilled men like Munro of the difficulties involved. He begged the women to take the advice of 'experienced trade unionists. . . it was easy to take, it was simple to do what the men had done – to organise themselves into trade unions'.[8] Eventually, a Textile Operatives Society was formed with the assistance of William Walker,[9] but it was never to become a major force.

William Walker, a carpenter and delegate to the Trades Council from 1892, had been largely responsible for the one successful initiative in the heady days of 1891-2, the organisation of unskilled workers in the shipyards, principally platers' helpers, in the National Amalgamated Union of Labour. Success here owed much to the anxious tutelage of skilled workers, who did not want unskilled men in their own unions, but felt they would be a menace without the discipline of a union. Later in the decade Walker also assisted in the successful organisation of the municipal employees, a group which shared with NAUL an overwhelmingly Protestant membership.[10]

Even these distinctly selective advances soon caused a direct conflict of interest within the Trades Council. In 1893, as the recession deepened, wage cuts were imposed in the shipyards, and these had far more serious consequences for NAUL members, already on a bare subsistence wage, than for the highly-paid skilled workers. In an act of desperation NAUL members struck, demanding the minimum wage paid in the north east of England and, more embarrassingly, requesting status as direct employees rather than as employees of skilled men acting as subcontractors.

The Trades Council merely appointed an impartial delegation to seek 'an amicable conclusion' and secured an offer of fifteen shillings and sixpence, far short of the men's demand. This was cause for celebration by Samuel Munro who described it as 'a very important step in the history of the labourers' association'. The NAUL members disagreed and remained on strike, eventually suffering bitter defeat.[11]

For the rest of the decade, the direct spotlight in the shipyards shifted to the skilled unions, which were involved in three prolonged disputes. From October 1895 to January 1896, engineers were on strike, trying to re-establish their primacy within the United Kingdom shipbuilding industry; between July 1897 and January 1898 they were locked out as employers sought to reassert their control, and in 1899-1900 the carpenters were out for eight months.[12]

Unskilled workers, who were simply laid off as a result of these disputes, suffered acutely and yet little positive action was taken by skilled unions to alleviate their plight. In 1895 William Walker was one of the few to intervene, arguing that the Trades Council 'should not wait until these starving ones came to them and asked for help, the council should proffer their aid at once'. The Trades Council accepted this, but rejected Walker's more radical proposal for a demonstration by the unemployed.[13]

In spite of this display of understanding for the plight of the unemployed, Walker and other labour activists were inevitably chiefly preoccupied with the actual disputes and the hope that they would effect a radicalisation of the skilled men. The combination by the employers in 1897-8, in an attempt to smash the engineers, seemed momentarily to be achieving this, but the effect was substantially weakened by the defection of William Pirrie, of Harland and Wolff, from the employers' side in favour of 'a progressive and advanced policy'.[14]

It was against this essentially discouraging background that the small minority of socialists such as Walker had to work to secure their own power base within the trade union movement. In Walker's case, his link with the Amalgamated Society of Carpenters and Joiners was crucial, culminating in his appointment as full-time local organiser for the union in 1903, a position which gave him freedom to engage in wider labour activity. However, in spite of his long and active association with the union, he did not necessarily have a radicalising effect upon it – as late as 1906 only one of the nine or ten ASCJ branches in the city had bothered to affiliate to the Trades Council.[15] In this respect the ASCJ was no worse than other powerful skilled unions which, although they represented the majority of trade unionists in the city, were consistently under-represented on the Trades Council, as compared with a variety of much smaller and weaker unions. This abstention was a reflection of their strength in their own industrial spheres, but also of disinterest in or even positive distaste for wider labour organisation.[16]

Walker's natural identification with the interests of the joiners could appeal to a general audience amongst the skilled elite. He therefore spoke for all skilled workers when, as Secretary of the Trades Council, he explained the joiners' dispute of 1899-1900 – 'the *casus belli* is that whilst every other city in Great Britain of like size to Belfast can obtain substantial reductions in hours, with a corresponding increase of wages and generally improved conditions of labour, Belfast, simply because it happens to be in Ireland, is to be denied any advance or improvement'.[17] It was a common and feasible objective for Belfast's craft unions to seek in this way to abstract themselves from their Irish locale, while the unskilled, for whom this objective was unattainable, were barely represented on the Trades Council.

What is surprising is the extent to which, even at the height of his influence in the labour movement in the years up to 1907, Walker pursued the narrow interests of the ASCJ to the detriment even of unity amongst skilled unions. He resigned from the presidency of the Trades Council in 1905, rather than allow it to arbitrate in a dispute between the ASCJ and carpenters and mill-sawyers working on the new City Hall, provoking John Murphy, Secretary of the Council, to remark, 'it was a gloomy outlook for trade unionism if the spirit of co-operation was to be dropped, and the strong unions were to crush out the weak ones'.[18] A year later the ASCJ was again censured for failing to hold talks with the cabinetmakers in a demarcation dispute, and by July 1906 the Amalgamated Society of Engineers was accusing Walker of being 'an informer' in seeking the sack for one of its members in a shipyard dispute.[19]

If this was an unedifying record of petty disunity, there was one area in which there was widespread, if purely theoretical, agreement on the Trades Council in the years leading up to 1907, and this was on the folly of strikes, the view expressed by Walker in his presidential address to the ITUC in 1904. For skilled workers, this reflected a reaction to the prolonged and largely unproductive strikes of the 1890s, and a recognition of improvements readily gained in the headlong expansion of heavy industry in the early years of the new century. The smaller craft unions had long favoured, for quite other reasons, arbitration in all disputes up to international level; their relative industrial weakness led them to rely heavily on the negotiating authority of the Trades Council.

Unfortunately the new peaceful strategy of the Trades Council did not in practice live up to the high hopes expressed in it. Early in the century the Trades Council set up an arbitration scheme in conjunction with Belfast Chamber of Commerce and even subscribed £5 towards the cost of it. However, in 1903 it was forced to ask for its money back after several successive refusals by employers engaged in disputes to go to arbitration.[20] From 1903 to 1907 the Trades Council consistently relied on the petitioning of notables and the sending of delegations to employers. During a major textile strike in 1906 the bankruptcy of these tactics was clearly revealed. Four delegates, including William Walker, visited the Lord Lieutenant, Lord Aberdeen, and appealed to him to intervene. This he did with great effect, advising the strikers to surrender. It mattered little that the Trades Council then passed a resolution accusing Lord Aberdeen of 'betraying' the strikers. As John Murphy said, it did not seem 'possible to succeed in the matter in the way indicated by Mr Walker'.[21] Certainly in this record there was little to encourage the by now long-dormant ranks of the unskilled and unorganised to take action.

If any major crisis in the trade union sphere did develop, there was another aspect of the labour movement which was of potential significance, and that was its wider political role. While the apparent strength of the trade union movement in Belfast concealed deep structural weaknesses, the same was true of its campaign for independent political representation.

Belfast had played a pioneering role when in March 1892 its Trades Council had established the first Labour Electoral Association in Ireland, and in 1896 no less than six Labour candidates triumphed in the local elections against the background of the typhoid epidemic and engineering lockout – they were the first Labour councillors elected in Ireland. Three years after the setting-up in 1900 of the Labour Representation Committee in Britain, Belfast became the first Irish centre to follow suit. At the ITUC,

Belfast delegates, led by William Walker, were the driving force in persuading Congress to support the LRC in that and following years.[22]

Once again appearances were deceptive. This initiative for separate labour representation did not arise because the movement in the north was in any way more politically advanced than that in the south. In the south the Irish Parliamentary Party acted as an effective channel for labour discontent. Thus J.P. Nannetti, a former President of Dublin Trades Council, was elected as a Nationalist MP and acted as liaison officer between his party and the labour movement. In the north labour spokesmen wrote to Unionist leaders, asking them to carry out a similar function. They did not even receive the courtesy of a reply.[23]

Northern labour leaders made it clear that they did not object to the labour record of the Irish Parliamentary Party, only to its Nationalism. Thus John Murphy, proposing the LRC resolution at the ITUC Congress in 1907, said 'he had no fault to find with the Irish Party, but they did not represent entirely the views of the voters of Ireland. There were Unionists as well as Nationalists, and he contended they should have a distinct Labour Party.'[24] Other delegates to Belfast Trades Council were even more explicit in their support of the 'labour' programme of the Nationalists. In 1902 the Trades Council was debating whether to endorse the Independent Orange candidate Tom Sloan in the South Belfast by-election. Mr Harvey, a Protestant, argued that 'they must admit that the best members they in Ireland had in the House of Commons were the Nationalists, and he did not see for a moment how Mr Sloan could go into the same lobby with them when he was ridiculing them from one year's end to another'.[25] In 1906 the question of endorsing Joe Devlin, Nationalist candidate for West Belfast, arose. In what must be a classic expression of the contradictions of northern labour politics, Mr Dyson explained that, 'while admitting himself to be a strong Conservative, he could not withhold his support from Mr Devlin in the face of the strong Labour programme he had outlined'.[26] In short, if the majority of northern voters had not been Unionists as opposed to Nationalists, there is little doubt that they would have been just as satisfied with labour representation through the Nationalist Party as were the majority of their southern compatriots.

As it was, the attempt to compromise with the Unionist machine remained a constant theme in northern labour politics. In 1893 the

Trades Council backed Murray Davis in a city council election, but some members of the Trades Council spoke for the Unionists. Davis himself produced a clergyman to prove that he was not a Nationalist, and not a socialist. The Unionists won, and four days later the Trades Council congratulated McCammond, the successful Conservative, as 'the workers' best friend'. In 1896 Robert Gageby (who by 1907 had become a father figure of the labour movement in Belfast) had been elected as a Labour candidate in tandem with a Conservative, F.C. Johnston, who was an ex-Secretary of the Trades Council.[27]

The central figure in the efforts to obtain labour representation in the new century was to be William Walker. His early record suggested a more radical perspective. Along with John Murphy, he had established a branch of the Independent Labour Party as early as 1892, and from 1892 to 1895 the branch, led by Walker, sought to preach the doctrine of socialism at the Custom House steps.[28] Walker's small band, although assisted by prominent English speakers, faced violent opposition, led principally by Arthur Trew, the city's most extreme religious demagogue in the entire pre-war period.[29]

Bruce Glasier, in his report to the 1907 Labour Party Conference in the city, recalled those stormy days and an occasion when 'the mob lifted him [Walker] shoulder high on the Custom House steps with the cheerful intention of pitching him into the river'. He added, 'both Pete [Curran] and myself also recollect visits to Belfast which somewhat seasoned us for after-day pro-Boer experiences'.[30] In fact by June 1895 the small ILP group had abandoned the steps and it was on this basis that the Belfast Protestant Association was later to claim a triumph for Trew in 'the overthrowal of the local society of Socialists'.[31] Also in 1895, the ILP activists suffered a further reverse when they failed dismally to persuade the Trades Council to adopt Pete Curran as a Labour candidate in a by-election caused by the death of Sir Edward Harland.[32]

These setbacks may have been the direct cause of the demise of the ILP branch by 1896, but it seems more likely that Walker and his associates deliberately chose to adopt more pragmatic tactics. In this they did not differ from British ILP members. The latter, in the years up to 1900, fully supported efforts to establish the Labour Representation Committee on the basis of a minimal commitment to independent labour representation, designed to win the support of the majority of trade unionists who still saw themselves politically as Liberals or Conservatives. Walker's pragmatism went further in that he now distanced himself from the advanced wing of the movement. This became clear at the meeting held to establish the LRC in Belfast in 1903 when Walker made it clear that the pursuit of truly independent representation was not for him a matter of immutable principle. When a resolution requiring LRC candidates to adhere strictly to a party pledge was proposed, Walker successfully backed an amendment, arguing that a party pledge for local elections 'would offend people they did not want to offend at elections'.[33]

The adoption of positions such as this helped Walker become the first standard-bearer for the LRC at parliamentary level. In June 1903 he was selected to fight North Belfast, narrowly defeating the more conservative Robert Gageby, and his approach to electioneering showed he was unwilling to put at risk the broad, if uneasy, coalition which had won him the nomination. When, in November 1903, Ramsay MacDonald suggested that he and Keir Hardie should speak at Walker's inaugural meeting and combine it with an Independent Labour Party meeting, John Murphy, Secretary of the Belfast LRC, replied on Walker's behalf that any such identification with the ILP 'would militate against Mr Walker's chances and at least neutralise the good results the committee hope to achieve by holding the meeting'.[34]

Thus, while labour leaders on the mainland were actively using the ILP as an instrument within the LRC to urge the latter in the direction of a fully-fledged Labour Party, no such process was taking place in Belfast under Walker's aegis. Indeed it was not until 1905 that an effective ILP presence was re-established in the city by others.[35]

If Walker distanced himself from his former ILP background, he could be more than ecumenical in other directions. In 1902 he suggested that the Trades Council should write to the city's four Conservative MPs and ask them to support Keir Hardie as a Labour candidate in an English seat,[36] and as late as 1906, during the textile strike in which he played such a disastrous role, Walker wrote for the Liberal *Ulster Guardian* rather than the *Belfast Labour Chronicle*.[37]

It would be a mistake to think that there was necessarily any contradiction in all this, for William Walker's philosophy in its developed form, and hence his 'labour' programme, was essentially the non-political programme of the Trades Council, and his main interest municipal reformism. Even in this field, his increasing northern chauvinism limited his ability to attack Conservatives effectively, a point borne out in his controversy with James Connolly in the columns of the Glasgow socialist paper, *Forward*. Writing in 1911, Walker said:

> We have moved fast to municipal socialism, leaving not merely the other cities of Ireland far behind, but giving the lead to many cities in England and Scotland. We collectively own and control our gas-works, harbour works, markets, tramways, electricity, museums, art galleries, etc., while we municipally cater for bowlers, cricketers, footballers, lovers of band music (having organised a police band) and our works department does an enormous amount of 'timed' and 'contract' work within the municipality. With the above in operation we, in Belfast, have no need to be ashamed of being compared in municipal management with any city in the United Kingdom.[38]

In writing thus, Walker was defending the doubtful record of an overwhelmingly Conservative Corporation, on which there had never been more than seven Labour councillors.[39]

Even the Tory press was prepared to praise Labour politics of this limited kind. Thus, in 1899 the *Belfast Evening Telegraph* commented, 'The Labour Party, as they are sometimes called, have every right to claim that they have comported themselves with credit to themselves and benefit to the artizans of the community.'[40] Indeed, as late as 1902, the *Belfast News-Letter* positively favoured labour representation, arguing that Belfast Conservatism should concede it 'either through its own machinery, or to support proper candidates put forward in the name of the working man'.[41] More serious still, non-Labour groups were quite capable of stealing the scanty Labour clothes. In 1907 Labour lost every seat it contested while a newly-formed and middle-class Citizens' Association won every seat it contested on a platform of municipal reform.[42] It would be wrong to underestimate the difficulties and sacrifices made by the early Labour pioneers, but even before the crisis of 1907 their political weakness, in the non-controversial sphere of municipal reform, was evident.

There was, however, another and uglier side to labour politics. The description of the Labour Party as 'a body which represents men of all shades of religious and political opinion',[43] covered a multitude of sins. In spite of this claim of a non-political position,

Belfast labour activists had taken decisions which were, albeit unconsciously, of a political nature; the decision to affiliate to the British LRC implied a very definite view of the relationship between the Irish working class and the Empire. In October 1905 the *Belfast Labour Chronicle* enthusiastically quoted Ramsay MacDonald: 'The best way to get rid of the Jingo Imperialism which has been fostered so much of late years is to awaken the workers to a sense of a nobler imperialism of which they are the masters.' The following month the *Chronicle* responded in similar vein: 'Imperialism is but the transition stage to the international union of the proletariat the world over.' In April 1907, weeks before the strike, Arthur Henderson visited Belfast to speak of 'one unbroken imperial family'.[44] It was quite clear that Belfast labour saw itself as part and parcel of the British Empire.

In spite of this clear stand, Home Rule was viewed as a 'political' question and, as the Ulster image of the word 'political' often meant religious or sectarian, Home Rule was considered to be an issue of private or almost religious conscience. The banishing of a view on Home Rule to the realm of private conscience enabled many labour candidates to spend more time emphasising the sectarian nature of their private consciences than explaining specific labour policy, and the higher the stakes the more this was so.

Between 1905 and 1907 William Walker contested North Belfast three times – in the by-election of 1905, the General Election of 1906 and the further by-election of 1907. These were the only parliamentary contests fought by Labour in this period. All three campaigns were coloured by Walker's ever-narrower vision, and were marked by a squalid opportunism for which he was principally responsible. As a major part of labour resources in the three years were devoted to these campaigns, they tended to mark the Labour candidates as representing the Protestant section of the working class alone.

In the first by-election of 1905 Walker stood against the Lord Mayor, Sir Daniel Dixon. In his election address he described himself as 'a Unionist in politics', and his election leaflets were almost entirely devoted to proving that he was not a Home Ruler.[45] In the last week of the campaign Walker felt the need to go even further than this. The Conservative candidate had avoided the Belfast Protestant Association which wished to get answers to a series of highly sectarian questions. Walker had already made use of a BPA

> ## TO
> # THE CATHOLIC VOTERS
> ## OF NORTH BELFAST.
>
> # WALKER
>
> The so-called Labour Candidate, BROAD-MINDED (save the mark), in answer to some questions submitted to him by the Belfast Protestant Association, has given the following replies:
>
> **(1). WALKER will oppose**
> any attempt to abolish or alter the Statutory Declaration which the Sovereign is compelled to make against Transubstantiation upon his accession to the Throne, whereby he calls the Catholics Idolators.
>
> **(2). WALKER will oppose**
> the Repealing of the Law that prevents a Catholic holding the Offices of Lord Chancellor of England and Lord Lieutenant of Ireland.
>
> **(3). WALKER will try**
> to secure the Inspection of Convents and Monasteries.
>
> **(4). WALKER will oppose**
> Fair Play to Catholics in University Education.
>
> ## Catholics of North Belfast!
> BIGOTED PRONOUNCEMENTS. HOW CAN YOU SUPPORT THIS MAN? WALKERS Socialism consists in **INSULTING CATHOLICS** in their cherished ... and ... **he would deny a Catholic obtaining employment** in a high ... Walker would, if he had the power, **prevent a Catholic Working-man from earning his daily bread.**
>
> ## CATHOLICS OF THE NORTH DIVISION
> *DO NOT BE MISLED by this sham, narrow-minded bigot, who calls himself a Labour candidate.*

The price Walker paid for his answers to the Belfast Protestant Association, in this case probably at the hands of Unionist black propagandists (Central Library, Belfast)

hall for his election committee meetings, and was more easily cornered.[46] He now agreed to oppose any Catholic succeeding to the Monarchy, becoming Lord Chancellor or Lord Lieutenant of Ireland. He agreed to oppose Home Rule in any form and to attempt to secure a redistribution of Irish seats to increase the representation of Protestant areas at the expense of Catholic areas. Finally, when asked, 'Will you in all things place the interests of Protestantism before those of the party to which you are attached?' he replied, 'Protestantism means protesting against superstition and hence true Protestantism is synonymous with Labour.'[47] Walker's replies caused a major crisis within the Labour organisation, and almost led Ramsay MacDonald, who was acting as Walker's agent, to resign. He voiced his despair in a letter to Thomas Johnston, saying, 'I was never more sick of an election than that at North Belfast, and then the religious replies at the back of it knocked everything out of me. I am afraid these answers will make it impossible for Mr Walker to win the contest.'[48]

MacDonald's assessment of the electoral damage was astute enough. Walker's replies were widely publicised, were made the subject of an anonymous poster distributed at Catholic chapels,[49] and almost certainly lost him a substantial proportion of the small Catholic vote in the constituency, enough to provide the narrow 474 vote margin by which he was defeated.

Walker also faced immediate criticism nationally for using the term 'a Unionist in politics' in his election address. The issue was raised by Pete Curran at the executive of the Labour Representation Committee in London. Walker's defence was based on the quite correct assertion that he was pledged to the LRC programme which excluded any position on the Home Rule issue.[50] Publicly the LRC endorsed this position, stating that 'Mr Walker has broken no provision of the LRC constitution', but privately there were reservations and 'the chairman was asked to express the feeling of the executive that it was improper to accentuate religious strife during the contest'.[51] In Belfast disagreement was similarly suppressed. Thus Harry Stockman, who wrote to the *Belfast Evening Telegraph* defending Walker's position, also wrote privately to MacDonald speaking of Walker's 'selling himself to that intolerant Protestant clique'.[52]

All those who might otherwise have debated the issues more publicly were subject to the constraint that a General Election was expected shortly. In the event it did not occur until January 1906 when Walker once again contested North Belfast. On this occasion he again emphasised his opposition to Home Rule in his election address, but in less controversial terms than during the previous contest, and he came even closer to winning, losing by a bare 291 votes. In defeat one issue, as always, was central to his thoughts, and he ascribed his failure to the Liberal upsurge which 'brought Home Rule into the arena'.[53]

At the Labour Party conference in January 1907 Walker exuded renewed confidence and was 'wildly cheered by the audience' when he said 'neither he nor the Labour men of Belfast would rest till they won every seat for the Labour and Socialist cause'.[54] Soon after the departure of the Labour delegates such rhetoric was put to the test when the death of Sir Daniel Dixon precipitated a further North

Belfast by-election. Far from rushing to the fray, Walker was at first unwilling to stand again, and from the point of view of labour activists the direction in which he appeared likely to throw his influence was even more alarming. An anxious Thomas Johnston wrote to Ramsay MacDonald describing a meeting of the Trades Council executive and representatives of the North Belfast and other Labour clubs, held to discuss the situation, and he reported Walker's view that the candidate 'must be a local man – an imported candidate would be useless – and that a local man can be found *and the money too*'. Johnston commented, 'this means that a Liberal will be run – or an unconnected Labour man financed by the Liberals and A.M. Carlisle, Pirrie etc. This will be disastrous to the cause of independent Labour.'[55]

In the end Walker was prevailed upon to stand, but quickly dispensed with any assistance from Transport House. Ramsay MacDonald wrote to him on 27 March, asking, 'are you wise in refusing the services of half a dozen trained agents?' and was told in reply that Walker had men 'familiar with the "peculiarities" of Belfast'. MacDonald also received back a large supply of Labour Party leaflets which Walker said 'would, I am afraid, be a "white elephant" in Belfast'.[56]

In fairness to Walker, he faced a campaign of special virulence. The Unionists were by now thoroughly alerted to the danger in North Belfast and, whereas Sir Daniel Dixon had been a classic 'dead head' candidate, his successor, G.S. Clark, was an effective exponent of the new aggressive approach of the Ulster Unionist Council. In addition to impeccable Orange credentials, he could exert substantial influence as a major employer in the area, using his connection with the Workman Clark shipyard to the full. The Orange card was soon played, as in this popular election song:

> Now, brethren keep your powder dry,
> Have your swords all shining bright,
> Brave Walter Long your general is,
> Close your ranks up round him tight,
> With him, Craig, Moore and Orange Clark,
> You're sure to take the field,
> Rome's hellish crew will find lots to do,
> Pressed by your Orange steel.[57]

It was a campaign in which, according to Harry Stockman, it was impossible to refer to nationalisation because it was immediately misunderstood as Nationalism. Walker did not propose nationalisation of the shipyards but, when talking about Harland and Wolff, he innocently used the words 'take Harland and Wolff for example', and was promptly denounced for advocating the immediate seizure of the yard. Then there were the anonymous leaflets for which the small but crucial Catholic section of the electorate was once again a target; they received one which read, 'Socialism has pillaged France's church, broken up our holy images with military force, and put to the point of the sword her bishops and clergy.'[58]

These indeed were local peculiarities, but Walker's own enquiries made to Labour Party headquarters indicated that his response was to engage in the unlikely task of attempting to overtake Clark on the wilder shores of loyalism. One of his queries was about the 'Home Rule proclivities of the present and past Clark family', and he asked for the 1886 division list because, 'I am informed that my opponent's father, who sat for a Glasgow division, voted for the Bill'. He also wrote to the King, pointing out that Clark was using the Royal Standard on his election wagons, and was gratified to receive a reply agreeing that such use was unauthorised. He attacked the Unionists from the sectarian right: 'Unionism seemed to be synonymous with Protestantism in the old days of 1886, but at present they found Orange Lodges passing votes of confidence in Roman Catholic candidates for Parliament.'[59]

Walker's election address made his priorities very clear. On all social issues he merely commented that, because of the previous elections, 'it is unnecessary now to do more than say that my programme remains unaltered', but he continued, 'Still I feel that as we are on the eve of legislation affecting the future of Ireland, I must again declare that *I am, as I always have been, a supporter of the legislative union.*' Although he did not aspire to an Orange mantle, his polling cards were suitably tailored for an evangelical audience, embellished as they were with suitable religious verses rather than items of Labour policy.[60]

It was to no avail: Walker was defeated by 1,800 votes, the largest margin of all in his three North Belfast contests. It was a defeat that caused no great sorrow in advanced Labour circles. As Thomas Kennedy in the Social Democratic Federation paper *Justice* put it, 'What was called "abuse" and "misrepresentation" by the Tory press was really a statement of Mr Walker's own intrigues with religious factions for electoral support. When Socialism was attacked and misrepresented neither the candidate nor his supporters had the courage or the ability to affirm a definite principle or policy.'[61]

The attitudes expressed by Walker in his three North Belfast campaigns were not his alone. They were faithfully represented in the *Belfast Labour Chronicle,* a joint publication of the Trades Council and the LRC in the years 1905 to 1907. After Walker's defeat in 1905 the *Chronicle* eulogised, 'Mr Walker believed in the Union between Great Britain and Ireland as in the union between one man and one wife in spirit and fidelity. Is Sir Daniel's belief in Unionism as broad and deep?'[62] After Walker's defeat in 1906 the *Chronicle* commented, 'The supporters of our slobland king raised the hypocritical cry of Union, as if Walker would not have been far the most capable friend had the Union been in danger.'[63]

Like Walker, the *Chronicle* was concerned with the sectarian fears associated with Home Rule rather than with any social or economic consequences. In October 1905 the Republican Dungannon Clubs issued a manifesto in which, amongst other things, they advocated separate Irish trade unions. The *Chronicle* retorted, 'Do they suggest that the international principles of Irish trades unionism should take refuge under the banner of Nationalism and the Upas Tree of Rome's priesthood?' It went on to accuse the manifesto of sailing 'dangerously near the borderline of treason and Fenianism when it advises that Irishmen should not join the British army, but leave England to fight her own battles'.[64]

Even the simple trappings of Trades Council demonstrations revealed the identity of the movement. Thus the 1902 Trades Council demonstration was led by the Cromwell, Kane Memorial, Ballymacarrett Conservative and G.W. Wolff flute bands. The *Belfast News-Letter* was able to comment: 'The display of Union Jacks and other loyal flags was an exceedingly creditable one, and it was noticeable that the music played was confined to loyal and military airs.'[65] It is, however, unfair to suggest that all Labour opportunism was in one direction. When, in 1905, a rare foray was made into Falls Ward, normally the territory of the United Ireland League, the *Chronicle* said of the Labour candidate, 'We are putting forward a candidate who, while a good Catholic and a sound Nationalist, can be relied upon to look after the interests of the working-class electors of the ward.'[66] No doubt religious and cultural differences helped to make men like William Walker chary of entering Catholic areas, but these barriers were compounded by class differences. In 1908 the Belfast correspondent of Glasgow *Forward* explained why Labour would not contest Court Ward, saying that 'the large slum element in this ward makes it almost hopeless to contest from the Labour standpoint'.[67] Let it be said that these Labour aristocrats viewed the 'slum element' of both Catholic and Protestant areas with disdain, but in Protestant areas at least the lumpen proletariat was watered down by a skilled element. In Catholic areas this skilled element was much smaller in relation to the whole electorate, hence there was less temptation to enter Catholic areas.

What was the legacy of this record of parliamentary and municipal struggle? There was no indication that the activities of Labour were encouraging the withering-away of sectarian differences. On the contrary, the more desperate the attempt to obtain seats, the greater the degree of capitulation to sectarianism. It was quite clear that Labour had prepared no firm base from which to give the working class a lead in times of political or social crisis. In Protestant areas Labour swam in the Orange tide, hoping to be washed onto a parliamentary shore. In Catholic areas Labour rarely put a foot in the water. In neither area did Labour challenge existing conventions on a broad front.

In the face of these weaknesses, Walker and Belfast Labour could enlist the broader authority of the British movement. There were two elements involved in their enthusiasm for the leadership of the British LRC. In the first instance, close links with the LRC and the British trade union movement enabled Belfast Labour leaders to pose Labour Unionism against Conservative Unionism. In this case, Belfast Labour leaders were not concerned with any distinction between right and left in the British movement. It was sufficient for them that it was British, but in any case the Belfast Labour leaders were far more in sympathy with the British labour leadership than with the British left. Walker was attracted to the evolutionary and parliamentary road to British socialism which he hoped to extend to Ireland. These methods and objectives seemed realistic to the skilled workers of the north who enjoyed conditions of work, pay rates and trade union rights equivalent to, or in some cases better than, those in Britain.

Otherwise, however, conditions in Ireland and Britain were different. The vast mass of unskilled workers in Ireland was appallingly paid by British standards and, whereas in Britain unskilled unions had established an effective foothold, in Ireland the unskilled were unorganised, and the very notion that they should be unionised was anathema to both the employers and the authorities. In Britain the Labour Party had fifty-two parliamentary seats and was an established force. In Ireland distinctive Labour political organisations had fewer branches than British Labour had Westminster seats. Above all, in Ireland there was a far clearer tradition by which the authorities dealt with dissent through force or the threat of force.

The illusion that Walker's strategy might succeed could be preserved only by keeping Labour activity within the strictest confines, and confines of interest to a skilled working-class minority. The strength of other strands of working-class political activity reflected the irrelevance of much Labour activity to the masses. Certainly in early 1907 there was little sign that Labour was prepared for a rising of the unskilled workers in Belfast, much less equipped to lead it. Indeed, any such development threatened existing concepts of Labour organisation.

4

Orange dissent, Nationalist factionalism

The nature of working-class society in Belfast, allied with the shortcomings of official Labour, helped to ensure the continued importance of channels of working-class dissent within the Nationalist and Unionist camps. This dissent emerged in a more clearly-articulated form within the Protestant community. Protestant workers were ruled by a Protestant ascendancy and class strains were bound to develop. Catholic workers viewed the Protestant ruling elite as their chief agent of oppression and were thus far less likely to develop specifically working-class opposition to their own middle class which, whatever its faults, was in no sense a ruling class in the north.

When in 1902 the Independent Orange Order broke away from the old Order, its creation represented the fruition of nearly forty years of Orange working-class dissent against the ascendancy. Much of this frustration had been expressed in theological terms – low church against high church, evangelical against episcopalian. Protestant workers tended to feel that what was wrong with the ascendancy was that it was not Protestant enough. From its beginnings in 1902 through to 1907 the Independent Orange Order made it increasingly clear that the dispute was based on social and political factors as well.

The first major schism occurred as far back as 1867. At that stage the Orange Order was viewed as an unruly influence by important sections of the landed gentry and by the captains of industry in Belfast, and Orange processions were still banned.[1] The Fenian threat led to growing resentment amongst the Orange rank and file at this ban, and in 1867 William Johnston, of Ballykilbeg, led 10,000 Orangemen in an illegal demonstration. Johnston was jailed and in the following year stood as an Independent in South Belfast where, with the support of the Liberals, he routed the Conservatives.[2]

Johnston was also supported by the United Protestant Workingmen's Association of Ulster,[3] and at Westminster he was the only Ulster Conservative MP to back measures such as the Ballot Act.

It was for this vague association with reforming causes that a vote of condolence was passed at Belfast Trades Council on his death.[4] However, Johnston's reputation stemmed principally from his identification with popular Orangeism, an enthusiasm maintained by coups such as a visit to Canada from which he returned with a Mohican chief suitably converted to the Orange cause.[5] Johnston was no radical, even within the Orange and Conservative context. He helped reunite the supporters of the Protestant Workingmen's Association and the traditional Conservative organisation in the early 1870s on the basis of an agreement by which one of the two Belfast seats should go to a representative of the Conservative working classes and the other to a representative of the employers. In 1878 Johnston was saved from bankruptcy when he received minor Ministerial office under Disraeli, and he returned the favour in the resulting by-election by betraying his former supporters and backing the candidature of William Ewart, an employer.[6] Hence, from the late 1870s it was left to others to take up the cause of Orange dissidence. Prominent amongst these was Dr Richard O'Kane, a Belfast clergyman who helped to whip up the first great anti-Land League scare in the early 1880s. In terms of the size and status of the Orange Order, O'Kane's tactics were successful. His views were at first derided by the establishment but by the time Randolph Churchill spoke of 'playing the Orange card' in 1886 the establishment was flocking to the Orange Order. In the last years of his life Dr O'Kane voiced doubts that these developments had actually served the Protestant working class. He asked in 1898 whether 'there are not other ways of killing Home Rule besides the rough and rather barbarous way of killing at the same time the loyalty and confidence of their [the Government's] own supporters'.[7]

Working-class Protestant militants did not learn from these experiences quickly. In 1902 the issues which divided them from the ascendancy were still ones of sectarian purity. They condemned Balfour's Irish policy of 'amelioration' as pro-Papist; they protested against the banning of a demonstration at Rostrevor; they rejoiced when Horace Plunkett, a founder of the co-operative movement and progressive Unionist, was defeated in South County Dublin; and they demanded the inclusion of provision for the inspection of convent laundries in a Government Bill. It was from the last, unlikely, issue that schism developed.

At the Twelfth of July demonstration in 1902 disaffected members of the Orange Order heckled Colonel Edward Saunderson MP, the

Grand Master, on the issue of convent laundries.[8] The attack was hardly entirely spontaneous, led as it was by one Thomas Sloan who actually climbed onto the platform. Sloan had a substantial track record, first as an evangelical preacher at lunchtime meetings in the Harland and Wolff shipyard, but latterly as the main speaker for the Belfast Protestant Association at the Custom House steps, a role he had taken over following the jailing of Arthur Trew for incitement to riot in 1901.[9]

Tensions arising from the 'Twelfth' incident might well have died down if it had not been for the death almost immediately afterwards of William Johnston, the hero of '68 and MP for South Belfast. In so far as there was a citadel of Orange 'democracy', this was where it was to be found, and Thomas Sloan was soon tempted to allow his name to go forward in opposition to the official Conservative candidate. In a curious re-echo of Johnston's famous campaign in 1868, it seems highly probable that Sloan received the secret support of the Ulster Liberals, now led by William Pirrie, himself a significant defector from Conservative ranks.[10]

There was very little of radicalism in Sloan's campaign. He set out to assume the mantle of William Johnston and announced that he was 'prepared to go through again the Battle of the Boyne'.[11] He did have to raise some of the social issues which concerned his working-class supporters, and was soon denounced by the mill owner William Ewart as 'a socialist'.[12] True, he represented himself as a worker and has subsequently been portrayed as such, but he could more properly be described as a small subcontractor engaged in the cementing of ships' floors, or, as the *Northern Whig* put it, 'he is a worker himself, and employs other workmen'.[13] The Trades Council did discuss the possibility of endorsing him, but was dissuaded by the evident dominance of his sectarian views over any concern for labour issues.[14]

Now in 1902 the Conservative candidate Charles Dunbar-Buller faced a trail of wrecked meetings, and Sloan won a convincing victory. From that point on, a bitter war within the Orange movement became inevitable as the existing Orange and Conservative leadership sought to isolate what they viewed as a dangerous renegade. In October 1902 Sloan was suspended from the Order for two years; in June 1903 his appeal was rejected and six lodges which had supported him had their warrants withdrawn. The dissidents had failed to hold their own within the Order, but those who had secured their expulsion soon had little cause for celebration. A few days later, on 11 June 1903, 8,000 people attended a mass meeting at which the breakaway Independent Orange Order was formally established.[15]

In order to justify its separate existence, the Independent Orange Order required a greater motive force than the dregs of sectarian controversy. All too often the Orange and Conservative leadership had proved willing to capitulate to popular demands on sectarian issues. Indeed it soon turned out that Colonel Saunderson had, in fact, supported the inspection of convent laundries, and in 1903 Sloan and Saunderson together requested legislation on the issue.[16]

The creation of the Independent Orange Order made necessary a clear statement of the full demands of Protestant workers, including their attitude on social questions, and it was here that the old Orange establishment could not give an inch. Thus it was in this field that the Independent Orange Order began to establish its separate identity. In 1904 it published *Orangeism, its History and Progress: A Plea for First Principles*. This attempted to give Orange radicalism a basis of tradition by emphasising the more progressive aspects of the work of Johnston and O'Kane, a task possible only through highly selective quotation. Although there were clear factual difficulties in creating retrospectively a 'golden age' of Orange radicalism out of such material, the actual analysis of what had happened to the Orange Order in the 1880s and 1890s was acute enough. The Independents argued that 'in 1880 and succeeding years, numbers joined the Orange Order as offering a vantage ground from which to fight the Land League and protect their lives and properties'. These new recruits, who 'had been openly hostile to Orangeism in former times had only one clause in their Orange creed – "the existing rights of property"'.[17]

The 1904 document argued effectively the case of the Protestant 'democracy' against the Protestant ascendancy, but this theme rested uneasily alongside a crudely stated defence of Protestant supremacy in every field. In line with this, the political objectives of the Independent Orange Order were to be expressed through an 'Independent Protestant Parliamentary Party'.[18]

One man, Lindsay Crawford, was responsible for carrying the Independent Orange Order beyond this confused position. Born in Lisburn in 1878, he moved to Dublin and in 1904 was editor of the *Ulster Protestant*.[19] Crawford realised that any successful campaign for independent Protestant working-class representation was bound to introduce an element of political instability in the north, and that in that situation the Catholic community simply could not be ignored. Protestant radicals had to accept that there were social demands held in common by Orangemen and Nationalists, and that if necessary they could ally to wrest basic reforms from the government. Crawford did not argue this merely for tactical reasons. Working in Dublin he became friendly with Owen Sheehy Skeffington and other Nationalists and, if he did not immediately become a convert to Nationalism, developed a far greater understanding of its secular advocates. With his strong Orange background, he was acutely aware of the enormous difficulties in creating a basis for co-operation between Orangemen and Nationalists in the face of the close links between Catholic clericalism and Nationalist politics. He hoped, by edging the Independent Orange Order in a more truly independent direction, to strengthen the secular forces within the existing Nationalist movement.

His opportunity came in his year of office as Grand Master of the Independents in 1905. In June of that year a sub-committee of five was set up to produce a constructive policy for the institution.[20] The manifesto was written by Crawford and signed by four members of the committee, including Tom Sloan.[21] It appeared without warning at the Independent demonstration held at Magheramorne on 13 July 1905,[22] hence the name, *Magheramorne Manifesto*.

It was indeed a remarkable document. It opened on the traditional theme of the Battle of the Boyne, but with a very new interpretation of its relevance, saying:

> The Anniversary of the Battle of the Boyne seems to us a fitting opportunity to address our countrymen – both Protestant and Catholic. . . [the Independents stood] once more on the banks of the Boyne, not as victors in the fight, nor to applaud the noble deeds of our ancestors, but to bridge the gulf that has so long divided Ireland into hostile camps, and to hold out the right hand of fellowship to those who, while worshipping at other shrines, are yet our countrymen, bone of our bone, flesh of our flesh.

King William's victory was interpreted not as a victory for Protestantism but as a victory for modern ideas on democracy and justice, and a Nationalist historian was quoted to prove the point. The Catholic Church was attacked not because it was enthusiastic about Nationalism but rather because it had always proved the worst enemy of all that was best in Irish Nationalism.

The position of Northern Protestants without property was summed up with brutal clarity: 'No people suffered more at the hands of landlords than the Protestant tenant farmers, and none have done more to rivet the chain around their own necks by the return to Parliament of landlord representatives.' Clear conclusions were drawn from this. The Independents no longer trusted either of the English parties 'on any of the questions that divide Ireland... [thus it was] high time that Irish Protestants should reconsider their position as Irish citizens and their attitude towards their Roman Catholic countrymen; and that the latter should choose once and for all between nationality and sectarianism. Both should reconsider their positions, and in their common trials unite on a true basis of nationality.'

The *Magheramorne Manifesto* was not universally greeted as a progressive document and was, for example, condemned by the *Irish News* as the 'cloven foot of militant Orangeism'.[23] The *Irish News* could hardly support a manifesto which called for a diminished role for the Catholic clergy in Irish life; the paper was, in any case, responding to the known past associations of the Independent Order. However, in the manifesto the call for a reassessment by Protestants of their position was not made dependent on the adoption of secular attitudes by Catholics although the latter development was seen as highly desirable. In any case, the document called into question what had been the fundamental certainties of militant Orangeism in the previous years, a point soon recognised by young Nationalist idealists like the Sinn Feiner Patrick McCartan who wrote to veteran Fenian Joseph McGarrity in New York in October 1905, saying of the Independents, 'they have taken a long stride in the right direction. They see the interests of Ireland and those of England are opposed to each other, that the interests of Irish Protestants and Irish Catholics are identical. They appeal to join hands across the Boyne. They are democratic. But they are yet Unionist.'[24]

The *Manifesto* also ran quite counter to contemporary developments in Unionist politics. Earlier in the year the Ulster Unionist Council had been formed, committed to an aggressive stance at Westminster and to militant Protestant mobilisation at home. The Independents had at the time dismissed the development as being of little significance, but in the *Manifesto* they made it clear that they intended to forego competition with the new Unionist leadership in stirring up traditional sectarian gut feeling, and instead were offering leadership in quite another direction.

The methods employed to introduce the *Manifesto* to the Independents themselves indicated that Crawford was well aware of its controversial nature and hoped to minimise subsequent damage. As one critic put it, it was 'surrounded by plenty of Protestant padding';[25] and in speeches over the 'Twelfth' both Crawford and Sloan condemned the selection of Denis Henry KC, a Catholic, as Unionist candidate for North Tyrone, while more generally traditional Orange rhetoric flowed alongside the new radical plan.[26] This, in turn, had hardly yet been discussed; when finally considered by the Grand Lodge it was approved with one vote against. The members, however, provided valid comment on the undemocratic tactics used in introducing it by voting to change their rules of procedure to ensure that no document could in future be introduced to the Order without full prior discussion.[27]

There were also demands from the rank and file for fuller debate and these led to a mass meeting in Belfast, attended by more than 1,000 members. Here too the storm was weathered with only a few dissenting voices raised.[28] What remained to be seen was how the Independents would fare now that they were clearly linked to the *Manifesto*.

It has indeed been argued that the *Manifesto* was of little more general significance because the Independents ceased to be a significant force soon after its introduction.[29] This is a view apparently borne out by Thomas Carnduff, a former Belfast Protestant Association member and later an Independent, who recalled that 'bickerings amongst the members in regard to the *Manifesto* brought the progress of the movement to a standstill', while at the same time 'the fierce opposition of the parent order was beginning to wean the weaker individual members from its ranks'. Yet Carnduff was writing many years later, with benefit of a hindsight also available to present-day historians. The Independents were, in fact, far from finished as a significant force, and Carnduff himself was one of those who enthusiastically supported Crawford's strategy.[30]

The immediate outlook was certainly unpromising because, in the months leading up to the January 1906 General Election, a more serious test of organisational allegiance to the principles of the *Manifesto* was to occur. This centred round Thomas Sloan who, as the Independents' only MP, had, in South Belfast and more particularly Sandy Row, the most evident power base within the Order. He was a man whose politics were instinctively those of Protestant populism and, while at times he voiced working-class resentment against the ruling Conservative oligarchy in Belfast, he was soon prepared to co-operate with their MPs at Westminster. Now, with an election approaching, he sought to retreat to the safe ground of straightforward Unionism. Clearly, the *Manifesto* was a millstone round his neck in any such movement and he soon dissociated himself from those parts of the document which 'opposed the settled policy of the Unionist Party in Ulster'. He went further, agreeing to 'loyally co-operate' with Unionist members, not just on matters related to the Union but 'on the general policy of the Party', and finally he announced his intention of appearing on the platform at a Unionist rally in the Ulster Hall. He hoped as a result of this to be allowed an unopposed return in South Belfast.[31]

It was a form of backsliding which faced the Independents with grave difficulties. How could they discipline their most prominent leader in Belfast when he above all justified his actions in the rhetoric of Orangeism? It was a problem rapidly resolved by direct action from the rank and file, itself evidence of support for Crawford's strategy. The Ulster Hall rally, which Sloan had intended as the occasion for his re-entry to the Unionist ranks, was disrupted by Independents and Walkerites,[32] and the Unionists, already none too keen to allow Sloan within their fold, were thus provided with the perfect excuse to oppose him at the election.

Sloan now had to fall back on his Independent support but, to ensure that he got it, he had to accept the censure of the Grand Lodge and withdraw his pledges to the Conservatives.[33] As it turned out, he had underestimated the independence of his electorate and easily retained his seat.

Although Sloan was still no true convert to Crawford's views, the latter's position was unassailable in early 1906, a reflection of successes elsewhere, in spite of the *Manifesto*. T.W. Russell and R.W. Glendinning, at the time non-party candidates but soon to become Liberals, won rural seats in the 1906 election, largely on land reform issues. Glendinning's victory in North Antrim was particularly significant because the Independents played a crucial part in the campaign and, in so doing, helped secure the defeat of one of the leaders of the new Unionism, William Moore.[34] Such victories renewed confidence and over the Twelfth of July period Independent demonstrations were not only well attended[35] but had the *Magheramorne Manifesto* as a major feature of speeches. Crawford's growing importance was recognised in other quarters. In September 1906 he was appointed editor of the Ulster Liberal paper *Ulster Guardian*.[36] Lord Pirrie, now the backbone of the revitalised Ulster Liberal Party, saw Crawford as the ideal recruiting agent to win Protestant workers for the Liberals. Another development, signifying the apparent strength of Crawford in the Order, was the change in its relationship with the extreme Belfast Protestant Association. In 1905 the BPA still acted virtually as the electoral arm of the Independent Orange Order[37] but after the victories of Sloan and Joe Devlin in the 1906 General Election BPA members stoned the Independent Hall in Great Victoria Street.[38] By early 1907 it was a disciplinary offence for an Independent member to belong to the BPA.[39]

There was no evidence of organisational decline and by 1906 the Independents could count upon sixty-five lodges, twenty-five of these in Belfast and the vast majority of the remainder in County Antrim.[40] They represented a strong new undercurrent in Protestant working-class life which could prove to the advantage of Labour in any crisis. Crawford at least had attempted to make the membership face up to wider political realities in a way that often contrasted with the abject narrowness of outlook of some of the Labour leaders.

Nevertheless, the Independents were in no way formally organised in the labour arena, and they were still weak beyond the main areas in which their original breakaway had occurred, a point of which they were forcibly reminded in November 1906 when Crawford contested a by-election in North Armagh, formerly the seat of Colonel Saunderson, an old adversary of the Independents. Any hopes of storming this citadel of the 'old Order' were quickly dismissed in flurries of stones as Crawford's meetings were systematically smashed up. A heavy defeat ensued.[41]

Catholic politics in the years leading up to 1907 had also undergone an upheaval. However, although important issues were involved, this was basically a contest within the leadership of the community, rather than a challenge by Catholic workers to the nature of that leadership.

In the 1890s Catholic politics had reflected the political demoralisation of the community following the successive defeats of two Home Rule Bills and the Parnellite split. Nationalist activists in the city were, as elsewhere, divided by the Parnell issue, and the Catholic hierarchy, which had intervened decisively in that dispute, had assumed control of the community's principal newspaper, the *Irish News*, and of its political expression, through the Catholic Representation Association, directly headed by Bishop Henry.

The main emphasis of the association was on securing Catholic rights within the city, and in this field a notable success was achieved in 1896 with the reorganisation of ward boundaries to provide for the almost automatic election of eight Catholic councillors in the new wards of Falls and Smithfield. Political activists had assisted in this campaign; thus the young Joseph Devlin, a former barman, was a member of the CRA committee and helped to draft its case for the creation of the new wards. Disagreement now arose over the consequences of the victory, which was viewed by Bishop Henry as an opportunity for the extension of clerical patronage in the political field and the pursuit on a wider scale of a highly parochial Catholic conservatism.

Devlin and others had hoped that the availability of the new council seats would provide the opportunity for a more democratic and outward-looking Nationalism. The overbearing approach of Bishop Henry soon brought about an alliance under Devlin's chairmanship of former Parnellites and anti-Parnellites to contest the CRA's dominance.

It was a battle carried on with increasing bitterness until 1905. Devlin's position was strengthened by the formation in 1899 of the United Ireland League which became the basis of the reorganised Irish Party under John Redmond in 1903. Devlin was now able to portray himself as a key figure in a national movement, and yet in 1904 the CRA still held the upper hand in the council elections, a superiority retained through its control of electoral registers and the ruthless use of episcopal patronage within the Catholic community.

Devlin's ultimate victory in the battle for control came about in 1905, not because of the triumph of a new elite over an old one but rather because, in the context of the Nationalist politics of the time, Bishop Henry's stance had become an embarrassing anachronism even to erstwhile supporters. His defeat was heralded by a challenge from twenty-two of his own priests, condemnation from Archbishop Walsh and the defection of that key section of Belfast's small Catholic business class the Licensed Vintners' Association. It was for these reasons that the CRA was dissolved in May 1905 and, although a fanatical rump of Henryites continued as the Catholic Defence Association, Devlin captured the old machine largely intact.

From the beginning Devlin was aware that he had to work with the highly conservative elements once to the fore in the CRA. Hence he avoided too close an association with atheistic socialism or secular liberalism, but at the same time he understood well the needs of his working-class supporters and accordingly held relatively progressive views on labour issues and favoured most liberal social legislation. His underlying strategy was to maximise the pan-Catholic vote in West Belfast, and his undoubted efficiency in doing so tended to stifle any alternative developments in Catholic working-class politics.

Devlin's relations with other political forces outside the Catholic ghettos were again largely determined by pragmatic factors. The West Belfast seat, even with a united Catholic vote, hung on a knife edge in terms of a purely sectarian head count. In 1906, therefore, Devlin was prepared to see himself characterised as one leaf of the three-leaf clover of opposition in the Belfast seats,[42] no matter that the other two leaves, Walker and Sloan, were bitterly opposed to Home Rule. Devlin approached Protestant members of the Trades Council to solicit votes for him.[43] The wrecking candidature of A.M. Carlisle, put forward by the Liberals to win Protestant votes from the Unionist, assisted him, but the Unionist papers reckoned that Devlin gained directly at least 200 Protestant or 'Sloanite' votes.[44]

Devlin's weekly paper, the *Northern Star*, showed a rather different face. It represented the worst of the gut politics on which Devlin depended in his West Belfast base. Militant Labour might well have taken offence from these words on socialism and trade unionism: 'Catholics cannot be socialists. That is certain; they must choose between the Catholic Church and socialism, and if the trade unions are to become socialist organisations then every Catholic must choose between his trade union and his Church.'[45] The paper was viciously sectarian and carried anti-Protestant articles each week. Thus, on 3 August, readers were offered an article headlined:

THE RELIGION OF THE MUCK-RAKE.
PROTESTANTISM FEEDS GREEDILY ON GARBAGE.
CHRISTIAN (?) LITERATURE DOING THE DEVIL'S WORK.

Each week there was a proselytising article entitled 'Why I became a Catholic', by some suitable convert.

The paper was not only sectarian, it reflected strongly a shopkeeper, small businessman mentality in articles like 'How Millionaires Have Made their Money: Wise Words to Readers on Increasing Their Incomes'. Here wealth was gloried, as in the passage, 'The pleasure of seeing the banking account and the income that is started from practically nothing grow day by day until it reaches colossal proportions is a pleasure that must fascinate all.'[46]

The only group which in any way represented radical opposition to Devlin was the organisation of Dungannon Clubs. Named after the Dungannon Convention of Irish Volunteers in 1782, the movement was set up in March 1905 by Bulmer Hobson, a young Quaker. Hobson was just one of a number of middle-class Protestants idealistically attracted by Nationalism in the period. In 1900, with William McDonald, he had formed the Protestant National Society and then the Ulster Literary Theatre. They made little effort to link their romantic idealism to concrete working-class interests, and were numerically insignificant. In Belfast the Dungannon Clubs had from forty to fifty members. For six months they published a paper, the *Republic*, but ran out of money.[47]

Bulmer Hobson and his associates did not differ from Devlin on social policy, and later in the decade Hobson was to prove a bitter enemy of Connolly, Larkin and the labour movement in the south. Disagreements with Devlin arose over Home Rule or independence and how to achieve it. Devlin wanted to achieve Home Rule through the British parliamentary system; the Dungannon Clubs supported abstentionism and ultimately a republic and were to merge with Sinn Fein in 1908.

5
The battle begins

Whatever the complexities and difficulties of Belfast as an arena for the labour organiser, it did not take Larkin long to make an impression. He went first to the work he knew well – the holding of street-corner meetings at those points where casual dockers assembled each day to seek employment. No record of those early speeches remains, but years afterwards men remembered the impact of Larkin's words. William Long, who first heard him in Corporation Square, recalled 'as fine a speech as ever I had or as ever I heard', while Joseph Cooper summed up his feeling thus: 'half a dozen words from Jim Larkin and you were all together'.[1]

Soon there was tangible evidence of progress. By 16 February Larkin had recruited 400 men to the NUDL;[2] in March he organised a conference on the problems of the dockers.[3] By April union membership had topped the 2,000 mark,[4] and separate offices had been established for members at the deep-sea docks and the cross-channel quays.[5] On 4 April this breadth of organisation was reflected when Larkin and four other delegates, John Quinn, Walter Savage, John Morrow and John Davidson, representing the various sections of the trade, presented their credentials to the Trades Council.[6] By the end of the month these developments were sufficiently remarkable to attract the interest of the press – the *Belfast News-Letter* noted 'there is a movement on foot amongst all the dock labourers to join the Docker's Union',[7] and police reports went further, suggesting that 2,978 dock labourers had joined and that the infection was spreading to the 1,500 carters.[8]

What of Larkin's immediate impact on the existing labour movement in the city? On the face of it, there was little that was evidently controversial in his message; thus Larkin, like the other labour leaders in the city, accepted the distinction between politics and trade-union activity, arguing that 'along with the purely industrial side of the trade-union system they ought to have a purely political side'.[9] So he provided firm support for William Walker in his North Belfast by-election campaign in April, with the cry 'their watchword should be Walker – London',[10] and his first arrest in Belfast took place following a fracas at the count in the City Hall, where he was much to the fore amongst Walker's supporters.[11] Larkin further confirmed his credentials with local labour activists during a hard-fought English by-election campaign in Jarrow in June and July when he backed the Labour candidate, Pete Curran, against an Irish Nationalist. Indeed, at the time it was suggested that Larkin could assist in punishing the Nationalists by becoming a prospective Labour candidate in West Belfast against Joseph Devlin.[12] Larkin, however, was not to be tempted into arousing unnecessary antagonisms and, in any case, accepted the prevailing Trades Council policy of supporting candidates providing they were reliable on non-political matters, whatever their other politics. This was the basis on which the Trades Council had endorsed Joseph Devlin in the 1906 general election, and on which Larkin now argued that 'Mr. Devlin was a working-class member and he was determined to maintain his hold on the constituency';[13] and it was in the same context that Larkin saw no difficulty in recruiting Michael McKeown as Secretary of the new NUDL branch, in spite of his position as a United Ireland League councillor on the Corporation.

If there was an immediate difference between Larkin and others, it was that he pushed the cause of independent labour representation with a new purism and indeed optimism, and there were soon indications that this could lead to tensions in significant quarters. In March an aldermanic by-election arose in Dock Ward, at the centre of the area in which the NUDL was now organising. The Trades Council decided not to contest the vacancy, but Larkin persuaded John Murphy, Secretary of the Council, to contest the seat for Labour with the support of the NUDL. Both Robert Greig, President of the Trades Council and local organiser of the National Amalgamated Union of Labour, and Alex Boyd, organiser of the Municipal Employees, wrote letters to the press supporting the Conservative candidate. Boyd at least was subsequently censured by the Trades Council.[14] So the representatives of the only two existing unions with significant unskilled membership made their stand against the assertiveness of the new union. In doing so they illustrated that unskilled organisation in the city had until then been achieved only in restricted areas, under the tutelage and within the perspectives of the older and more conservative skilled unions.

Both Greig and Boyd were soon to be affected in different ways by the sea change that Larkin was bringing about in the aspirations of the unskilled generally. By April, groups of workers quite outside the realm of the docks were approaching Larkin for advice. Larkin, already heavily committed with the dockers, could not take on others, but it was already evident that his message, well understood in an English context, was having far-reaching effects in Belfast. At the same time, employers were aware of what was going on and, dependent on cheap unskilled labour and unused to the very concept of unskilled unions, had no inclination to compromise.

All these factors were revealed in the first skirmish of the coming battle. On 26 April unskilled workers at the Sirocco Engineering Works struck for more pay.[15] The men were not even union members and, although there is no evidence that Larkin was in any way directly involved, it seems possible that Thomas Johnston, with whom he had close contact, may have offered encouragement.[16] Certainly this was not forthcoming from Robert Greig of NAUL, the most appropriate union for these workers – he now argued that 'they had been unorganised and therefore could not obtain the benefits of the Society'.[17]

The Trades Council was equally unhelpful. John Murphy, the Secretary, did write to Samuel Davidson, the employer, but in terms that virtually conceded defeat, saying, 'your men acted most unwisely in leaving before giving your firm a reasonable opportunity to consider their grievances, real or imaginary'.[18]

Davidson's response was indeed uncompromising; he viewed the men's action as 'a sort of spring cleaning, but the carpets now out in the open air will not be brought back', and he also threatened to transfer the works to Germany.[19] Such was the attitude in a firm described by the *Northern Whig* on 29 April as 'more like a big family party than an industrial concern'. The strike collapsed by 1 May with all the men, except the ringleaders, allowed back, provided that they agreed not to join a union.[20] The document the men had to sign was characteristic of others that were to appear in the coming months:

> I the undersigned am now entering the employment of Davidson and Co. Ltd., Sirocco Works, and hereby undertake to cancel my membership with any Labourers' Society or any Union of which I am a member, and that so long as I am employed by the firm of Davidson and Co. Ltd., I will not join any Labourers' Society or Union.[21]

The strike had received considerable attention in the press because of the wider agitation amongst the unskilled – in the words of the *Belfast News-Letter*, it was feared that 'all supplies and all shipments [to Sirocco] would be stopped by a combination of unskilled labour in the city'.[22] It may be that hopes of this kind had encouraged the strikers, but while the older unions were unwilling to intervene, Larkin was in no position to take premature action as his priority was to strengthen and consolidate the NUDL's base at the docks. However, even as the Sirocco dispute came to an end, the dockers were getting involved on their own account.

At Kelly's coal quay, Samuel Kelly attempted to dismiss union members on 26 April. In response, almost his entire workforce walked off the job. Kelly stated very clearly the prevailing view of Belfast's employers when he said, 'the situation at issue had no reference to wages whatsoever; it was merely as to whether the dockers should associate themselves with a union which he considered should not embrace such a class of employment'.[23]

Meanwhile the cross-channel shipping companies were making their own preparations. At the end of April, W. Chambers, the Secretary of the Ulster District Office of the Shipping Federation, had written to his London headquarters. The wording of that letter is not known but the reply makes it clear that representatives of the Belfast shipping companies had met in anticipation of a dispute:

> Dear Sir,
> I am in receipt of your letter of yesterday reporting the result of your committee meeting in reference to the conditions of local labour. As you appear to anticipate a local dispute, we are sending through on Monday (6th May) Mr Irving our general Labour superintendent who will thoroughly investigate the situation, and we shall then be prepared to act immediately should the necessity arise.
>
> Yours faithfully,
> Michael Brett (Secretary)[24]

This pre-emptive arrangement of support by the Belfast shipping companies was no small matter. The Shipping Federation had practical experience in organising armies of blacklegs throughout western Europe wherever need might arise.[25] As the hostilities were opening in Belfast, thousands of Shipping Federation blacklegs were finishing off a mass strike in Hamburg.[26] Later in the year, the same organisation was to be bloodily engaged on the streets of Antwerp.[27]

The opportunity for springing the trap in Belfast did not take long to arise and stemmed from the euphoric enthusiasm of the men for their new union. It was on 6 May that Thomas Cupples, one of the union delegates, approached the foreman on the Belfast Steamship Company ship SS *Optic*, to complain about the refusal of one 'Mug' Magowan to join the union, and about his abusive behaviour. When there was no response the union men walked out on strike.[28]

They had chosen an unfortunate target. The Chairman of the Belfast Steamship Company was Thomas Gallaher, one of the city's best known self-made men, Belfast's 'tobacco king', who had made Gallaher a household name throughout the United Kingdom. Like many such men of his generation, he was devoted to his work and, although a supporter of charities,[29] was unlikely to be amenable to any arguments of public interest relating to his own firm. He was a firm Unionist in politics,[30] not that this necessarily affected his attitude to his employees. For them he was not just 'king' by reputation, he expected unswerving loyalty and viewed any effort by the unskilled to organise as a direct assault on the principles on which industrial success was founded. He was to be cruelly affronted by the suggestion that he was anything other than a good employer, but his attitudes were to make him an able and bitter opponent of the dockers.

Larkin immediately recognised that a serious tactical error had been made by his men, and took immediate steps to try to rescue the situation, first with the men and then with the Belfast Steamship Company's legal representative, Alex McDowell. As far as the men's action was concerned, he admitted 'this was a mistake' and accordingly he immediately 'instructed the men to return to work'. He suggested to McDowell that the matter could be settled 'amicably', although he also warned that 'in the present feverish condition of the men, in consequence of the Kelly lockout the troubles might extend to other ports'. McDowell might well have taken this as a threat to the Belfast Steamship Company's operations in Liverpool, also the NUDL base, but Larkin made it clear that this was what he wished to avoid.[31] After meeting McDowell, Larkin again met the men and sent Michael McKeown back to McDowell with a message confirming that the men would definitely return to work. According to Larkin, McDowell 'after hearing Mr McKeown's message did not condescend to reply to him'.[32]

It may at this point have been open to the men humbly to petition for return on their own behalf, the plight to which the workers at the Sirocco Works had been reduced a few days earlier. As one police report later put it, the Belfast Steamship Company 'was perfectly willing to treat with the men directly. . . but would not recognise any outsider [i.e. union representative]'.[33] Recognition was the crux, and as far as Larkin was concerned, however unfavourable the circumstances, it had to be fought for. The era of humble petitioning was over.

There was still one possible compromise option, one that side-stepped the main issue, and this was for the men simply to return to work the following morning in the hope that no questions would be asked. Larkin's decision to adopt this approach indicated his anxiety to avoid conflict at this stage. It soon proved a forlorn hope.

The men reported for work on the morning of Wednesday 8 May and were confronted by the SS *Caloric*, docking from Liverpool with fifty-three blacklegs aboard.[34] Larkin's prior intelligence that the Shipping Federation had been considering an offensive against the union was now borne out. As he put it, 'we believe this matter has been forced upon us for the purpose of smashing the Dock Labourer's Union'.[35]

The Steamship Company soon had disturbing evidence that it was not going to be as easy as that. Another 140 of their men immediately walked out in sympathy with those already locked out. This reverse, although easily overcome with the importation of a further 100 blacklegs on the following day, was indicative of changed times.[36]

It was on this morning of 9 May that the employers discovered that the new union, far from being simply snuffed out like others before it, was a new and formidable adversary. Events began to move first at Kelly's coal quay, where the NUDL men, in spite of a temporary shift of attention to the Belfast Steamship Company, were still locked out, and blacklegs were also at work. Shortly after 9 am NUDL men advanced on them:

> The carters and fillers at work on the quay were first tackled, and compelled to cease work. Some of the latter attempted to seek the shelter of the boat, and rushed for the gangway, but were inter-

cepted and peremptorily ordered to leave the wharf. A warlike spirit was now rampant – the men on the boat continued their work despite cries of 'come to — out of that' – and then from all quarters, stones and lumps of coal were hurled at them. Many of the missiles fell with ominous thuds on the bridge of the vessel and others thrown with unerring aim, found their way into the holds, and fell among the labourers, causing them to scatter in all directions.[37]

After this triumph, the union men crossed the river to the Belfast Steamship Company sheds on Donegall Quay. They overwhelmed the Harbour Police, invaded the sheds and drove the blacklegs onto the boats. These men had already seen the fate of the other blacklegs at Kelly's, and had little appetite for resistance. After a tense parley with the NUDL men, they ceased work at 11.30 am.[38]

The strikers then held two mass meetings, one in Scrabo Street and the other in the Municipal Employees' Hall at 11 Victoria Street. The very availability of this meeting place indicated that Alex Boyd, organiser of the municipal workers, and only recently in dispute with the dockers, was one of the first of the existing union leaders in the city to recognise the importance of the dockers' fight. At the meeting held there, reformed blacklegs were the prize exhibits. They had been recruited in Liverpool and offered one pound ten shillings a week with one shilling per hour overtime after 6 pm. Now in the strikers' hands, they did their best to present their experiences in an innocent and unjustifiably heroic light:

> I arrived here on Wednesday morning and when I landed I found there was a strike on. I did my best to get away then, but the police were there, and I had to wait for an opportunity to get away. I didn't do a stroke of work, and there were a whole lot more like me. We were kept like men in a prison. We could have gone ashore but at our own risk. The gates were barred and we could not get out. At one o'clock today I saw my opportunity and came away with three others.

The union was intent on making the maximum capital out of such defections, and that night when all the blacklegs departed for Liverpool, having downed tools, they were serenaded by strikers accompanied by the Ravenhill Amateur Flute and Drum Band.[39]

The events of 9 May were too much for Sam Kelly. The next day he capitulated, giving recognition to the NUDL, and granting pay increases ranging from sixpence to five shillings a week. A victory march followed, headed by a man with a Union Jack, and as the NUDL men passed the offices of the bitterly anti-trade-union *Belfast Evening Telegraph* they sang 'Britons never shall be slaves'. The nature of the march was a reminder that the men at the coal quays and the cross-channel quays were Protestants almost to a man and certainly no disloyalists.[40] Events such as these were soon a matter for wider concern, and the Lord Mayor, Lord Shaftesbury, reflected a widespread view that the situation should not be allowed to deteriorate further when he took steps to contact the NUDL on 13 May. He was agreeably surprised when Larkin assured him that the union would be glad to put the issue to arbitration.[41]

Now Gallaher showed his hand, making it clear that he would not negotiate – not for him any petty short-term considerations. He was engaged in a wider struggle against trade unionism and socialism. In this he was supported by the *Belfast News-Letter* which, in an editorial on 13 May, called for the use of force by the police, echoing Gallaher's cry that 'what we think we have a right to complain of is a lack of police protection'.

Larkin replied in kind, assailing Gallaher as 'an obscene scoundrel' and adding that 'although St. Patrick was credited with banishing the snakes, there was one he forgot and that was Gallaher – a man who valued neither country, God, nor creed'.[42] This was no isolated thrust made in the heat of the moment, for a few nights later Larkin told his supporters, 'the man they were fighting would not be hanged for no honest rope would do it'.[43]

Larkin had clearly concluded that no easy settlement was possible with Gallaher. His rhetoric served a number of functions – to isolate Gallaher, to warn other employers of the public pillorying they could expect if they allied with Gallaher, but perhaps above all to cement the morale of the NUDL men, now involved in their first major dispute, on which the survival of the union depended. Larkin's attacks certainly removed any remote possibility that may have existed of an amicable settlement, but they amazed and delighted his men, on whose morale any prolonged struggle depended.

The immediate point of confrontation remained the Belfast Steamship Company sheds at Donegall Quay. There fresh drafts of blacklegs now worked behind a regular cordon of between 175 and 300 members of the RIC.[44] The blacklegs were billeted at night on the

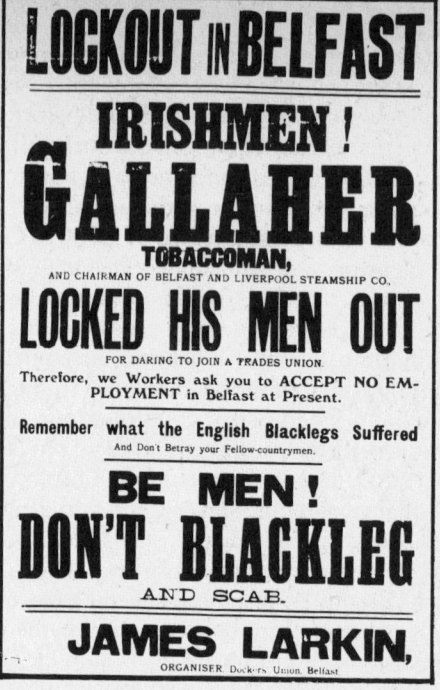

(Central Library, Belfast)

SS *Caloric*, but even here the company had to take extraordinary precautions – in the early days of the strike NUDL members had launched a seaborne attack on the ship, using hired boats. From then on, the SS *Caloric* steamed out each night to moor in relative safety in the middle of Belfast Lough, although each morning she had to run the gauntlet of the shipyards where the young William McMullen, later a significant labour leader himself, and other workers pelted her with 'an avalanche of rivets, nuts and bolts'.[45]

More legal methods were also used in an attempt to undermine the security of the blacklegs. Labour members of the Corporation raised the conditions of billeting at a meeting of the Public Health Committee. However, a subsequent inspection gave little satisfaction – the SS *Caloric* was licensed to accommodate 356 men and only 250 were aboard.[46]

Stalled at Donegall Quay, Larkin soon showed that he was prepared to move elsewhere. At lunchtime on 16 May he held a meeting in Earl Street, outside Gallaher's Tobacco Factory, and urged the mainly female workforce to join a union. In the afternoon his message was more far-reaching: 'there was a strike of quay labourers at New York and Montreal, and before long it was not improbable that there would be a general strike all over the United Kingdom'. Regardless of this wider message, his oratory was very clearly giving a new sense of power to the unskilled – that night police had to use batons to disperse a crowd of 2,000 in Corporation Street.[47]

Tension was immediately heightened on the following day with the news that Gallaher had set out to call what he saw as Larkin's bluff by dismissing seven girls from his tobacco factory for merely attending Larkin's lunchtime meeting the previous day. He also announced that 'he had arranged to start two additional factories in England where work could be done that is now done in Belfast'. Following this, 1,000 girls walked out of his factory and marched to the afternoon strike meeting in Corporation Square. Larkin accused Gallaher of 'white slavery' and at the end of the meeting the crowds did not disperse.[48] In the words of the police, 'later on in the evening their conduct became very bad. They commenced stone throwing and had to be dispersed several times by the police. A number of street lamps were broken and also the plate glass windows in five business establishments.'[49]

These disturbances were not in themselves particularly serious, but there were rumours, never substantiated, that shipyard workers were planning to march and assist the dockers in seizing the sheds at Donegall Quay.[50] In these circumstances, the Lord Mayor, Lord Shaftesbury, panicked and requisitioned 200 men of the Royal Sussex Regiment from Victoria Barracks 'for the purpose of preventing an apprehended attack'.[51]

The attack never materialised. Strikers marched past 'shouting and jeering, waving Union Jacks and flourishing sign boards adorned with the skull and cross bones and bearing the words "Down with Blacklegs"' but that was all.[52] The episode was nonetheless revealing – however unpopular Gallaher might be, he had sound tactical sense and could bring others into line. On 13 May he had rebuffed the Lord Mayor; now three days later the Lord Mayor was playing his game.

By any standards, the introduction of troops was premature. Barely 200 dockers were on strike, and the business and commercial classes were by no means convinced that confrontation was either necessary or desirable. This was a view forcibly expressed by the *Northern Whig* on the following day:

The bringing in of the military, as was done yesterday, we must regard as a serious mistake. There was no evidence that the resources of the police were exhausted. Unfortunately the appearance of the military on the streets of Belfast for such a purpose as this recalls memories which are not agreeable, and is apt to be an incentive to riot.

The military authorities were equally displeased – Brigadier-General Vesey Dawson, in charge of the northern garrison, protested to Dublin Castle, saying, 'in my opinion it is very undesirable that troops should be called out to do police duty in a town like Belfast' and adding that, in spite of Belfast's self-proclaimed reputation as a haven of law and order, this was the third time troops had been called out in a year.[53] The episode did much to discredit Lord Shaftesbury with Dublin Castle and was to have serious consequences for effective communication at a much more critical stage later in the year.

Yet the troops were there, and were to remain on duty, albeit often hidden behind the scenes, until September. That was one victory to Gallaher, and on 17 May he had further cause to celebrate – the girls from his tobacco factory had to return to work.[54] The NUDL could not take them on, nor apparently could any other union and, more to the point, no financial assistance was available to them from any source.

Even in the ranks of Labour, there were still reservations about the situation. This became evident on Saturday 18 May when William Walker, making his first appearance since his defeat in the North Belfast by-election, was positively conciliatory: 'Mr Gallaher never tried to pay less than the joiners' union stipulated should be paid, or to work longer hours than the maximum laid down. If Mr Gallaher could work harmoniously with joiners and members of skilled unions, surely there was nothing to prevent him doing the same with the dockers.'[55]

The most charitable interpretation of Walker's intervention is that he intended to direct attention away from Larkin's vitriolic attacks on Gallaher, but he certainly revealed how far he, as Labour's leading public spokesman, had failed to understand the difficulties faced by the new unskilled movement.

Even in early June there were others prepared to offer their services as intermediaries, such as Alderman George Doran, victor of the Dock Ward by-election in April. His intervention was no doubt self-interested in that his constituents were those most affected by the dispute, but it genuinely reflected conventional wisdom on how unskilled workers should seek redress. Doran wrote to the Lord Mayor, asking him to intervene once more because 'there are at the present moment thousands of wives and families who feel acutely the pinch of hunger and many a starving child is hushed to sleep without a pick of food'. Doran went on to assure the Lord Mayor that, if he could assist, 'I am sure the poor will thank you from the innermost portion of their hearts'.[56]

Michael McKeown's reply on behalf of the dockers rejected such maudlin and exaggerated pleading. He pointed out that some dockers were actually receiving more in strike pay than they had earned by casual labour – 'there are hundreds of men on the quays and docks of Belfast whose incomes in their normal state do not average the weekly allowance of the single, unencumbered man who gets ten shillings a week of locked out ailment'.[57]

Such exchanges, although devoid of any fruitful potential, reflected a lessening of tension in the weeks following the night of 16 May. This lull in the level of activity in turn arose from the success of the Belfast Steamship Company in protecting its blacklegs at Donegall Quay. The main potential for trouble now arose when groups of blacklegs broke the rules, laid down by the company for the men's own protection, and sought the pleasures of the town. William Long, a docker, later recalled chasing one such group – 'I never seen better running in my life... I don't think they tried it after.'[58]

Incidents of this kind had very little significance for the main battle over the working of the quays, but one was to have serious consequences for Larkin, and to lend new colour to the attempts of the employers generally to characterise him as a violent agitator. Pay day for the blacklegs was on Friday, and it was on Friday 31 May that ten blacklegs, including one Richard Bamber, made their way to the Stag's Head at the corner of North Street and Rosemary Street. As soon as drink was ordered they were confronted by dockers, and in the ensuing flight Bamber became separated from the others.

Bamber, now alone, proceeded down Waring Street towards the docks, but at the junction with Victoria Street he had to pass the strike headquarters. Some fifty dockers were gathered outside and, as Bamber attempted to pass, he was attacked. He drew a knife and stabbed three men. Larkin witnessed all this from an upper window and arrived on the scene at this critical point. He lifted a heavy stone and threw it, hitting Bamber on the head. Bamber, after a further running battle, was finally knocked senseless by a coalman's shovel in the appropriately named Tomb Street.

Both Larkin and Bamber were charged, but inevitably all public interest focused on Larkin, attention encouraged by Larkin's publicly-expressed view that Bamber had got what he deserved and a further allegation that Gallaher had offered £500 to any policeman who ensured a successful prosecution of Larkin.[59] Larkin's success in getting the case transferred to Dublin, on the grounds that he could not obtain an unprejudiced trial in Belfast,[60] delayed resolution of the matter until January 1908. It also laid him open to the accusation that he could secure special treatment while other arrested dockers had to face swift and painful justice in Belfast's magistrates courts.

In spite of the prosecution of Larkin and the successful defence of Donegall Quay, the operations of the Steamship Company were far from restored to normal. Usually, much of the firm's cargo work was handled outside Donegall Quay, but attempts to renew operations beyond its narrow confines had proved disastrous.

As early as 11 May the *Caloric* was moved to York Dock, but was repelled by fusillades of stones flung by dockers who clambered onto surrounding ships in spite of the efforts of 175 policemen.[61] The insecurity of operations at York Dock had been made more evident on the same day by a highly damaging fire, apparently caused maliciously, in a dockside shed adjacent to the Belfast Steamship Company ship the SS *Optic*.[62] Two days later, an attempt to unload the SS *Logic* at the Dublin Steampacket Quay had failed when dockers there simply refused to handle the ship.[63]

If tension had slackened at Donegall Quay because the Steamship Company was now impregnable there, the same was true at York Dock and elsewhere because the union had forced the company to curtail its activities. In this case Belfast Steamship Company could not look for effective assistance from the authorities. There were 1,000 RIC men in Belfast and, of these, between 175 and 300 were involved day by day at Donegall Quay. The provision of a further 175 men had proved inadequate to protect the SS *Caloric* at York Dock, and the police estimated that to protect this larger area would require 300 men, which would not leave adequate reserves to deal with any trouble elsewhere.[64]

This was a weakness on the employers' side soon to be put to a more general test for, as the weeks passed through May into a blazing June, there was no sign of the ferment amongst the dockers slackening.

The early success at Kelly's coal quay encouraged other coal-heavers, and on 11 June they put in a combined demand for an additional two shillings a week, giving a four-day ultimatum. Four firms capitulated immediately, and on 17 June the other firms gave in when 500 men refused to start work.[65] On Friday 14 June it was the turn of the Dublin Steamship Company and a short-lived strike brought dockers an increase of a penny an hour.[66] Five days later, men at the Antrim Iron Ore Company followed suit, winning 'a substantial increase' and, as some of their men had already benefited by the coal settlement, they were in the enviable position of receiving two increases in a week.[67]

It was obviously in the interests of the NUDL to standardise these demands, and the continuing stalemate with the Belfast Steamship Company provided an added incentive to do so. If the NUDL could establish its position firmly in the rest of the port, it would be the Belfast Steamship Company which would be left isolated, rather than its locked-out employees. Encouragement to hold out on Donegall Quay had already come from two key quarters, with official backing for the dispute from NUDL headquarters on 30 May[68] followed by the full support of the Trades Council on 6 June.[69]

A further encouraging element in the situation, from Larkin's point of view, was that further disputes were developing spontaneously in areas far beyond his organisation. On 11 June sailors and firemen employed by local firms in the coastal trade presented an ultimatum to their employers,[70] and by 18 June men on Head Line ships were on strike and others were threatening to come out.[71] Meanwhile another major dispute, initially unrelated to the dockers' strike, threatened to have a significant impact on the developing situation. On 31 May 500 ironmoulders struck for a two-shillings-a-week increase[72] and by 27 June their action had led to the laying-off of 3,000 to 4,000 men in the shipbuilding and engineering industries.[73] The workforce in the shipyards had already shown sympathy with the striking dockers, at this stage principally their coreligionists, whether by showering passing ships with 'shipyard confetti' or by works collections. Now a large and discontented mass of men from the yards, already noted for its fighting reputation, was thrown onto the streets just as matters began to reach a new level of crisis in the docks dispute.

6
General strike

Further escalation in the dockers' dispute was not long in coming. On 20 June the NUDL submitted a claim to all the cross-channel shipping companies. Now, in addition to recognition, the union was demanding a minimum wage of twenty-seven shillings and sixpence and a reduction of the working week to sixty hours.[1]

What was the reasoning behind the new demand? To a substantial extent it represented a rationalisation of the spontaneous claims put forward by various groups of dockers in the preceding days, a rationalisation encouraged by Larkin. He may well have taken the view that the union could not sustain for ever the stalemate in which his men remained locked out by the Belfast Steamship Company. The only alternative was to widen the battlefront and to hope to deal with the Steamship Company in the context of a more far-reaching victory. Certainly, the long-term future of the union in Belfast depended on the achievement of widespread recognition.

From the point of view of the men and their representatives, the general demand of 20 June represented an entirely reasonable aspiration. As Michael McKeown put it, 'they asked only for what was conceded by the vast majority of employers, the right to organise, and that freedom of action that was the heritage of all men'.[2] However, the decision to take on all the cross-channel companies had implications stretching far beyond the quays of Belfast. This was evident simply in terms of the ownership of the various routes. The Fleetwood steamers were owned by the London and North Western Railway Company and the Lancashire and Yorkshire Railway, while the Midland Railway owned the Barrow and Heysham steamers.[3] The Belfast dockers were therefore taking on the great railway companies of the British mainland.

The next day, a meeting in Belfast gave the dockers a clear demonstration of their new-found opponents' attitude to labour relations. Members of the Amalgamated Society of Railway Servants were discussing the continued failure of the railway companies generally to grant recognition even to their own direct employees.

According to the visiting speaker, Mr W.G. Maunders, such rights as the ASRS enjoyed had since 1897 'been practically frittered away'. Six hundred ASRS delegates were due to meet in Birmingham on 24 and 25 June to consider industrial action, but there was no guarantee that this would take place. The local speaker, Robert Gageby, 'was glad to learn by the tone of Mr Maunders' statement that they did not anticipate a strike'.[4] Larkin, by contrast, may well have hoped that the dockers' action in Belfast would encourage more militant action by the ASRS.

For a brief period the importance of the dockers' challenge to the railway companies did not become apparent. The dockers did not immediately act on their demand that a reply be received by Friday 21 June, perhaps because Larkin was temporarily involved in other advances elsewhere. He was an active participant in the action by seamen employed by the smaller Belfast-based cross-channel and coastal cargo companies, and here the employers soon capitulated, granting increases of five shillings a month on 25 June.[5] It was a victory which added to Larkin's aura of invincible strength, and boosted the morale of his men on the docks who were about to face a far sterner test.

There were already straws in the wind with regard to the dockers' general demands. The *Northern Whig* reported on 24 June that the shipping companies were considering the claim 'to some extent at any rate in concert'. The following day the 'Labour World' correspondent of the *Belfast Evening Telegraph* suggested that they could be seeking to compromise by recognising the union as acting for casual workers but not for regular employees.

By that evening it became evident that the employers were, in fact, divided. Seven of the smaller firms were inclined to settle but, on the other hand, the Belfast Steamship Company had now won powerful allies in the great railway companies who refused to give way on the Barrow, Heysham and Fleetwood services. Resistance from this quarter now had to be faced.

On the morning of Wednesday 26 June all the dockers at the Heysham, Barrow and Fleetwood berths came out on strike, and there was soon new evidence of the seriousness of the situation when the Lord Mayor requisitioned 500 men of the Royal Sussex Regiment to guard the quays.[6] Cordons of armed soldiers stood shoulder to shoulder in front of the sheds, a presence maintained with additional dramatic flourishes. The *Belfast News-Letter* reported:

It really seemed as if military tactics were in active operation when one saw a corps of flag signallers and heliographers in constant communication with the Victoria Barracks. At the Custom House Steps the men were in touch by these means with a relay station at the harbour end of Corporation Square from whence transmission was simple on the direct line to the barracks in North Queen Street.[7]

All this was precautionary, thus once again the Lord Mayor had failed to meet the proper criteria for calling in troops. However, if there was no actual violence, there was soon a war of words and on 27 June the shipping companies stated bluntly that 'they were determined to fight to a finish'. They were now encouraged in doing so by the decision of the ASRS delegates in Birmingham the previous day not to take strike action on the recognition issue.[8] The railway companies in Belfast hammered the point home, stating that, 'as they do not recognise the ASRS, which has a membership of some 84,000, they flatly refuse to treat with the strikers through the union and will not re-employ the men who left work'.[9]

That night Larkin retorted: 'the railway servants were afraid to tackle the English companies, but the Belfast men had taken them on, and what was more would beat them'.[10] Thus, despite his rhetoric, Larkin was under no illusions as to the immensity of the task in hand. However, in commencing battle with the shipping companies which had railway links, he could report one psychologically useful victory; the seven smaller shipping companies, which had already shown signs of weakness, had seen enough when they realised that the NUDL was prepared to take on the larger firms, and by Friday 28 June all had settled on terms favourable to the union. Typical of these settlements was that at the Ayr Steamship Company where the men obtained a one-shilling-a-week increase, and the *Belfast Evening Telegraph,* commenting generally on these gains, admitted that they represented 'a substantial victory for the men, who, in addition, have had their union recognised'.[11]

No such weakness was evident among the larger companies. By the evening of 27 June thirty blacklegs had arrived from Dublin, and the following morning a further 150 came in with two new depot ships. These men were not recruited from the doss-houses of English and Scottish seaports like those who had come earlier to assist the Belfast Steamship Company. As the *Northern Whig* put it, 'they are not imported labourers in the ordinary sense, being men employed by the different railway companies who are drafted over for special duty'.[12] They were men well capable of doing the strikers' work and were unlikely to defect, for if they did so they stood to lose their permanent jobs and their pension rights with the railway companies.[13]

However, these companies, ever with an eye to economy, evidently viewed the employment of their permanent men on the Belfast quays as an expensive luxury, and soon sought to recruit cheap labour locally. On the first day of the strike 'posters were distributed through the city asking for labourers'.[14] This was ground that the NUDL could more readily contest. Already, in the earlier dispute with the Belfast Steamship Company, union posters had been seized by police as far away as Londonderry.[15] Now in Belfast, according to police reports, a substantial propaganda operation got under way to neutralise the advertising of the employers:

> Twelve men are employed by Mr McKeown, bill-poster, with wheel boards going through the streets with these [union]

A wheelboard (*Irish Independent*, 5 August 1907)

notices posted on them. The men with those wheel boards either go before or after men who are wheeling boards with notices offering employment to labourers at the Fleetwood, Heysham and Liverpool steamers.[16]

Such tactics were, however, of limited value if no access to blacklegs who had already started work could be obtained. Larkin had found to his cost the difficulties of addressing even his own men within the harbour area. On 19 June he had been arrested for trespass on the property of the Harbour Commissioners and, to add insult to injury, he had at the time been engaged in dissuading 150 deep-sea dockers from taking strike action.[17]

In a speech on the night of Thursday 27 June Larkin made plain his frustration on the access issue:

> The soldiers had refused to allow their pickets through the cordons, although it was contrary to the Trades Disputes Act. The next day they would force their way through and if Mr Haldane [the Minister for War] wanted fighting he would get his belly full of it, and the blood would be on his head.[18]

In the event, the only bloodbath was one of mixed metaphors, for Larkin had fully ascertained his rights under the new Act, and the following morning his manoeuvres were entirely legal. Larkin, armed only with a copy of the Act and accompanied by pickets wearing union badges, presented himself at the cordon fringing Albert Quay, and demanded access.[19]

This unexpected action caused some consternation. District Inspector Edward Clayton, who led the Belfast detective branch, noted: 'The Lord Mayor was of the opinion that such pickets should not be permitted... but the Commissioner of Police, believing that Section 2 (i) of the Act of 1906 authorized such pickets, allowed 24 men to pass through.'[20] Commissioner Hugh O'Halloran Hill was later to comment: 'It became apparent that the powers given to the pickets... were great.'[21]

This confrontation was the first test of the Act, and in the ensuing weeks both sides sought to wring the greatest possible advantage from it. Larkin had considerable assistance from British labour leaders who advised him and also put pressure on the Liberal Government to ensure that the Act was applied fairly. For the Government, studied impartiality on the matter compensated for unwelcome publicity on the premature use of troops.

Even with the provisions of the Act ritually observed on the quays, Larkin had no great confidence in it as a measure benefiting the labour movement – a view coloured perhaps by the pyrrhic nature of his victory on 28 June when it had proved impossible to persuade any blacklegs to defect.[22] Now on Sunday 30 June he told his followers that the Act would be better described as the 'Trades Act folly',[23] a jaundiced view shared by Alex Boyd who argued on the following night that 'if they were given their right to peacefully persuade the imported labourers, they would end the strike in 24 hours'.[24]

The chief obstacle to any freedom of action by the strikers, whether peaceful or otherwise, was the presence in overwhelming force of the military, and on Monday 1 July the issue was raised at the meeting of the city council by Labour councillors. This in itself caused no alarm amongst the huge Conservative majority, but Larkin's supporting tactics did. Without warning, dockers assembled at Victoria Street and set off to march on the City Hall, which at the time was guarded by no more than a couple of constables. The men were 'marshalled in a long column of fours, and headed by Mr Larkin they marched in military order through the streets gathering an immense crowd at their heels'.[25]

At the City Hall hasty agreement was reached to allow a deputation from the dockers to enter the council chamber, and to permit others access to the gallery. It was a foregone conclusion that in the actual debate the Lord Mayor would refuse to change his mind on the use of troops, but a cry from the gallery – 'the Lord Mayor is no use. I'd shoot the Lord Mayor' – confirmed for uneasy councillors that there was a new and bitter anger amongst the unskilled.[26]

Once again the NUDL had achieved dramatic effect and yet made little progress. Indeed, if no other options had been open to Larkin, the effect of the general strike on the cross-channel quays would have been simply to create a larger and more debilitating re-run of the original stalemate with the Belfast Steamship Company. It soon became evident, however, that he had another powerful weapon to hand, and it is unlikely that Larkin would have taken on the great railway companies without certain knowledge of his ability to stretch them further.

The first evidence of the new weapon was revealed only a day after the dockers started their general action. Some of the carters at the Fleetwood quay came out in sympathy, and it was rumoured that those employed by the Midland Railway Company at the Heysham and Barrow boats would follow. On the morning of 27 June they duly did so.²⁷

Any question of the slightly higher status of the carters proved irrelevant on the quays run by the railway companies because dockers and carters suffered under the same employers. More surprising was the readiness of carters employed by independent firms to join the fray. The various members of the Master Carriers Association had received a letter from Michael McKeown, warning that 'if your carters in any way assist the Fleetwood, Heysham, Barrow or Belfast steamship companies in their attempt to smash the Dockers' Union, our members will everywhere regard them as blacklegs, and refuse to load or unload them',²⁸ but they barely had time to consider a response before carters themselves at two of the largest independent firms, Wordies and Cowans, refused to cart to the strike-bound quays.

If matters were proceeding at breakneck speed on the union side, the employers were little slower. Indeed, before the carters had taken any action, the companies had already taken steps to secure protection for the importation of blacklegs²⁹ and, as their men stopped work, Wordies and Cowans were ready with replacements brought in from Glasgow. This enterprising effort to snuff out action by the carters in its infancy was to prove a disaster, for it soon became clear that it was one thing to employ blackleg dock labourers in the relative safety of quayside sheds while it was quite another to introduce them as carters onto the streets.

As soon as the first cart manned by a blackleg emerged it was surrounded by 'a jeering crowd' and by the time High Street was reached it was being followed by 'two or three thousand people'. In the face of such opposition, only three carts ventured forth on behalf of Wordies and Cowans all day, and by afternoon the Glasgow men were demanding to be sent home.³⁰ An angry letter to Dublin Castle from all the railway companies complained that the imported carters 'were followed and interfered with by large crowds and their efforts to perform their duties rendered impossible'. This merely confirmed the effectiveness of the strikers' hold on the streets.³¹

The episode greatly increased the enthusiasm of the carters for action, and on 28 June a general claim was submitted on their behalf, bearing striking similarities to that put forward earlier by the dockers. The carters were now demanding a wage increase to twenty-six shillings a week and a reduction to a sixty-hour week.³²

The Master Carriers, shaken by the debacle of their attempted use

> **NATIONAL UNION OF DOCK LABOURERS.**
>
> # LOCK-OUT
> ## OF
> ## DOCK LABOURERS IN BELFAST.
>
> **IRISH TRADES CONGRESS, Dublin, 1907.**
> The following Resolution was unanimously adopted at this Congress:
> "That this Congress expresses its sympathy with the Locked-Out Dock Labourers of Belfast, and would recommend their case to all Trades Unionists. We strongly condemn the action of Mr. T. GALLAHER, 'The Tobacco King,' and Chairman of the Belfast Steamship Company, in importing hundreds of Foreign Blacklegs into Belfast for the purpose of trying to smash the Men's Union."
>
> ### Trades Unionists and Friends of the Oppressed !
> put your principles into practice by supporting Home Manufacturers, and those firms in Ireland which do not import Foreign Blacklegs to take the places of our fellow-workers.
>
> **JAMES LARKIN, Dockers' Organiser.**
>
> Irishmen, are we going to build up Irish Industry on the sweated and degraded bodies of Irish Women and Men ? It is Men and Women we want in Ireland, not Millionaires of the type of Gallaher !
>
> Are you aware that a Crippled Irishwoman who worked for twenty odd years for Gallaher, and never earned more than 10/- per week, was dismissed for attending a Trades Union Meeting ?
>
> *The way to stop this Tyranny is to Smoke only Tobacco manufactured by*
> MURRAY, Belfast ; CARROLL, Dundalk ; GOODBODY, Dublin ; SPILLANE, Limerick ; and LAMBKIN, Cork.
>
> ní h-é an bodac a ceartuiġear uaione.
> már "ġallobcor" in Éirinn. Síad na haoine muincuire.

One of the posters referred to Dublin Castle with a view to prosecution
(SPO 1908 CSORP 20333)

of blacklegs, now belatedly sought to extricate themselves from the growing storm, and on the evening of Saturday 29 June agreed to offer the carters two shillings a week extra.[33] They also sought to drive a wedge between the carters and the dockers, a spokesman for the employers arguing: 'It is difficult for anyone in our business to conceive why the carters should have thrown in their lot with the dockers who, in my opinion, are an entirely different class of men altogether.'[34] The Master Carriers used the same ploy in negotiation. Thus when Larkin called with them on the afternoon of Saturday 29 June, they snubbed him by sending a hand-delivered letter to R.J. Moore, Secretary of the Carters' Society.

The letter itself was calculated to make the carters reconsider any action. The employers had decided 'that a small deputation of our representatives should meet a similar number of yours' to consider any offer, but crucially this was 'conditional, and the conditions are, that the carters connected with the various firms who have ceased work shall resume same on Monday' and that carters would cart 'wherever they might be sent, including cartage to and from the various cross channel steamers and railways'.[35]

In addressing the letter to an official of the Carters' Society the employers were attempting to stem the wholesale defection of their men to the NUDL, and they were doing so at a time when the organisational relationship between dockers and carters was highly fluid, and had by no means been settled to the NUDL's advantage.

The Carters' Society had a substantial and bona fide history as a trade union, having affiliated to the Trades Council as early as 1892 with 500 members. In 1899 one Samuel Campbell had represented the carters at the Irish Congress of Trades Unions,[36] and as late as June 1902 they had been represented on the Trades Council.[37] By 1907, however, even the police doubted the society's effectiveness. As District Inspector Clayton put it, 'only a few men belonged to it, and it had fallen practically into desuetude and was of no real value to its members'.[38] Perhaps for this reason Alex McDowell, the employers' chief spokesman, was later prepared to heap praise on it, saying that it 'had been conducted in a most responsible way – the carters in the old association were perfectly willing to do carting from those steamers that had been boycotted'.[39]

The Carters' Society was, however, still very definitely in existence, and on Monday 1 July it was evident that the organisational situation had still not been fully resolved. In the evening a public meeting was held in Corporation Square, followed by a joint meeting of dockers and carters in the Exhibition Hall, but then a further private meeting of carters was held. The proceedings of this private meeting are not known, but even on the public platform earlier in the evening the strains of the situation had been evident, as Alex Boyd had revealed:

> When it became known to them that there was some prejudice against Mr Larkin on personal grounds he had at once said 'I want this case settled, and I will not stand in the way if the employers will meet any of the men's representatives – Mr McKeown, Mr Gageby, or Mr Boyd.'[40]

Gageby too offered advice befitting an influential moderate, advising the men 'strongly to carry on their work while these negotiations were proceeding'.[41]

The following day it was clear that no firm decision had been reached. The *Northern Whig* reported how Larkin had spoken 'vaguely of bold action being taken next week or the week after' — a significant retreat from earlier confident assertions that the carters would be out *en masse* from Wednesday 3 July. Indeed, on the afternoon of 2 July, negotiations with regard to the carters' position actually got under way. The Lord Mayor was visited by the Master Carriers who explained that their outstanding difficulty was the necessity to cart to the strike-bound quays. Meanwhile Robert Gageby, who had also been in contact with the Lord Mayor, organised matters on the other side, and arranged a deputation of three dockers and three carters, ready to take part in further negotiations on the following day.[42]

Larkin may well have felt that the initiative was being taken from him, and in particular that the full support of the carters, which was absolutely crucial if the dockers were to have any chance of success, was being undermined. Accordingly, on the night of 2 July he dramatically made an issue of his leadership by announcing his resignation from the role:

> He was there to vindicate his position that night and was willing to stand before any tribunal to answer any charge. It was said that he was the great dictator who wished to exercise his own will. He did not desire to keep them back, and if his presence was any hindrance to negotiations he was willing to stand on one side. It was not his own benefit, his own personal ambition, but the betterment of the men of Belfast that he was fighting for and he would not interfere for a moment in what was best for the men. It was not a question between Catholics and or Protestants; it was a question for all men who were employed on the docks or in carting... from that night he resigned his position as leader of the strike, but he would be there to give his advice if necessary. A Protestant in the person of Mr Alexander Boyd would be at the head of the men of the union. He retired now until the matter was settled but he would be there fighting in the ranks, and give them all the help and information he could.[43]

It was a speech calculated to ensure a wave of sympathy for his position. Few, if any, of the strikers had considered the possibility of continuing the strike without his charismatic leadership and, even in practical terms, it was difficult to see how dockers could hand over the leadership of their own strike to officials of other unions.

Larkin may have hoped to thwart the efforts of moderates to undermine him but, equally importantly, he hoped to provide a full opportunity for dealing with the dangerous sectarian allegations now being made against him, albeit from predictable quarters. As early as 19 May he had been driven to refute the suggestion that he was related to Larkin, the Fenian Manchester martyr,[44] but a more sophisticated attack had appeared in the Presbyterian *Ulster Echo* on the morning preceding his resignation speech. This attack combined social prejudice – the paper wished to preserve 'the city from the dictation of irresponsible vulgarians' – with ugly sectarian innuendo, purportedly put forward in the interests of 'Protestant dockers'.

> What is behind all this is not the mere question of wages. It is the question in whose hands will the employment of the men rest? We all know what manner of man Mr Larkin is. We know what his peculiar political and religious opinions are. . . If Mr Larkin was master of the employment of the dockers in Belfast, how many Protestant dockers would be left in the city at the end of the first twelve months?. . . Mr Boyd is being used as a catspaw of Messrs Larkin and McKeown. Both these men are extreme and rabid nationalists and Roman Catholics.[45]

As it happened, the events of 3 July rendered Larkin's spectacular gesture almost superfluous. The incipient disagreements amongst the labour leaders might well have been damaging, but the actions of the employers soon made unity imperative.

During the morning Gageby's non-contentious deputation of dockers and carters stood by while the Lord Mayor met all the employers. The employers then met separately for two hours before announcing that they were 'unable to see their way to take part in the proposed conference'. The Master Carriers, very much at the beck and call of the shipping companies, now took their cue from them and announced that unless the limited group of carters already on strike returned to work all other carters would be locked out.

The attitude of the employers dismayed even those not necessarily sympathetic to the trade-union movement, thus the *Northern Whig* expressed a very general feeling when it stated, 'It was a sore disappointment to all concerned, and to every citizen who had been hoping against hope that a way out of the dilemma would be found and the menace that threatens the city removed.'⁴⁶

The employers' decision had an electrifying effect on the trade-union movement. That night, at another mass meeting in Custom House Square, Alex Boyd caught the mood when he said 'it was now war to the knife'. There was now no room for division at any level. 'The result of that struggle concerned not merely the unskilled but the skilled workman. It was the principle of trade unionism that was being attacked.' Boyd now denied that Larkin had ever resigned the strike leadership. His offer to stand aside in any negotiations had been 'misrepresented in the press'. Boyd also replied directly to the sectarian smear campaign:

> There was a deliberate attempt to work on party feelings on the eve of the July the twelfth celebrations. They had first tried to get at the Protestants by saying that Larkin, a Roman Catholic, was leading the strike; now they were trying to turn the Roman Catholics against him [Boyd].

As far as Boyd was concerned, however, in the crisis of the hour any such difficulty had been overcome and 'the men of both faiths concerned in the strike were determined to stand together against the common enemy, the employer, who denied the right of the workers to a fair wage'. Indeed, as the struggle widened it had a new implication: 'that dispute had done more to bring the men of opposite beliefs together than all the wirepulling of the past fifty years'.

Larkin, the last speaker at the meeting, was received with rapturous applause. The action of the employers earlier in the day had removed any doubts about his central importance. There were, however, new arrangements – Alex Boyd would now be 'grand adviser on the lines of communication' and there would be a wider strike committee involving the leaders of the Trades Council and representatives of other unions.[47] The changes were designed to strengthen the position of the dockers and carters, and reflected recognition of the unprecedented dimensions of the dispute. However, at the same time they inevitably curtailed Larkin's power to engage in inspired and independent action.

Now, on Wednesday 3 July, Larkin's main concern was to issue instructions for the following day and to ensure that 'no carter's wheel of any union man would turn on the streets of Belfast'. There could be no doubt about the men's response – as the *Northern Whig* commented, 'We are on the eve of an experience something akin to that which has paralysed Russian cities during the last couple of years.'

7
Strangest Twelfth

On the morning of Thursday 4 July the remaining 1,000 carters employed by the sixty firms of the Master Carriers Association came out almost to a man.[1] The most dramatic evidence of the new action was a lack of incident. Very little moved, and at the quays the soldiers were allowed to stand easy.

The particular quiet at the docks reflected the widening of the strike arena. The strikers' attention had shifted to the streets of the city and to any attempts to undertake carting. Fanning out from the strike headquarters in Victoria Street, pickets watched every thoroughfare. Some had union badges, but the large numbers who had joined the union in the previous weeks could not get theirs because, as Larkin explained, even supplies of union badges were now strike-bound and locked 'in the Fleetwood shed'.[2]

The previous night Larkin had told the men, 'they had assured Lord Shaftesbury that there would be no violence'.[3] By and large this assurance was kept, and the few carters who did venture forth were dissuaded by large groups of strikers who argued fiercely with them. It was a style of picketing which had already been used in the limited strike at Wordies and Cowans from 27 June. Commissioner Hill reported to Dublin Castle that 'there were very few cases of destruction and, beyond some occasional booing, no violence' and yet he was still of the view that 'the carters were intimidated'.[4]

One incident on the first day of the all-out strike, in which a cart was smashed into a lamp post in Waring Street and had its shaft broken, was made much of by the employers. Hill was less concerned, arguing that 'considering the excitement, and the small force of police available, very few incidents of the sort described. . . have occurred'.[5] If for the moment no blood ran in the streets, the employers were under no illusions about the serious implications of the carters' action. It had been all too apparent from the commencement of limited action on 27 June how effective this could be, and as early as 28 June the Belfast Steamship Company had admitted that 'with the carters joining the strikers the situation is made much more difficult'.[6]

(*Nomad's Weekly*, 20 July 1907)

The *Northern Whig* on 1 July had effectively summed up the situation: 'In the earlier stages the efforts of the dockers were concentrated on striving to make it impossible for the companies to load and unload their boats; now they assert they do not care how expeditiously this is performed so long as they are unable to distribute the goods through the city.' With an all-out strike by the carters, these problems were immediately compounded and the employers could not obtain ready assistance from the authorities. On 28 June the Belfast Steamship Company had demanded the assistance of cavalry, a request which received an unenthusiastic response from Commissioner Hill who argued, 'I do not consider that this would be advisable.'[7] However, on 1 July Lord Shaftesbury, who in his capacity as Lord Mayor had legal power to do so, requisitioned 500 cavalry, thus ignoring the advice of both Hill and General Dawson.[8] Shaftesbury's credibility in Dublin Castle was already at a low ebb following the premature call-out of troops in May, and Chief Secretary Augustine Birrell made his contempt for the new application clear when he advised his Under Secretary, Sir Anthony MacDonnell, that 'the government have nothing to do with the application and should avoid assuming any responsibility'. The administration was legally bound to respond to the requisition, but it could hope effectively to nullify it by procrastination, and the nearest available cavalry at the Curragh hardly moved with alacrity. Indeed by 2 July the Lord Mayor was reduced to pleading for 100 men.[9] In the event 120 men of the 3rd (Prince of Wales's) Dragoon Guard did arrive[10] but they were not used. Here, in addition to the opinions of military and police, Lord Shaftesbury may have been influenced by Larkin's arguments – on the one hand he was prepared to give assurances that the pickets would not use violence, on the other hand he made light of any assumed threat from the cavalry, saying that he 'would like to see any cavalry charging on the hard square setts – they would kill more horses in a week than the British Government could steal in a year'.[11] With the collapse of this dramatic but inappropriate security solution in a welter of indecision, the strikers retained the upper hand on the streets and it was an outcome viewed not unsympathetically in Dublin Castle where Sir Anthony MacDonnell, forwarding a memo from Commissioner Hill to the Chief Secretary, added his own marginal comment that, 'You will notice deadlock is due to refusal of employers to consult Trades Union leaders.'[12]

The consequences of that deadlock soon began to pile up: on 5 July local agents for the Barrow and Heysham Steamers put restrictions on the goods they could carry,[13] and a week later all the main shipping companies ceased to carry any goods that could not be delivered and collected by the consignees.[14] The *Irish News* commented on 6 July, 'That perishable goods are suffering from delay in delivery is proved by the great quantities which have been destroyed by the authorities recently as unfit for human consumption', and, four days later, noted the overpowering stench of rotting food on the quays. As far away as Poulton-le-Fylde in Lancashire 200 wagonloads of perishable goods quietly disintegrated in the summer heat. The *Belfast News-Letter* on 6 July noted a few 'amateur private van-men, kid-gloved and fashionably dressed', and described a scene of desolation on the 11 July, saying, 'It was remarkable to see the stagnation which existed from the Custom House to the Clarendon Dock. With the exception of an isolated van or lorry driven by the obvious amateur, there was scarcely a sign of life or movement.'

All this was reflected in the Harbour Commissioners' statistics for cross-channel and coastwise trade. Up to 1 July trade of this kind had shown an increase of 9,000 tons over the previous year; by mid-July the figure was 7,000 tons less than the amount for the previous year.[15] It was a situation summed up on 13 July by *Nomad's Weekly*, a virulently anti-trade union journal, which published a special supplement on the state of trade in the city, consisting of two blank pages.

In spite of the undoubted impact of the carters' strike, there was little evidence of any weakening of the employers' position. The sole victory won by the men in the first week of July was the decision by A.M. Carlisle, works manager of Harland and Wolff, to reinstate carters initially dismissed for failing to cart to the strike-bound quays,[16] but on the employers' side this was viewed as the predictable defection of a political maverick of known Liberal or even Nationalist views. The imposition of a general strike by carters actually resulted in a loss of ground. The union had hoped that the smaller steamship companies, with whom settlements had been achieved at the end of June, would put pressure on the other employers. Instead, finding their operations disrupted by the carters' strike, they chose to abandon their independent position and line up behind the larger companies.[17]

From the employers' point of view, one of the few encouraging aspects of the situation was that threats by the strike leaders to spread the strike movement still further did not materialise. This in turn may have reflected the dilution of Larkin's role within a wider strike committee. The dynamic development of the dispute was now replaced by a degree of tactical inertia, an inertia which, while it did not immediately have adverse effects in a situation where the strikers had the upper hand, was to become cumulatively more damaging. In his statement of 3 July, Larkin had threatened to bring the men at the coal quays out again. Other strike leaders made even wider threats, and Joseph Harris, speaking on the Custom House steps on 4 July, said that 'other trades unions would join them in their actions and it would be a bigger contest than the masters ever anticipated if they took in the whole of the men employed in the city. . . it would not only operate in Ireland, but would extend, if the present opposition were maintained, throughout England and Scotland'. There was a threat to call out the printers, even the firemen were expected to come out,[18] and Alex Boyd threatened to 'leave Belfast in absolute darkness'.[19] None of these things was done. It was a case of rhetoric rather than action. Police Commissioner Hill, describing a meeting held on 11 July, accurately summed up much of the content of the mass rallies in the first weeks of July when he said, 'The speakers at the meeting last night did not speak of the strike. They spoke of socialism and generalities.'[20]

Threatening talk merely served to warn the employers of areas in which they were vulnerable, and the coal employers were all too willing to take a hint from Larkin. They met on 8 July; two days later the *Northern Whig* reported a rush for coal, and on 11 July the coal employers issued lockout notices.[21] For the moment it did not much matter that it was the employers who took the initiative and locked the men out, rather than the men who came out on strike. This development did, however, indicate that the employers were prepared to take decisions where the strike leaders dodged them.

The latter were now increasingly emphasising the moral force of their case rather than its actual force, while the employers had no such scruples. What the labour leaders neglected was the danger of a situation in which moral argument cut no ice and they were left engaged in an indecisive war of attrition, which the employers could weather better than unskilled workers short of funds.

It was, however, a battle being waged with increasing vigour on the streets by rank-and-file strikers and their supporters from all parts of the city. Shipyard workers were much to the fore on 9 July when, armed with their traditional weaponry of rivets, they attacked and burnt one van and threw another into the harbour, while that afternoon they made up a substantial proportion of a crowd of some 2,000 who stoned the police. On the same day eight or nine vans were destroyed elsewhere in the city.[22] Two days later equal militancy was shown on the Catholic Falls Road when carts attempting to get through to the Catholic-owned Hughes Bakery were systematically attacked.[23]

The strike leadership was not overawed by the new coal lockout. Larkin said he 'was glad that the fight was developing, and now they saw where the employers were'.[24] A union spokesman confidently told the *Belfast Evening Telegraph* on 15 July: 'The action of the coal merchants is playing into our hands; the want of coal will rouse manufacturers and everyone, and public opinion cannot be withstood even by the employers. This action will bring about a climax and the employers will have to give way.'

A factor which might in ordinary circumstances have favoured the employers was the timing of their ultimatum: immediately preceding the 'Twelfth' holiday, a time when workers were likely to spend their all, and depend on a return to work; a time also when sectarian tensions were at their height and most likely to disrupt any labour agitation.

The strike leaders were well aware of the dangerous potential of this Protestant and Orange holiday. Joseph Harris, referring to the 'Twelfth' on 7 July, said the men 'would differ on one day of the year but their interests were the same for the other 364'.[25] The divisive threat of the 'Twelfth' was always one likely to misfire for the employers because, as the *Ulster Guardian* had noted, the majority of strikers were Orange and Protestant.[26] Now, in the week prior to the 'Twelfth', there were indications in the correspondence columns of the *Belfast News-Letter* that any attempts to use the 'Twelfth' as an occasion for schism were going to fall on unusually stony ground. Thus 'Protestant Carter' wrote on 5 July, 'There is no use trying to bamboozle us, Mr Editor, there is plenty of work for us all at double our present pay in Canada and West Australia. You and the class who hire you have held us in contempt for long but we are beginning to understand the way we have been wronged and we are determined to secure for ourselves a living wage.'[27]

Mr Walter Savage, of Ohio Street, now an NUDL delegate to the Trades Council, wrote of those. . .

who have been trying all through this dispute to stir up the old spirit of bigotry and hatred that has kept the labouring classes of this great city so long under the heel of their masters and made them white slaves, and even worse than slaves, for no slave had to work the hours that we had to work... from 6 in the morning to 9.30 at night for the first five days in the week and on Saturday from 6 in the morning till 11.30 at night, and a good many of us had to turn out and work a half day on Sundays for the miserable sum of 1s.... being even deprived of the right of attending our place of worship. I would like to know where the Orangeism or Protestantism of our city comes in? Or what Orangeism or Protestantism has got to do with men fighting for their just rights, when the issue lies not in religion but is a question of bread and butter, and shorter hours and better conditions which we should have had 20 years ago... I can get 1,000 Old Orange Order Orangemen who belong to the Union to sign this letter. Our fervent prayer is that James Larkin may long be spared, by the help of God, to work for the emancipation of the unskilled workers in his native land.[28]

On the 'Twelfth' itself Larkin did not, as in some fanciful accounts, lead or address Orange demonstrations,[29] but there was marked support for the strikers on both processions. The Independent Orange Order gave them official backing, while many of the men in the ranks of the Old Order demonstration displayed their strikers' badges and otherwise showed their support for the strike movement. About two dozen lodges took part in the Independents' march to Shaw's Bridge – the turnout was smaller than in the previous year but at least 1,000 people took part. Lindsay Crawford made the main speech, describing the Old Order as 'the dust-bin of the Carlton Club and the tool of place-hunting lawyers'. He said:

It was humiliating to reflect that when the farmers of Ireland became trade unionists and combined to force concessions from the British Government, Ulster, with a few exceptions, was the black-legger of the land strike, and it was still more humiliating to reflect that at that period the Orange Institution was the dumping ground for the harassed landlords, who at once turned the Institution to their own purposes, turning the lodges into rent agencies and pressing the rank and file by tributes of gold into their service as emergency men, crow-bar brigades, process servers and bailiffs.

Tom Sloan, Independent MP for South Belfast, always the weathervane for Protestant working-class opinion, spoke in typically muddled fashion, although it was clear that he was aware of popular feeling in favour of the strikers:

> While the dock labourers and carters might not all be right, no man could convince him that they were all wrong, and if there was any combination amongst the masters to safeguard their interests, the men had an equal right to combine to protect their interests. He understood that the men were asking for the right to submit the matter to arbitration, and the masters denied it. In that case he thought that the sooner the men put their backs against the wall and faced the situation, the sooner their courage and pluck would win the battle.

The Rev. J. Calvin, the clergyman presiding, made clear the non-sectarian message of the gathering: 'It was not the Catholics they were engaged in fighting; they were a democracy fighting for mere existence against an aristocratic and selfish monied class'. Alex Boyd, one of the strike leaders and an Independent, spoke on behalf of the strikers, and a resolution was passed in favour of trade-union rights. More than £80 was collected for the strike fund.

The *Irish News* reported the favourable reception which strikers received: 'A notable feature of the two demonstrations was the large number of strikers who took part in each and, as they were recognised at points along the routes, they were extended sympathetic greetings by the onlooking crowds.'[30]

Proof that the events of the 'Twelfth' had, if anything, lent encouragement to the strike movement came on Monday 15 July when, to the anguish of police and employers alike, the 800 coal quay men refused to work in the face of the employers' ultimatum. It was also on 15 July that the strike leadership launched a significantly extended campaign of popular mobilisation. This had been announced two days earlier at the Custom House steps meeting by W.J. Murray:

> ... they intended to begin a new policy and during the week would hold two meetings daily. At noon each day they would hold a demonstration in that square, and at 7.30 another

meeting would be held but in different parts of the city. Hitherto they had held all their meetings at that square, but now they would visit every part of the city and strive to promote a spirit of brotherhood between the Protestant and R.C. workers.[31]

Just as the strike had extended from the quays and then, following the carters' strike with attendant picketing, onto the streets throughout the city, so also the strike meetings had extended and expanded, first from Corporation Square to the Custom House steps and now apparently to the residential areas of the city. The new scheme for meetings could be seen as a logical parallel to the ever-widening theatre of strike activity, but it had an added significance not appreciated at the time. It marked the extension of the movement from one within strictly industrial confines to one aiming at a wider mobilisation. This too was reflected in the rhetoric of the strike leaders who now spoke of a more general social transformation as well as immediate strike objectives. They did not for the moment perceive that they were moving into an arena in which they, as union leaders, could no longer exert direct control, or that their new and broader objectives brought them more directly into a wider political environment. These were factors which would help to ensure that the 1907 crisis was to be one on a scale out of all proportion to the number of men ever actually on strike.

The first of these meetings took place at Tennent Street at the foot of the Protestant Shankill Road on the night of Monday 15 July. The speakers were Alex Stewart, Alex Boyd and Larkin. The *Belfast News-Letter* reported that speeches were 'somewhat interrupted by a drumming party', but both the *Northern Whig* and the *Irish News* reported that the speakers had received a friendly reception. Larkin dealt with his attitude to religion, saying, 'He had never denied his religion and he did not think that if any of his hearers went up the Falls Road they would deny theirs either. Religion or nationality did not enter into the present question. They were only concerned with a man's work and his right to be treated as he should. Let them stand fast together in the fight for their rights.'[32]

Crawford did not speak at Tennent Street, but made his first speech from the strike committee platform in Queen's Square. His was already a wider message: 'Stand firm, out of this movement will spring not only the strength of organised labour but also the realisation of that hope which Ireland has been longing for, the unity of all Irishmen.'[33]

There were now three strike meetings a day, the July holidays were in full swing and crowds numbering thousands turned out. On Tuesday 16 July there was a noon meeting at Custom House Square at which Larkin read a letter from the Rev. S. Simms, the minister at Agnes Street Presbyterian Church, which read in part, 'The insane actions of the coal merchants have brought the matter to a crisis. The battle is now between the classes and the masses, and the masses will ultimately win. Not one pound of coal shall I purchase from the federated employers any longer.' Then in the evening Larkin, Boyd and Crawford spoke at a meeting at the end of Templemore Avenue. After that there was a further meeting at Custom House Square.[34]

The strikers carried their message to the Falls Road on Wednesday 17 July when a huge crowd, including many from Sandy Row and the Shankill, gathered at Clonard Gardens. Alex Boyd told his audience that,

> He was proud of the fact that he could come to Clonard Gardens and address a meeting in his official capacity as the representative of Sandy Row (cheers) and moreover, he was glad to tell them that he saw before him some members of his own constituency, Sandy Row (applause)... his friend Lindsay Crawford (cheers) and a few others had set about to unite the people of Ireland in one strong band of friendship.[35]

The following night, Thursday 18 July, the speakers went to Sandy Row where Lindsay Crawford was the main speaker, focusing on a recent report of the Inspector of Factories which was 'a damning indictment of brutal commercialism... it would be better that every mill and factory should be closed, and the grass grow on the quays, than that one little one should go down to the grave prematurely or become permanently stunted'.[36] The last of this series of meetings in working-class districts was held in York Road on Friday 18 July.[37]

The success of these meetings made it clear that the strike had mass working-class support in all areas of the city. The shipyard workers, in particular the boilermakers and engineers on strike, played a full part in the struggle of the carters and dockers. At the midday meeting of 17 July Larkin had to tick off the carters and dockers because the men from Harland and Wolff were being left to do all the picketing.[38] The *Northern Whig* described the attitude of the shipyard men on 23 July: 'Their presence in Custom House Square and along the approaches served to augment the crowds there. The Islandmen, to a very great extent, were no doubt sympathetic with the strikers.'

Meanwhile, the impact of the three major disputes was threatening to paralyse the city. The coal blockade had achieved dramatic effects. By Monday 15 July eight coal ships were waiting to unload,[39] and by Tuesday 5,000 tons of coal were held up. There were drastic consequences. Combe Barbour's works in North Howard Street, which employed 1,800, did not reopen on 15 July after the holidays;[40] part of Ewart's mill, one of the largest linen firms, closed on 18 July and the entire factory a week later. The Broadway Damask Company and the Suffolk Linen Company closed on the same day.[41] By 29 July the *Belfast News-Letter* estimated that at least 7,000 workers would be laid off in the city within a week.

The indirect effects of the carters' strike were becoming equally far-reaching. The deep-sea docks, not initially affected by the dockers' action, were rapidly crippled by the carters' strike; by 18 July, grain ships from the Black Sea and the River Plate, which normally took ten days to turn round, had been stuck for three weeks, and the *Irish News* reported on 19 July that 'the discharge of vessels at the low docks is now practically out of the question owing to the enormous quantities of material that have been collected in the sheds and on the quays'.

However, the employers remained active in circumstances which grew ever more alarming even to them. When they could not carry out normal carting they resorted to more imaginative tactics. The Midland Railway Company attempted to ship coal out to suburban stations for distribution from there, but one such train was attacked within the harbour area, while another was attacked at Balmoral and had to retreat unloaded.[42] Attempts by the Great Northern Railway to reroute goods via Holyhead and Greenore failed, thanks to the solidarity of workers on both sides of the channel.[43] An attempt was made to bring in a coke ship, the SS *Norman*, on 17 July, but the blacklegs working on her were scattered and the ship was driven out to sea with broken skylights and other deck damage.[44]

The employers now tried to deal with their main problem, delivering goods in the central area of Belfast, by the introduction of traction engines. Four of them arrived in Belfast on 9 and 10 July and were rapidly fitted with heavy metal guards,[45] but before they could appear on the streets the question of police protection had to be faced again. At the time of the carters' lockout on 4 July the police had argued that to extend full protection would only create an unnecessary crisis, but the action of the employers in locking out the coal quay workers on 11 July had created that crisis in any case. Commissioner Hill and his successor from mid-July, Acting Commissioner Morrell, were forced to retreat onto much weaker ground in resisting demands for protection. They first relied on hopeless optimism with regard to the likely course of events and then, as things got worse, simply claimed that, because the police were fully engaged, they could do no more.

Thus Commissioner Hill was not at all alarmed by the coal lockout and reported to Dublin Castle on 11 July, 'I would not be surprised if there was a settlement this week owing to want of funds on the part of the men', and again on 12 and 13 July reported that the coal men were likely to submit to the employers' ultimatum. When the coal men came out in face of the ultimatum, Hill suggested that this new trouble could be used as an excuse to 'postpone' any action over the protection of blackleg carters.

The increasing evidence that the police were not doing anything because they were impotent, rather than for any nobler tactical reason, strengthened the employers' hand. They were now able to represent the situation in Belfast as an actual breakdown of law and order, and the pressure on Commissioner Hill was stepped up. On 11 July he informed Dublin Castle: 'I am being pressed by the employers for the protection of motor lorries, and the only way I see to do it is by cavalry.' Hill had earlier opposed the use of cavalry and was not himself convinced now. He mentioned the matter to give the authorities an opportunity to intervene. Dublin Castle was, however, as intent on dodging controversy as was Commissioner Hill. When Commissioner Henry Morrell, from Armagh, took over as Acting Commissioner in Belfast on 15 July, as a result of Hill's illness, he continued the earlier strategy of playing the situation along from day to day. On 15 July he resisted pressure to extend police protection to York Dock, and told Dublin Castle that 'nothing could be better than the outlook at present'. On 16 and 17 July he sent similarly optimistic communications,[46] but on the evening of 17 July, at a conference attended by Lord Shaftesbury and General Dawson, he was forced to give in. Lord Shaftesbury had accepted the argument for caution over the 'Twelfth' holiday but this had passed peacefully. As President of the Chamber of Commerce, Lord Shaftesbury was also far more subject to direct pressure from the employers than was the Police Commissioner. He insisted that action be taken. After midnight on 17 July Morrell wired Dublin to explain that the police would give protection to traction engines from 22 July: 'Instead of affording protection by police to individual carters, a large part of the central part of the town is to be protected by the police and military at six points.'[47]

It appeared the employers had achieved one of their major objectives, to secure the intervention of the police and military authorities on their side. However, the implementation of the first part of the plan, the protection of traction engines by police, proved quite as difficult and disastrous as Hill and Morrell in their gloomier moments had suggested. The traction engines were first used on 19 July, and as early as 11 am a riot took place in Queen's Square. Throughout the day the traction engines were surrounded by large hostile crowds. At 4 pm there was a further riot in Chichester Street and five strikers were arrested.[48]

In the following days the strikers retained the upper hand as violence spread to east Belfast. William Hunter recalled:

> I saw a traction engine making its way to the ropeworks and when it reached the Connswater Bridge, which was a rise that it had to go up, it was stopped by a log dropped in front and it couldn't mount the log. Before they could get clear of it the half of the load was over into the Connswater River.[49]

Further evidence that angry support for the strikers was strongly based in the loyalist heartland of east Belfast came on 24 July when the police had to face riots on Ravenhill Road. The same day the vulnerability of the traction engines was revealed again when one was ambushed by 200 strikers at the junction of Limestone Road and Halliday's Road and both it and its load were destroyed.[50] The strikers were in no way overawed by the police; many were ex-soldiers and had justifiable confidence in their own knowledge of tactics. As William Hughes, a member of the carters' committee, later explained, 'The police was clever but us army fellows knowed the wrinkles... We made a charge at them, then the police run after me we'll say – well, there was another rearguard, they done the damage you see.' It was an easy enough matter for burly dockers and carters to overturn the typical light cart. As Hughes explained, 'As long as you take the stuff off the one side of the van and three or four of you get the other side you can coup it over.'

The men were sent out in groups from the strike headquarters and might act on information received or on personal knowledge of what their own employers were trying to do. John Orr, a carter with Wordies, described the process: 'You were told – often maybe tens and twenties – watch so and so. Well, we watched them and one of them was a clerk out of Wordie's, a fellow called Harry Hart. Well, we catched Harry with a load of shipping on and up-ended Harry, cart and all – put him over the body in Victoria Street.' The men were even out after dark and woe betide the employer who tried to slip a load through under cover of night. William Hughes recalled a struggle over one such cart leaving Hughes Dickson's flour mill on the Falls Road: 'I got knocked through a woman's door in the street and the woman came down screaming in her chemise and I said "Don't be ashamed missus – here's a bag of flour, hold your tongue, we're strikers".'

Women took an active part, especially when a woman was black-legging. It was the misfortune of a Mrs Moore from the Markets to drive a van past the girls leaving York Street Mill at the end of the

'Couping' a cart in Waring Street (*Irish Independent*, 7 August 1907)

day. 'They threw her off the van and tore all the clothes off her. There used to be puddles there – we called them ink bottles – well, they just rolled her in that.'[51]

The evident success of such rough and ready tactics spawned anecdotes such as these and, whether true or exaggerated it did not matter, they were symptomatic of a new and heady confidence – a spirit of euphoria maintained in the evenings at the strike headquarters in Victoria Street where entertainments were laid on and Hughie Hamill 'could give you a step dance' or Rea sang 'Hopping in the middle like a herring on the griddle'.[52] At the end of the night Larkin often bedded down in the empty hall, for now, in the latter part of July, his were more pressing concerns. The employers had failed to break any part of the strike and had put at risk the morale and discipline of the police in the process, but the strikers in turn had chosen a war of attrition for which they were ill-equipped and had found that the moral appeal of extraordinary working-class unity and determination counted for nothing. The strike leaders now had to choose between alternatives: escalation in an all-out bid for victory, with its contingent social and political risks; or negotiation. A turning point was at hand.

Women attacking a Hughes's bread van in Divis Street
(*Irish Independent*, 24 July 1907)

read-van on its rounds attacked by women.   One venturesome lady got into the van and made short work of its contents.   Sketched on the spot

8
Betrayal

As July drew to a close, dire financial necessity loomed as the greatest threat to the strike movement. As early as 6 July John Murphy had written to Transport House asking, 'Can the party do anything more for the men here? Funds urgently needed.'[1] By 14 July 1,000 men required assistance: this was costing £400 a week and there was only £600 left in the kitty,[2] but the coal lockout was only beginning to make an impact – by 24 July 3,500 men were seeking aid.[3] It was a time when, as Michael McKeown later recalled, 'they had to borrow sums of £100 and £25 from local gentlemen to pay the men who were clamouring for money, while many a Monday morning they were nearly £1,000 in debt'.[4] The symptoms of distress were also evident elsewhere, whether in increased poorhouse admissions[5] or in the large numbers of hungry and workless men who descended on Antrim, twenty miles away, and were reduced to begging.[6]

Alongside this came the collapse of the strike committee's most ambitious scheme for alleviating distress, based on no less an objective than the creation of an alternative economy to that now paralysed by strikes and lockouts. W.J. Murray explained their high hopes on 14 July, stating that the Co-Operative Society would supply Belfast with coal if the merchants would not and that, with 100,000 tons coming in, 'they could supply work for them [the strikers] at the quays in connection with the Co-Operative Society'.[7]

Much rhetoric was expended on this scheme and yet readers of the Belfast Co-Operative Society's magazine, the *Belfast Wheatsheaf*, were left in no doubt that such idealism was foreign to the Society's proceedings. The strike leaders were praised for displaying 'an exact knowledge of Co-Operative essentials and principles that is wholly admirable', but their exaggerated hopes were 'to say the least. . . indiscreet. . . To say that the Society can import on short notice, and in two or three days, 10,000 or 100,000 tons of coal is a bit wide of the mark. The Belfast Society cannot perform miracles.' Unable to perform miracles, the Society intended to do what any other capitalist firm was striving to do in the same situation, 'to take full advantage of the resources at its command to enable it to keep its own members fully supplied and to overtake as much other trade as possible'.[8] In fairness to the Co-Operative Society, it was inconceivable that extra ships could have been hired at short notice in a market controlled by the very shipping companies at the centre of the strike. In spite of this, additional loads of coal were successfully shipped in, but they carried an extra humiliation for the strike leaders. The coal men refused to distribute the coal on the grounds that the Co-Operative Society was charging prices too high for their working-class customers.[9] The ultimate contribution of the Co-Operative Society to the strike movement was in the end pitifully small. A donation of £50 was given to the strikers and they were permitted to place their collection boxes on Co-Operative premises. A more radical suggestion, that strikers should be allowed extended credit, was never formally acted upon.[10]

This reflected the difficulties of raising funds locally. The strike committee and, in effect, the Trades Council set itself a target of £4,000.[11] Unions such as the Linen Lappers and the Bakers donated £50 each, while William Walker's ASCJ made a more formidable contribution, placing a three-shilling levy on all its 2,300 members and helping to organise collections in the shipyards.[12] Efforts also extended far beyond formal union circles, with 150 women engaged in door-to-door collections from 17 July,[13] and fund-raising may well have been one of the motives for the citywide meetings after the 'Twelfth'. The message was also sent further afield but often with disappointing results, as when at a meeting of Dublin Trades Council a donation of £3 was approved, but an amendment to increase the amount to £5 was ruled out of order.[14] The end effect of all these endeavours was that a sum well short of the original target was raised.

The inadequacy of these efforts was highlighted by a further finely calculated turn of the screw applied by the city's employers. The notion that they would be disgusted at the behaviour of the coal employers was well buried by a new flurry of lockout notices. Members of the Power-loom Manufacturers' Association issued lockout notices to come into force on 27 July,[15] and all men working on the tram system were issued with lockout notices to apply a day earlier.[16]

It was common knowledge that the strikers were short of funds. Alarm naturally grew among new masses of workers now threatened with unemployment themselves. On 22 July Alex Boyd tried desperately to allay fears in a way which must have sounded to many like the knell of doom. He announced that the rumour that 'some of the works were to be closed [was] only an attempt to frighten the workers, because, if some of the firms shut their doors, they would never open them again'.[17]

It is perhaps unfair to say that the strike leaders were indecisive in the period 6 July to 25 July. In the light of the Co-Op experiment, it is fairer to say that in the midst of crisis they tried to build part of the peaceful road to socialism, to find a middle way between the perils of Larkinism on the one hand and the desertion of the unskilled workers of Belfast on the other.

By the latter part of July it had become clear that there was no middle way. This did not necessarily imply a split between Larkin and the more traditional local labour leaders – the latter were appalled at the way they too were now blackguarded as extremists. Nor was there any difference of opinion about the next necessary step – the financial crisis made the involvement of British trade union leaders a necessity. There was perhaps a difference of motive, with Larkin hoping for financial assistance while others wanted, in addition, a hand to pull them back from the edge of the abyss, a magic talisman to ward off the threat of ever-extending conflict.

The arrival of James Sexton, General Secretary of the NUDL, on 19 July with news of the full backing of the union's executive brought immediate encouragement. Now he told the strikers that he was 'prepared to recommend to his society that if necessary every penny of their reserve fund of £20,000 should be spent for the benefit of the locked out men'. Alex Boyd, standing side by side with Sexton, went further: 'He had had some concern about the finances, but that had disappeared that night because of what he had heard from his friend Mr Sexton. They would have £48,000 by noon on Tuesday next from the trade unionists across the water.'[18]

They were words roared to the echo by men who that week received four shillings and sixpence strike pay.[19] They were not to know that Sexton had brought a mere £200 from Liverpool with him.[20] However, at this stage, even those aware of his actual contribution had no reason to doubt his promises, for he was unequivocal in his support for the strike movement. He saw a 'singular analogy' between his own formative experience, the Liverpool strike of 1889, and the Belfast strike of 1907, for in both situations 'all the employers were arrayed against the men, the police and military were called in to shoot them down and bludgeon them if necessary, and every influence was brought to bear in order to crush and starve out the dockers'.[21] Sexton did not question the use of militant tactics, for 'if men were half starving and [there was] plenty of food in the city, the responsibility for any violence that occurred would be on the heads of the railway companies which had brought about the intolerable state of affairs that existed in the city'.[22]

If Sexton was momentarily caught up in the mood of the strike meetings, his caution and instinct to preserve the finances of his union were soon to reassert themselves, a process which began with the arrival the following day of two representatives of the General Federation of Trade Unions, a body set up under TUC auspices to provide mutual assistance in the case of major disputes. In its public guise, the GFTU could be party to statements which appeared to be tailor-made for the Belfast situation. In 1905 they had issued a pamphlet referring to employers who 'will not permit outside, that is, trade union interference' and arguing that 'this treatment too often means the most sinister form of intimidation, dismissal or boycott or both'. Such attitudes had, according to the GFTU, led to strikes which had been effective due to 'their suddenness and to the completeness of the stoppages'.[23]

Yet Sexton was already aware of the far more cautious policy actually applied by the GFTU. The NUDL's first application for assistance for the Belfast strikers, made early in June, had, much to Sexton's irritation, been turned down,[24] and now the two GFTU representatives who were joining him in the city were far from inclined to provide immediate backing for a potentially escalating crisis. Alderman Allen Gee, JP, Vice-Chairman of the GFTU and an official of the Yorkshire Textile Workers, had only a few weeks earlier, at a meeting of the GFTU General Council, emphasised the organisation's role in settling and preventing disputes and had expressed the hope that 'this part of the work of the Federation will grow rather than that we should have to pay out of funds for the purposes of disputes or lockouts'.[25] Hardly more adventurous was his colleague, Alderman Isaac Mitchell, of London County Council, who was serving his notice as Secretary of the GFTU before becoming a Board of Trade official. This defection was to earn him acid comment from George Lansbury in a letter to Ramsay MacDonald in which he said of Mitchell that he was 'suggested by our opponents as he always is when they wish to represent labour as being against us'.[26]

These men lacked even Sexton's affinity with the strikers and, as the book-keepers of the British movement, were alarmed by what they saw. As it was, the GFTU and the NUDL faced heavy burdens. It was a position that could rapidly worsen, given Larkin's willingness to fight on an ever-broader front and the employers' evident readiness to announce new lockouts. Added to these practical fears was the generalised disinclination of 'responsible' English trade unionists to become over-involved in Irish troubles.

All this did not imply an immediate instinct for surrender; it did imply the urgent pursuit of compromise, but, in pursuing this cause, with whom could they exercise moral authority? They could do so with the Belfast labour leaders, for whom they were now the only possible adequate source of finance and who, in any case, tended all too uncritically to venerate anything associated with British trade-union leaders. By contrast with the strikers, the Belfast employers had already shunned the efforts of other influential intermediaries and had remained unflinching in the face of a mass movement.

The first essential for the English delegates was to open lines of communication to the employers and, if this required the dropping of all preconditions, that was preferable to failure at the very beginning of their mission, with the incalculable results that would follow. For the employers, refusal to negotiate was not an immutable principle if the terms were right.

The initial signalling was undertaken on 20 July when Gee, Sexton and Mitchell met first Robert Gageby, then the Lord Mayor and some leading merchants. The merchants were not the employers engaged in the dispute but they could act as suitable messengers. The possibility of progress, from the employers' point of view, soon leaked as far as the press, and the *Belfast News-Letter* accurately predicted that, 'It is quite possible that some method may be arrived at by which masters and men may be brought to a friendly conference' and further observed that 'pressure will be brought to bear on the representatives to strengthen the argument for a resumption of work on the old terms, pending a reconsideration of the wages and hours of work'.[27]

The main disputes of the dockers and carters were hardly under discussion yet but the English delegates were soon deeply involved in what they viewed as a damage-limitation exercise involving the two most recent, and in themselves serious, extensions of the dispute, those affecting the coal quay workers and the ironmoulders. If Gee and Mitchell lacked a full appreciation of the linkage of all the disputes, the employers, for their part, scented the possibility of an important tactical victory. It was no doubt for this reason that when Gee and Mitchell met the Lord Mayor on 25 July Alex McDowell, the official representative of the employers, was present for the first time. Meanwhile the strikers' direct representatives, Larkin, Boyd, Alex Stewart and even Sexton, were banished to the Grand Central Hotel. Later Mitchell, as negotiator-in-chief, addressed a mass meeting of strikers at St Mary's Hall, at which he announced a successful settlement of the coal dispute. He then returned to the City Hall with Gee to sign the settlement both of this dispute and of that relating to the ironmoulders.

The ironmoulders' dispute was not directly linked with the other strikes. However, the settlement achieved for them by Gee and Mitchell showed how far the British labour leaders were prepared to go to force a settlement over the heads of the strikers in Belfast. The men had struck for an increase of two shillings a week to the existing wages of thirty-eight shillings a week for the sand moulders and forty shillings a week for loam moulders. On 2 July the employers had expressed willingness to go to arbitration. The men rejected this suggestion and also rejected a proposal from the employers that an English official of the union should be brought over to consider the arbitration proposal. The GFTU delegates, when told of this, proceeded to inform the union of the state of affairs and the President of the Ironfounders' Society, Mr Joseph Maddison, promptly travelled to Belfast and ordered the men on strike to accept a one-shilling-a-week increase or to forego strike pay.[28]

The coal settlement was far more disastrous. The terms agreed upon were humiliating for the coal men themselves. It was not until 5 August, nearly two weeks later, that Alex Boyd admitted 'they had been caught to some extent in a trap when they settled the coal dispute. The employers got the better hand of them for the reason that nothing had been committed to writing.' The position may have been even worse than that, because there does appear to have been a written agreement which the Belfast leaders did not see. H.R. Stockman, writing in *Labour Leader* on 9 August, described the episode as one of 'trickery' for which Isaac Mitchell was principally responsible. It was only after the discovery of this document that Larkin spelt out the tactical consequences of a separate settlement for the coal men: 'They had, as it were, withdrawn one of the wings of their army and allowed the employers to surround the rest.'[29]

Whatever the terms of the settlement, the tactical consequences of the coal men's return were disastrous. For the first time a group of strikers had accepted a piecemeal settlement. Now the dockers and carters were bound to ask should they not attempt to get back while they could. The carters, in particular, had refused generous terms offered at the end of June and had rejected out of hand overtures made by Gee and Mitchell in the period 19 to 25 July, precisely because neither offer included the dockers.[30] Larkin and other leaders had always emphasised the importance of solidarity; Larkin in particular had stressed the value of the sympathetic strike. The strikers had come to understand the principle of 'one out, all out' and its corollary, 'one back, all back'. Now the strike leaders, under pressure from the British leaders, had abandoned that principle.

More extraordinary and misleading was the attempt to dress up the settlement as a victory. On the night of 25 July Alex Stewart spoke of 'the first honours of war'. Larkin claimed that the coal men were to go back to work next morning with full recognition of their organisation, 'and their demand as to wages conceded to an extent which would mean an increase of eleven shillings per week to every man's pay'.[31] The *Belfast Evening Telegraph* the following day accurately described Larkin's claim as 'absolutely wrong'. Most papers gave the details correctly. The coal men were to get the rates agreed six weeks earlier and the employers were to be allowed to employ whoever they wished as stevedores, provided these stevedores were not themselves merchants. It was by no means even clear that the union was recognised – the *Belfast Evening Telegraph* commented, 'We understand that one of the main points for which the masters have been contending is conceded... the right to conduct their business without interference on the part of the union delegates.'

The same day, Friday 26 July, the mood of false euphoria over the settlement, which was encouraged by all the labour leaders, was given an added boost by a massive demonstration organised by the Trades Council. This showed that the coal settlement was made at a time when there was massive support for the strike movement from all sections of the working class in Belfast. James O'Connor Kessack, a correspondent for *Forward*, the Glasgow socialist paper, described sitting enthralled in the top of a tram on the Shankill Road as the massive demonstration, two or three miles long, wound past.[32]

James Sexton later claimed that 200,000 took part.[33] The *Irish News* described the composition of the march:

> One of its most striking features was the manner in which it demonstrated the different stages of organisation arrived at by the various bodies of workers represented. The older established societies, preceded by banners, many of which were designed with much taste... marched two and two with almost military precision, whilst the members of the more recently organised unions were collected in an irregularly formed but solid body, sometimes 20 abreast, rendering a computation of the total number taking part in the demonstration practically out of the question.

The procession went through the main working-class ghettos of the city. It passed via Ann Street, Queen's Bridge, Ballymacarrett, Albert Bridge, May Street, Howard Street, Durham Street, Falls Road, through to the Shankill Road, Crumlin Road, Clifton Street, North Queen Street, York Street, down Royal Avenue and then to the City Hall. The crowd at the City Hall was so vast that four separate platforms had to be used to address the masses.

Larkin and others did nothing to dispel the optimism of the occasion. Larkin once again praised the coal settlement:

> They had won a great victory. Someone had questioned his statement that the coal men would benefit by the settlement arrived at to the extent of 11s.0d. a week. Well, he repeated the statement and the figures if produced would prove it. The fact was that £500 a week would be added to the wages of the men labouring at the coal quays in consequence of the dispute. It was true that there had been some difficulty. It was true that two or three of the masters wanted now to back out of the agreement, notwithstanding all the anxiety over it, and should that be the case he hoped the men would stand firm by their rights.

Local labour leaders were less euphoric by Monday 29 July when John Murphy, Secretary of the Trades Council, told the men at a Custom House Square meeting that they 'were in as good a position as before the strike and in addition they had won for themselves a prestige which would not easily be lost'.[34] Prestige was to prove a poor substitute for eleven shillings a week.

William Walker used the presence of the English delegates as an excuse to cool tempers over the situation on the coal quays:

> As they knew, negotiations had been going on with regard to the carters and dockers and a conference was to take place the next day. In view of that conference, he did not wish to say a single word which would militate against the men, and he trusted nothing would be said by any speaker on that platform which would give the masters a chance to say that the leaders of that movement were lacking in tact and discretion, and the qualities that would enable them to handle a difficult and complex problem.

A speaker from Dublin, Mr Stewart, illustrated the increasing caution of the strike leaders when he admitted merely that 'they gained some of their demands'. He too spoke of other more intangible benefits: 'A great victory had been won for the International Workers' Union by the fact that the men of Belfast had had the good sense to sink their religious differences in the struggle.'[35]

Larkin made it clear on 1 August that he no longer stuck by his original claim for the settlement:

> As a result of the envoys from London it was decided that work should be resumed on the terms of the status quo, and that they should hold good for a month. He did not interfere in the bringing about of a settlement, although he had told the two English delegates that in the interests of the workers he would abide by what they did, but if the employers allowed the irritation to continue he would again have a hand in it.

Larkin still stood by the agreement. All that was wrong was that the employers were not abiding by it fully.

Alex Boyd put forward the position of the strike committee:

> So far the men had adhered loyally to the agreement and the leaders advised them to do nothing contrary to it; but some matters remained to be smoothed down. The employers had to be watched and their foremen had to be located still more. In one or two firms the men had been referred to the employers' manifesto and told that they had got back under its terms. That occasioned irritation and rightly so because the statement was false. It was an attempt to make the workers break through the

agreement, and he again counselled them not to fall into that net.

The following day, Friday 2 August, Boyd was again reassuring: 'So far as the coal men are concerned the little differences which had arisen had been satisfactorily adjusted, and they were merely matters of misunderstanding.'[36] Not until 5 August did Boyd admit, as already quoted, that 'nothing had been committed to writing', and only then did Larkin admit that they had 'withdrawn one of the wings of their army'.

Larkin now spoke in fighting tone, two weeks too late:

> The trouble in the coal trade had been settled by three Englishmen in his absence who knew nothing about the situation, and who succeeded in spoiling his plans, which would, if developed, have resulted in certain victory. They were in the same position as they were 13 weeks ago but they were quite prepared to start all over again and fight the battle anew.[37]

Although from 5 August Larkin described the coal settlement realistically in Belfast, he was still playing quite another tune elsewhere. Speaking in Londonderry on 22 August, he told dockers that in Belfast wages had been raised by between twenty-five and seventy-five per cent and that the wages of coal men had been raised from twenty-three to twenty-eight shillings per week.[38]

The coal men did not need any belated call to fight the 'battle anew'. From the day of the agreement, 25 July, they had actively resisted what they knew to be a disastrous settlement. On Friday 26 July they refused to carry coal to establishments where workers were still out on strike. Gee and Mitchell intervened and persuaded them to do so. Larkin and Boyd were unable to attend the normal Custom House Square meeting on Wednesday 31 July because they were busy trying to placate the coal men.[39] On 2 August the *Irish News* reported that the coal men were planning to come out again on 3 August.

The men were refusing to work under stevedores selected by the employers. The Lord Mayor, Lord Shaftesbury, appointed arbitrator by the terms of the agreement, had given judgment in favour of the masters on this issue. The men had rejected his decision. On Friday 2 August Gee and Mitchell met the Lord Mayor for six hours and also gave judgment in favour of the masters. It is little wonder that, in the words of the *Belfast News-Letter* of the following day, the men 'questioned the authority of the officials of the General Federation of Trade Unions to make such an arrangement'.

Discontent continued. On Monday 5 August the men struck at the coal merchants Davidsons and on the quays of the Antrim Iron Ore Company. These disputes over stevedoring and tonnage rates were no sooner settled than the men at Kelly's walked out on 7 August, demanding a tonnage rate instead of a time rate. The dispute lasted most of the day before the men were persuaded to return.[40] There remained much friction which was to flare up later.

Such was the disastrous aftermath of 'victory'. The moderate labour leaders, who had looked to the English delegates to find them a middle way between chaos and defeat, were in the end horrified at the peremptory fashion in which they had been sold down the river. The strike leaders, Larkin included, were, however, the architects of their own discomfiture. Larkin had accepted the financial argument for the talks, agreeing 'to stand out of the way if they [the English delegates] could bring about a settlement of the matter and avoid the shutting down of mills and factories'.[41] He, like the other strike leaders, did not look sufficiently critically at the terms of the settlement and was, of all the leaders, the most excessive and specific in his praise of a non-existent deal.

Larkin was technically correct when he said on 6 August that 'the men did not say, and never had said, that they would work with non-union men, and, as for himself, he would never sign any document in his life binding him to work with non-union men'.[42] However, even if he acted out of loyalty to a strike committee which had to a certain extent shunted him out of the way in the rush to the negotiating table, he had spent two weeks persuading workers to go back to work under just such an agreement.

The coal settlement was the first concrete intervention of the British trade union movement in the strike. It was so disastrous that it came under fire even from W.A. Appleton, a later GFTU delegate. Writing in a Nottingham paper he commented:

> I cannot help feeling that the settlement of the coal dispute seriously affected the men's chances of success. In my opinion, the Federation should have insisted upon negotiating for the whole of the interests involved in the dispute or none at all. Had this been done I am sure and certain the whole matter would have been settled not later than Saturday [3 August]

because Belfast would have had neither fire nor light, and public opinion would have compelled the manufacturers at least to meet the men and discuss terms.[43]

Lindsay Crawford, who knew the problems involved and yet was independent of the strike committee, raised the question in the *Ulster Guardian*. He felt that too much faith had been placed in the British delegates:

> [It was] of course necessary for the Irish workmen to be linked onto the big unions across the Channel, and the interference of the English head officials was justified by the monetary backing they brought. At the same time we venture to suggest that no colour should be lent to the suggestion that the English officials stultified local trade unionism by carrying on independent negotiations with Irish employers with whom the men were in dispute. We fear Englishmen are too prone to regard Irishmen as inferior beings. We hope that it is not a mistake common to English Labour circles, for it is one which Ulstermen are bound to resent. If negotiations are to be done in future, let it be done through local officials responsible, and let English officials stand behind them with moral and material support. It would be disastrous for the cause of Labour in Ulster were the impression to be created in the minds of employers here that, in cases of dispute, they could go behind the backs of local officials to headquarters officials in England. Whatever has been gained in Belfast for the workers has been gained by their leaders, and their influence should not be weakened by any undue interference of officials from HQ.[44]

The active intervention of the British trade-union leaders was damaging enough, but as doubts spread in the wake of the coal settlement the continued inaction of one key union, the Amalgamated Society of Railway Servants, provided the pretext for some in Belfast to consider a wider capitulation. An unnamed 'prominent local labour leader' told the *Irish News* on 26 July 'that so far as the dockers were concerned the men were prepared to go as far in the direction of a compromise as they reasonably could' and that he believed they would 'temporarily waive' their claim to recognition, because the ASRS 'intended to raise the question of the recognition of [their] union in England in September'. Once it had been hoped that this development would take place in June, now it was

September and, in the event, the ASRS's capacity for evading any struggle was to prove more extensive still.[45]

Instead of unity in action between Belfast dockers and English railway employees, there was a sordid dispute over the alleged use of ASRS members as blacklegs on the quays in Belfast. A resolution condemning the ASRS on this count was passed in early July at a meeting of Belfast Trades Council.[46] Larkin alleged that 'all the blacklegs are... members of the ASRS, one being a branch secretary',[47] a claim later supported by H.R. Stockman in modified form in his Belfast column for the *Labour Leader*, where he claimed that 'at least 32 are members of the ASRS'.[48] Stockman also argued that these men 'would be only too glad to get away from Belfast if the ASRS would take up their case'. The matter appeared sufficiently outrageous for the *Labour Leader* to assert in an editorial on 19 July that it 'demands an explanation from the executive of the Railwaymen's Society'.

Richard Bell MP, Secretary of the ASRS, responded from the safe distance of Dublin that he knew of no such 'scabbing' in Belfast. However, by 2 August the union had sent its Irish organiser, Mr Mear, to Belfast to offer union assistance to any blacklegs wishing to defect.[49] If the ASRS was belatedly willing to make minimal efforts to stop railwaymen, whether union members or not, blacklegging in Belfast, it implied no enthusiasm for the dispute. Richard Bell made this clear when he said that he hoped the Belfast dispute would be settled 'in a manner just and fair to both sides'.[50]

However, the main impact of the British trade-union movement remained the intervention of the GFTU whose delegates had, in turn, encouraged the pragmatic and cautious instincts of James Sexton. They failed to meet more than the most basic financial needs of the strike movement although this was a key basis for their authority. The NUDL was to spend less than £5,000 on the entire Belfast dispute, and the GFTU a bare £1,692. Indeed, the strike committee's income from all sources during the dispute was to amount to no more than £8,922, a far cry from £48,000.[51] The immediate price paid by the strike movement for this less than wholehearted commitment was a serious tactical setback.

What was worse for the Belfast labour leaders was that this reduction in the scale of the dispute failed to ward off the evils of the political and national questions they dreaded so much. These matters were now to erupt in a particularly dramatic form as a direct and inevitable result of a widespread strike movement in the city.

9

Police mutiny

As part of their offensive to drive the strikers to the negotiating table, the employers had persuaded the police and military authorities to provide increased protection for blackleg carters from 18 July. This extra strain on the increasingly demoralised police force helped to spark off a police mutiny.

Rank-and-file policemen had serious grievances of their own. There had been two enquiries into their conditions but, in the words of the *Constabulary Gazette*,[1] one made 'paltry recommendations that had never been put into effect. The other, confined to Belfast, has been kept by the State as a secret document.' The first enquiry had been held in 1901 and applied to the whole Royal Irish Constabulary. Although the Inspector General of the RIC, Sir Neville Chamberlain, had recommended the implementation of its proposals on four separate occasions, nothing had been done. The second enquiry applied only to Belfast and was held in 1906. It stemmed from a case the previous year in which a man had been wrongly convicted of counterfeiting, and there was evidence that police officers had connived at his conviction. The enquiry found that 'a deep and widespread feeling of discontent exists in the Belfast police force on the subject of promotion'. Both the report and its recommendations were suppressed as a direct result of the Inspector General's opposition to the whole enquiry and, in particular, to its strictures on the organisation of the Belfast force.[2]

Policemen in Belfast were not well off. Pay varied from seventy-eight pounds, eight shillings per annum to sixty-two pounds, sixteen shillings, that is roughly thirty shillings a week down to twenty-four shillings a week.[3] They were better paid than the bulk of the strikers, but policemen were expected to live in the more respectable parts of the city, a heavy burden for constables drafted in from outlying areas. The police were supposed to get one shilling extra if they were on continuous duty for more than eight hours, but complained that they were being continually taken off duty after seven-and-a-half hours in order to prevent this payment.[4] It was against this background that a More Pay Movement had been flourishing in the Belfast ranks for some time.

There were only 1,000 men in the Belfast force and the strikes put an enormous burden on them. As early as 11 July the *Northern Whig* reported, 'The strain on the police is daily increasing and yesterday between fifty and sixty members of the force from Henry Street barracks alone were on duty from six am to 6 pm.' On 29 June a letter to the *Northern Whig* made clear the difficulties faced by the police. The correspondent complained, 'The spectacle to which we were treated yesterday of a wagon load of goods going to the quay under the protection of a score of constables is a singular one indeed. Of course on that basis it would require half the entire force of the RIC to protect the traffic to and from Belfast Harbour and the Railway Terminus.'

Strikers and their supporters were aware of their impact on police morale: as Bob Getgood later recalled, 'The children attacked their children and their wives were getting into trouble – they were getting into trouble at home, at the barracks and on the job.'[5] The first mention of police discontent on a strike platform came on 7 July when a Mr Jones of Birmingham, speaking at a Belfast Socialist Society meeting on the Custom House steps, commented, 'The police themselves had been badly overworked from six in the morning till eleven and twelve at night, and he saw no reason why they should not bind themselves into a trade union.'[6]

Evidence that this hopeful socialist proposition might have some substance appeared on 10 July when a letter signed 'Willing to Strike' appeared in the *Irish News*. This referred to 'the screeches of the capitalist newspapers in Belfast for the past few days over what they term the gross neglect of duty by the police force of this city in not attacking and batoning the unfortunate "strikers" who are merely looking for justice from their employers', and went on to argue, 'The strikers are, as ourselves, trying to better their conditions, and if we work together we will wring from the government what I trust the strikers will soon wring from the capitalists – more pay.'

'Willing to Strike' wrote again on 16 July, this time in sarcastic vein:

> Of course we should slaughter all before us to settle this strife for the capitalists, who hate us as much as their unfortunate workmen. When they failed to turn the strike into a sectarian

business, they thought it would be a good idea if they got the police and 'strikers' into conflict.

This letter also forecast organisational developments and, in doing so, indicated that 'Willing to Strike' was at least a leading organiser of the More Pay Movement in the ranks of the police, although this was not evident at the time, given that the *Irish News* had a reputation for publishing letters of doubtful authenticity. To the authorities, 'Willing to Strike's' new letter may well have appeared to be the elaborate fantasy of an imposter. However, to a mutinous policeman it may equally have appeared that the *Irish News* was the only paper likely to publish his letter.

> In a short time a circular will be sent to each of your barracks giving you instructions how to act. In the meantime keep cool, don't get into unnecessary conflict with the workmen: subscribe as much as you can for their support... and say nothing. Your officers will be against you in this movement and will look for victims.

The day after the appearance of this letter, Larkin referred to the situation of the police, who 'were working eighteen hours a day, and they would go on strike too – only they dared not'.[7] He hardly expressed confidence that they would do so, and it would be wrong to read any instrumental role into his brief comment. At a point in the strike when the police were pressing the picketers hard, and threatening to intervene more effectively, it was clearly in the interests of the strikers to play upon any sign of demoralisation in their ranks, with perhaps, at best, the hope that the authorities might reconsider the wisdom of extending the police role.

Certainly, as in the ensuing days the *Irish News* increasingly became the forum for the views of disgruntled policemen, some of their correspondence had a Larkinite flavour, but this is to say no more than that they had been affected by their recent experiences on the streets of Belfast and elsewhere in Ireland. 'Willing to Strike' continued his campaign on 22 July arguing that...

> RIC officers were doing all in their power to humiliate the Belfast police by turning them into 'blacklegs', to please their friends the capitalists. They tried to make us accept tea from these companies, and put us under an obligation to these

'English sweaters', but we indignantly refused to sell our independence.

In an editorial published on the same day the *Irish News* gave extracts from other letters it had received: 'It is shameful to see a uniformed police officer sitting under the funnel of a "Puffing Billy" or taking the other side of the car to the driver and getting hooted and jeered at through the streets. Walking after the prohibited wagons is bad enough, and sometimes one has to run a little.' Some policemen, aware of the unhappy nature of their role on the streets of Belfast, went on to analyse the role of the RIC in Ireland as a whole. The *Irish News* editorial on 22 July included the following extract from a letter: 'We have never shirked any task imposed on us by our pay masters no matter how odious it might have been. We have made evictions possible from Donegal to Cork. We have left nothing undone that was demanded or expected of us. We regret our past misdeeds.' 'Salve', writing on the same date, said:

> The RIC were not established and armed to police Ireland but to soldier it. They were established as a garrison to enable those arbitrary rulers and landlords to impoverish, enslave and wring rack-rents from the poor. The tyrants and landlords were the indirect employers and masters of the police. These masters have nearly all fled, owing to recent land legislation, and the few who remain have no interest in the country; they are merely waiting for their 'bonus'.

There were very contrary views expressed elsewhere, although they confirmed the existence of grievances. Thus an unidentified constable told the *Belfast Evening Telegraph* on 29 July, 'We cannot forget the abuse that was hurled on us from strike platforms during the early part of the strike, when we were told no decent man could wear our uniform, and we will get our grievances remedied without the aid of men whose motives for assisting us I, for one, am not sure of.' A sergeant on 1 August argued that Larkin 'may get his dockers to follow him but he will never be a leader of a unanimous body of constables'. Strong confirmation of the separate nature of the police agitation came from the *Belfast Evening Telegraph* which, although acutely hostile to the dockers and carters, was positively sympathetic to the police case on the basis that it 'had nothing whatever to do' with the broader strike movement, and indeed had support 'including the great city merchants and the direct ratepayers upon whom in reality the ultimate cost must fall'.[8]

The incident which sparked off the mutiny occurred on 19 July as a direct result of the decision to provide more active escorts for motor wagons. On that day Constable William Barrett[9] refused to sit beside a blackleg driver on a motor wagon. He was suspended from duty. The incident occurred at 11.55 am at the Heysham shed. Official statements taken from the officers involved made clear the nature of the situation. District Inspector Thomas Keaveney ordered Barrett to sit beside the blackleg. He refused and Keaveney appealed to Head Constable Fraser Waters who ordered Barrett to do as he was told. Keaveney later explained the logic behind his orders: 'Mr Kemp [the employer] told me that Mr Morrell, the Acting Commissioner of Police, promised him that a detective would sit with the driver of the motor.'

The *Constabulary Gazette,* commenting on the incident, made clear the feeling within the force:

> In the first place, if a policeman was necessary he should have been a uniformed man; and, in the second place, there is, we are informed, an order with which the officers ought to be familiar, to the effect that members of the RIC are directed not to sit with an obnoxious person when on protection duty, but rather to drive one vehicle behind them.[10]

Barrett, dispensing with these legal niceties, later discussed the incident in a letter to the *Irish News* published on 8 August:

> The precipitating cause of the police strike and subsequent trouble leading to the importation of over 6,000 soldiers into Belfast was due to the unwarranted conduct of the Acting Commissioner [Morrell] in having entered into an alliance with the railway companies and masters in order to defeat the carters and the dockers in securing the rights they are fighting for.

Three days after Barrett's suspension, on 22 July, the circular foreshadowed by 'Willing to Strike' on 16 July appeared and was published by the *Irish News*. The main body of it ran:

> Comrades. . . having regard to the letters which have recently appeared in the public press, and the feeling of indignation which we are all sure prevails in our midst, the hardships and

injustice which are lately becoming unbearable, the despotic rule which prevents us from ventilating this injustice, we cannot refrain any longer from making our views public.

The circular then referred to the 'exorbitant cost of living and the excessive difficult duty which we have to perform', and went on to say that the time was now ripe for 'a petition setting forth our views on this matter', to 'be submitted to His Majesty's Government for due consideration'.

The circular was moderate in tone: 'We have been told lately to strike but such is not intended if it may be avoided by granting us the justice which we deem necessary.' It concluded: 'Now, comrades, you are not required to do anything underhand or injurious to your position. The press is always willing to assist you. All that is required is justice and no body of men have remained so long waiting patiently for this as the police force.'

The circular gave detailed organisational arrangements for a delegate meeting to be held in Musgrave Street Barracks at 7 pm on Wednesday 24 July:

> On receipt of this circular you will please hold a general meeting at each station. An intelligent man will be appointed to represent the party, who will enquire carefully into the views of the men, and note same for the information of the general meeting. This man should be appointed by his comrades; he will sign first, the remainder of the party to sign after. Then the list of names should be taken possession of by the selected man.

The representatives were to bring 'their list of names, also a summary of views'. The resolutions to be proposed at the meeting were:

(1) A rise of pay of 1s. per man
(2) That our pension on leaving be calculated as three-quarters of pay
(3) To appoint a solicitor to draw up a petition in legal form, and submit same to His Majesty's Government
(4) To apply to the Inspector-General by wire for his permission to submit same
(5) General[11]

The day before the meeting, Tuesday 23 July, Acting Commissioner Morrell took steps to prevent it by issuing a circular headed, 'More Pay Movement'. This read: 'With reference to the circular which has been sent to several barracks in the city this morning asking the men to hold a general meeting, I have directed that you [the officers] remind the men that no such meeting can be held without the direction of the Inspector-General.' Supremely over-confident, he informed Dublin that he did not expect the men's call for a meeting to 'have much effect'.[12]

On the morning of the meeting 'Willing to Strike' replied in the *Irish News*. He confirmed that the dissident circular 'had been seized in a number of stations by those in charge on its arrival, and submitted to the Commissioners', and went on, 'Comrades, hold your meeting in Musgrave Street Barracks, as suggested, and if not permitted to hold it there, march in a body to Queen's Square and hold it there.'

That night, between 200 and 300 men defied the official ban and went to the meeting held in the reading room at Musgrave Street Police Station. An *Irish News* reporter attended the meeting and gave a full account of the proceedings. The room was crammed to the door, but before the meeting could begin a head constable appeared and said the meeting was banned. The men shouted, 'We will hold the meeting' and Barrett said, 'Let all the men who are with us stand here', pointing to a corner. Several men moved to the corner to the accompaniment of deafening cheers. Then from the stairs came a shout of 'Attention'. The men stood to attention and Acting Commissioner Morrell entered. He asked angrily, 'What is this, men? What is this I hear?' There was no answer. He then asked a constable, 'What service have you?' 'Seven years,' came the reply. Morrell then ordered, 'All men of twenty years' service come forward.' Shouts came from the assembled men, 'Not one of ye go forward, not one of ye don't.' Morrell proceeded to walk round the room threatening individual men. Barrett then spoke up:

> Let no man, let no man tell his service to anyone. We are here to hold a meeting. Why should we be prevented from holding a meeting? It is as much our right as any other men in the city. Don't allow yourselves to be bullied. If we can't hold our meeting here we can hold it outside. But in any case you must stand together. Stand together, comrades, and all will be well.

Morrell advanced towards Barrett and ordered, 'Constable, leave this room.' Barrett replied, 'No, I will not, I am acting perfectly properly in warning these men against interference. I will not.' Morrell and District Inspector Clayton rushed forward to arrest Barrett. The constable next to Barrett punched Morrell and he went down on the floor. Morrell then punched Constable McGrath and declared him suspended. McGrath replied, 'I don't care about you or your service. I can make as good a living anywhere else.' Then pandemonium broke out. Barrett pleaded for quiet and asked permission to reason with the men. He was again ordered out of the room. Barrett then ordered the men to fall in, two deep, and march to St Mary's Hall. 'Come on, I will show you a place where we can hold our meeting.'

The men ran cheering down the stairs and lined up two deep in the yard. Just as the gate was being opened Morrell shouted:

> I appeal to you for God's sake, don't go any further with this thing. Don't go outside that gate into the street. Don't make a disgrace of the policemen of Belfast. . . I am going into my office. Appoint five men amongst you and I will let them confer with me there. I give you ten minutes to consider this.

After brief discussion the men accepted the proposal and five delegates met Morrell.[13] They made arrangements to meet him on Saturday 27 July. Soon after this the men dispersed.

The *Irish News* account of the Wednesday night meeting created a sensation. The Tory press dismissed the account as malicious Nationalist gossip. The *Northern Whig,* commenting on the incident in which Morrell was knocked down, said 'all that happened was that his foot was trodden on'.[14] Other sources, however, confirmed the *Irish News* account; thus the *Constabulary Gazette* described how, 'When physical force was resorted to, resistance followed. County Inspector Morrell was knocked down and both he and Mr Clayton were driven from the room; tables and forms were overturned and the police cheered defiance to all authority.'[15]

The appearance in the press of accounts of the disturbances seriously embarrassed Morrell who had hoped to keep the whole matter hushed up. They horrified the Under Secretary for Ireland, Sir Anthony MacDonnell who, like the rest of the Dublin Castle staff, first learnt of the problems in Belfast from the press. MacDonnell broke off a tour of Roscommon and hurried to Dublin to demand an explanation from Morrell.[16] On Friday 26 July, once the story had broken, Morrell did issue a statement confirming that some disagreement had taken place, and saying, 'I have agreed to hear the views of the five men selected on Wednesday last, tomorrow evening at my office, and no more men are to attend unless I send for them.'[17] However, Dublin Castle required a more detailed explanation, and Morrell wired his description of events, saying:

> Two constables did become insubordinate and excited and I suspended them and ordered them to leave the room. A rush was made for the door by the whole party. No violence was offered to any officers. The only promise I made to any of the men was that I would not take any notice of any personal discourtesy offered in their excited state to myself, and would remove the suspension for the present.[18]

This was bad enough. MacDonnell commented that the Acting Commissioner, 'with a view to prevent a public scandal, seems to have informed them [the dissidents] that he would condone their conduct'.[19]

At the time, however, all elements of the Irish administration were equally anxious to minimise embarrassment arising from the events in Belfast, and, answering questions at Westminster on 25 July, Augustine Birrell was happy to take Morrell's line, arguing that. . .

> The circumstances seem to be greatly exaggerated. Some cases of insubordination occurred amongst a small body of men – not anything like 200 – but they yielded at once to the very wise treatment they received, and I am assured that all danger may at once be dismissed from our minds.[20]

This attempt to keep the lid on the affair, made as it was in the most public forum of all, was seen as deeply provocative by the men involved, and led Constable Barrett to break regulations and write a letter to the *Irish News*, which appeared on 27 July. It was to provide the eventual excuse for Barrett's dismissal from the force and ran in part: 'The question is whether Mr Morrell, who presumably is mainly responsible for the material put before Mr Birrell, as well as for the course taken by the press, or I, state the truth. I now give an emphatic contradiction to the reports alluded to and I say that every material fact and circumstance in the *Irish News* account, however obtained, of Thursday is absolutely accurate.'[21] It remained to be seen who would command the loyalty of the men in the immediate future.

10
The mutiny crushed

Any doubts which remained about the serious nature of the police troubles were quickly dispelled on Saturday 27 July. That morning the news had broken of the suspension of Constable Barrett, leader of the dissidents, but by mid-afternoon it was clear that others had not been dissuaded from attending what was now an illegal meeting at Musgrave Street Barracks.

> The crowd cheered vociferously as batch after batch of tall, broad shouldered uniformed men, most of them carrying canes or walking sticks and walking with a jaunty swing, approached from all quarters of the city, and proceeded to crush their way through the mass of people to the barrack square.[1]

More than 500, perhaps as many as 800, out of the Belfast force of some 1,000 men made their way to the banned meeting[2] and were quickly drawn up into ranks six deep within the square. When loyal officers attempted to close the gates to the barracks, dissidents prevented them, arguing that they 'wanted the public to see what took place inside',[3] though for the moment, with the exception of a couple of newspaper reporters, 'other civilians were kept out of the gates by men who had trades union buttons upon them'.[4]

The tension of the occasion was acute – fuelled by rumours that the military garrison in the city had been confined to barracks in preparation for action,[5] and that special trains were already being held in readiness to rush reinforcements from Londonderry.[6] More alarming still was the suggestion that dissident policemen in several barracks within the city had already taken steps to protect their own arms from seizure.[7]

Before any formal meeting could begin in the square at Musgrave Street Barracks, Acting Commissioner Morrell and District Inspector John Gelston came forward to be greeted by a mixture of cheers and boos. Morrell then proceeded to read a statement, his last ploy in the attempt to prevent a complete collapse of his authority. He now suggested that those who wished to hold a meeting should give their names and nominate time and a place, and that he would then communicate with the Inspector-General and recommend that it be allowed. He ended by saying 'You have got a fair offer from me, now return quietly to your barracks'.

His proposal was greeted by some cheers but more heckling. Constables shouted 'What about the threats?', or 'We have waited long enough.' At this point, Barrett stepped forward to appeal for quiet, but his commanding officers were not prepared to share an illegal platform with a suspended man and began to walk rapidly away. It was a turning point – the men shouted, 'Don't run away' and then roared for Barrett.

Barrett then explained how he had been suspended for writing to the *Irish News* and in effect for refusing to assist blacklegs, but his initial proposals were moderate in the extreme:

> All I just ask you to do is this – let each and every one return to his barracks. Do your duty loyally and faithfully until this evening week, and then we will hold a meeting.

With the one important distinction that he was now addressing a proscribed assembly, Barrett was suggesting little more than Morrell, and there was some unease in his audience with cries of 'Too long', 'We'll give them one hour to reinstate you' or even 'Wreck the barracks'.

Barrett replied, 'No, we will give them eight days to consider the matter and give us a definite answer'. There were of course perils in delay but Barrett and the other ringleaders were still committed to their petition as a means of seeking redress of grievances. Any petition required time to answer, and they had taken steps to ensure that it could not simply be ignored – 'your petition has been forwarded now to the Commissioner, and will be forwarded to the Inspector-General in due course. Another copy will be forwarded by me to the Chief Secretary, and a third one to a member of the House of Commons, so that there will be no hunker sliding.'

The petition contained the demands outlined in the circular advertising the initial Musgrave Street meeting and concluded: 'The urgent character of the demands now being made by the men necessitates their being urgently attended to and, acting on our instructions, we have to press strongly, and with the greatest possible respect, for a definite assurance within a week that our case will be favourably dealt with forthwith.'[8]

> The urgent character of the demands now made by the men necessitates their being immediately attended to; and, acting on our instructions, we have to press strongly, and with the greatest possible respect, for a definite assurance within a week that our case will be favourably dealt with forthwith.
>
> We beg to subscribe ourselves, on behalf of the men in the five City Districts,
>
> GENTLEMEN,
> YOUR OBEDIENT SERVANTS,
>
> *William R. J. Shaw. Const. 56030*
> *William Barrett Const 57754*
> *William Naughton Const 57446.*
> *John Lanner Const 58.837,*
> *John McGovern Const 57991*
>
> BELFAST,
> 26th. July 1907.

The mutineers' signatures on the copy of the petition sent to the Chief Secretary (SPO 1908 CSORP 20333)

The police loudly cheered Barrett's explanation, but a new factor immediately threatened his control of the situation as the evident excitement within the barracks became too much for the ever-growing crowd outside and the pressure on the gates overcame the few trade-union stewards. Within moments, a mass of civilian strikers and their supporters had poured into the barracks and become inextricably mixed with the dissident policemen. Barrett rose to the occasion in addressing his new and wider audience: 'We have been threatened, here in this yard, that they can put ten thousand men in our places. Well, we will have a hundred thousand loyal union men waiting out there for them.' Barrett then attempted to wind down the proceedings by reading letters of support from all over Ireland, announcing that the next meeting would be held at the Custom House steps, and asking everyone to disperse.

The heady momentum of the occasion rendered this a forlorn hope. Barrett was chaired and carried forthwith by a mixed crowd of police and civilians straight to the Custom House steps. Here it was evident, according to the *Irish News*, that 'the plan of campaign had not been definitely decided upon'. Barrett again urged dispersal, but was overruled by his supporters, and the assembly proceeded back into the barracks, marched out through the rear gate into Town Hall Street and went on to besiege the Police Commissioner's office. The sole restraining influence was provided by civilian strike pickets 'taking the part of peace officers and endeavouring to marshal the crowd in order'. The police delegates, including Barrett and supported by the roars of the crowd, now successfully sought admission to the Commissioner's office.

Acting Commissioner Morrell had earlier retreated there in some disarray. He had exceeded his instructions by speaking to the men assembled in the barracks at all,[9] and this to no avail – now he was surrounded in his own office. He wired Dublin in some panic saying 'the situation looks very bad',[10] and the authorities there were able to provide him with a pretext for staving off immediate confrontation. The Inspector General, already dubious of Morrell's ability either to assess or manage the situation, had taken the precaution some hours earlier of dispatching Assistant Inspector General Alexander Gambell to Belfast. Morrell was now ordered to stall pending his arrival and accordingly Morrell was able to meet the dissident delegates merely to inform them of Gambell's expected arrival at 6 pm – it was now a little after 5 pm.[11]

When the delegates announced this the crowd began to disperse, but with the clear intention of meeting later. Indeed, the delay gave Barrett and his colleagues time to ring round the various barracks in the city urging a maximum turnout that evening.[12] By 6 pm police and civilians were reassembling at Musgrave Street Barracks in, if anything, larger numbers. It was very evident that the crisis of the day remained to be resolved.

Meanwhile other parties had become involved. Conservative councillor F.C. Johnston met some of the policemen outside the barracks and agreed to intervene in order 'to try to allay the excited condition of the men'.[13] The labour leaders, whose Saturday meetings at the Custom House steps had been almost deserted by those attracted to events at Musgrave Street, were equally aware of the explosive potential of the situation. Strike pickets had already helped maintain order on the fringes of the police meetings, but the police leaders had shown their inexperience in organising their demonstration, and now police and civilian strikers were once more assembled within Musgrave Street Barracks. If any control were to be maintained over the situation it was time to take a hand. On this occasion Larkin could not be blamed for developments – he was in Dublin;[14] the decision to participate in the police meeting was taken by the moderate labour leaders.

All those gathered at the barracks faced a long wait before Gambell actually reached Belfast or could be contacted. The crowd was initially good humoured, but there were signs that matters could easily get out of hand – at an early stage copies of the *Belfast Evening Telegraph* and its sister paper, the sporting weekly *Ireland's Saturday Night*, were ceremonially burned – but once again trade-union influence was very evident in maintaining order. When one hothead raised the cry 'To the Liverpool sheds and throw the blacklegs into the dock', 'not a man of the many strikers stirred, and when the wild shout was repeated two of the pickets seized the shouter and hustled him through the gates into the street'.[15]

The key development of the night did not take place in the barracks, rather at the nearby Commissioner's office where Gambell arrived shortly before 8 pm. Gambell, acting under instructions from Dublin, refused to see the dissident police delegates, but a hurried compromise was arranged by which Councillor Johnston, acting as an unofficial representative of the men, was admitted to hear the news that Barrett was not being reinstated.

Barrett now returned to the barracks where the news of his continued suspension was greeted with an angry roar. He did not, however, choose to capitalise on the mood of the moment, but made a plea for moderation and reminded the crowd of the tactics already adopted:– 'The question of the police grievances is now in the hands of the authorities and they have a week to consider matters. Go home and do your duty as disciplined and well-ordered men for the present.' He reserved any threat for the future: 'If I am not re-instated within the week, you will know what to do.'

Barrett was followed by an array of trade-union speakers, all of whom urged the crowds to follow Barrett's advice and return home. Much of what they had to say was calculated to reduce tension. The *Irish Independent* said of James Sexton, the dockers' leader, that 'after the excitement of the day his cool, measured tones fell upon his hearers like icy drops of water', and he was followed by Alex Stewart whose speech 'somewhat dampened the exuberance of the less determined spirits, for with pitiless clearness he pointed out the difficulties that lay ahead of them'.[16]

That is not to say that the labour leaders failed to offer encouragement to the dissidents. They did, but it was encouragement singularly remote from the needs of men deeply implicated in an illegal movement and attempting to promote a petition from that insecure ground. Thus James Sexton urged them to 'form a trade union and you will have fifty Labour men in the House of Commons behind you', and went on, 'There will be an important debate and that as soon as possible.' He then argued that policemen should have the right to compensation under the Workmen's Compensation Act 'because they had to encounter great danger sometimes in keeping the peace in Belfast'. This was a nice point when speaking to an audience several of whom had bandaged heads, but winning control of the situation required a determined, perhaps excessive, emphasis on solidarity. As Sexton put it, 'we do not recognise any distinction in the labour movement between the man who works with a baton and the man who works with a spade'.

Barrett had referred earlier to the support of 100,000 trade unionists to encourage his men to hold firm at the meeting; now a trade-union speaker, Mr Gambell, used their theoretical availability in the background as an argument for dispersing the meeting because 'if the police wanted any assistance they could turn out 100,000 trade unionists to aid them'. Alex Boyd, who spoke not as a trade-union leader but as a representative of the ratepayers,[17] suggested it was unlikely that this assistance would be needed anyway; instead 'he hoped that Sir Neville Chamberlain [the Inspector General] in whom he had every confidence, would investigate the matter to the bottom'.

No speaker suggested that, to secure their position, the dissidents might require more urgent action than a meeting one week later. The last speaker, Councillor Johnston, by his very identity encouraged the belief that the agreed tactics might be adequate; here he was, a Conservative, and, although 'it was quite against his wish that he spoke there', he did not mince his words on the injustice of police conditions – 'The government for the past twenty years has treated the police shamefully.' Many a dissident must have hoped that he was representative of a wider range of influential citizens who could act on their behalf. Johnston concluded the meeting with the oft-heard appeal that the police should return to their duties and the civilians to their homes. The series of meetings had now lasted some six hours. The repetition highlighted an increasing lack of momentum, exhaustion had set in and an explosive situation had for the moment been defused.

Assistant Inspector General Gambell doubted for how long. He telephoned Dublin Castle, warning that, if steps were taken against Barrett, 'I think you ought to expect the worst' and that if the men's petition received an unfavourable reply the police might well 'insist on striking and [would] probably march through the town accompanied by a large mob'.[18]

In Belfast the Unionist press no longer spoke of Nationalist scaremongering; on Monday 29 July the *Belfast News-Letter* said, 'When we say that these men numbered more than 500, that they met in defiance of orders and that they, or some of them, hooted their officers, it will be seen that the situation is serious enough and calls for prompt and decisive action on the part of the Government.' Perhaps because of the very seriousness of the situation the *Belfast Evening Telegraph* took a more conciliatory line, suggesting a 'practical' and 'moderate' course of action, namely that the Inspector General should meet the five dissident delegates and that 'he could do a great deal by way of recommending to the executive ameliorative measures'.[19]

The dissidents now found themselves powerless to do more than speculate anxiously over conflicting attitudes in the press. Their strongest card had been that they had acted when the authorities were powerless and, so long as that remained the case, radical letters to the press, insults to officers, and mutinous meetings had, if anything, strengthened their hand. It was, in the end, an advantage they had not chosen to make use of; instead they were now reliant on a 'legal' strategy in circumstances in which they had no legal rights. Indeed, in spite of the legalism of their petition, even its terminology was open to attack. The five dissident representatives had forwarded their petition with 'the greatest possible respect' but in stating that they were 'acting on instructions' they admitted that they were responsible to an illegal organisation within the force. They had also stated that their demands 'necessitated action within a week', an ultimatum which was hardly excessive in the heated conditions in which the petition was agreed, but was unlikely to win favour after the breathing space which they themselves had now allowed.

At first, even within the force, the signs were contradictory. In Belfast, Assistant Inspector General Gambell noted, 'Even the higher ranks have, I fear, some sympathy with the movement',[20] and elsewhere support came at a very senior level from Deputy Inspector General Heffernan Considine who sent Under Secretary Sir Anthony MacDonnell an unsolicited memorandum arguing that, while there should be disciplinary proceedings, there should also be 'conciliation in respect to what I am disposed to believe are demands made with some justice'.[21]

Such an approach struck no sympathetic chord with MacDonnell who, while tainted in Unionist eyes as a Catholic and principal advocate of the abortive devolution scheme of 1905, had been viewed as one of the few Catholics who could be safely appointed to the highly sensitive post of Under Secretary because of his impeccable record of imperial service and social conservatism. He was no liberal on questions of discipline, carrying with him from his Indian days the nickname 'the Bengal tiger',[22] one he was to live up to in his handling of the entire Belfast crisis. He was soon talking of dismissals, suspensions and transfers, and on 30 July, in a memorandum to Chief Secretary Augustine Birrell, was already highly alarmist, warning that 'the temper of the men is very bad; that there are doubts about surrendering their arms and ammunition'. By 2 August his enthusiasm for a purge was reaching awesome proportions as he argued, 'It is in the highest degree inexpedient to have some 200–300 insubordinate men in Belfast... if the 200 or 300 cannot be identified I may be driven to proposing the transfer of every constable in Belfast who does not give his word that he did not take part in the disorder.'[23]

It was an extreme reaction, perhaps coloured by MacDonnell's own wounded pride in failing adequately to predict the course of events in Belfast, and Birrell now had to urge caution, expressing the hope that 'the number will be restricted as much as possible as these men will be a doubtful factor and may affect the feelings of their future comrades'.[24] Before any disciplinary steps could be taken, Belfast had to be secured, and here the authorities acted with great rapidity and on an extraordinary scale.

There were normally two regiments stationed in Belfast and now elements of four more were rushed to the city. The Irish administration did not wait for a requisition from the Lord Mayor, representing the civil authority, as it was legally bound to do, but, as MacDonnell later explained, acted 'independently altogether of the municipal authorities in Belfast'[25] and Assistant Inspector General Gambell took the actual decisions, right down to recommending that the reinforcements 'should not be Irish regiments'.[26]

In quick succession, 500 men of the 1st Battalion Cameron Highlanders, 700 men of the Berkshires, the 4th Battalion of the Middlesex Regiment and the 2nd Battalion of the Essex Regiment rushed to the city, some 2,550 men in all, to add to the existing garrison elements of the 2nd Battalion Royal Sussex Regiment and the 1st Battalion of the Rifle Brigade, which since June had had the support of a squadron of the 3rd Dragoon Guards.[27] In addition to actual arrivals, there were other rumours. Thus the *Morning Post* heard of 'artillery and Gatling guns ready to be dispatched at a moment's notice to the capital of loyal Ulster'[28] and the more radical *Daily News* was one of the first English papers to express disquiet at the extent of preparations, commenting, 'It is impossible to imagine a dockers' strike at Liverpool or Hull producing such a tremendous marshalling of military forces, and to the ordinary mind such a display in an English city would be likely to precipitate rather than to divert any possible catastrophe.'[29]

For the moment, of course, the troops were there to overawe the dissident police, and on 30 July, the day on which the first 1,200 reinforcements arrived, Barrett and his colleagues had further cause for disquiet when a meeting of all district inspectors, head constables and sergeants was held and rumours soon spread that a list of the names of the dissidents was being compiled. 'Willing to Strike', in a letter published both in the *Belfast News-Letter* and the *Irish News* on 31 July, had to concede that these ill omens were having an effect and warned, 'Comrades the demon of dissension is amongst you. "Divide and Conquer" is the latest move.' Apparently, more moderate protestors were considering going back to square one and submitting a new petition, not connected with the stormy Musgrave Street meetings.

Time had, in fact, run out even for second thoughts of this kind, for the Irish administration had already prepared a rejection of the dissidents' demands. All that remained to be decided was the timing of its publication, a matter that had to be finely judged. Thus, in the early hours of 31 July MacDonnell sent Birrell a telegram in cypher, noting that 'as military preparations in Belfast cannot be completed before five o'clock today, Belfast military and police authorities decide that Government order should not be published until tomorrow morning [1 August]'.[30] At dawn on that first day of August nine men-of-war from the Second Division of the Atlantic Fleet moored at Bangor on the shores of Belfast Lough.[31] The Government's reply to the dissidents' petition was in similarly ironclad spirit and included the following: 'It is impossible for the Government to entertain a petition presented under such conditions of disorder and insubordination, and of which the concluding paragraph is of a threatening nature.' Before any representations were heard there would have to be 'complete re-establishment of discipline'. The petition was 'a serious discredit to all the constables concerned'. Constable William Barrett was dismissed and six other constables suspended.[32]

The dissidents were given little time to recover from this blow. At the meeting of head constables, district inspectors and sergeants, held on 30 July, a list of 278 dissidents had been drawn up. Of these men, 203 received notice of their immediate transfer on the morning of Friday 2 August. The majority were to leave on Saturday morning. The list of those to be transferred was haphazard and remained in doubt to the last. Some of those transferred had not even been in Belfast during the trouble, but officers now had an opportunity to pay off old scores.[33] The very rush of the arrangements and the random nature of the list were, paradoxically, an advantage to the administration. Dissidents as yet untouched knew that one further step out of line and they too would go. Others not yet involved were effectively warned of the dangers of dissent.

About the only encouragement for the policemen in Belfast came from the RIC in other parts of the country, in particular the far west. In Athenry seventy men met on Thursday 1 August and again on the following night when, in spite of the intervention of a District Inspector, they passed three resolutions:

(1) They objected to being made herds of
(2) They would stand by any strikers who were victimised
(3) They would support a strike

The strike movement also had support in Tipperary and Nenagh. Cork, however, was more typical of the general situation. On Thursday 30 July the men there almost unanimously agreed to apply to the Inspector General for permission to hold a meeting. All stations were circularised, but on Friday the Inspector General refused permission for the meeting, and the men decided to wait and see what happened in Belfast before taking further action.[34]

The support from the south and west raised new problems for the Belfast movement. The question now arose whether it was right for policemen in the north to strike and to unite with strikers and thus give encouragement to the peasants and the RIC in the far west to do the same. As the dock strike gained momentum, the question of British power and British support for the employers had been dimly raised but never articulated. Now the police mutiny made the issue crystal clear. The *London Standard* reported: 'The movement has been largely political. By this we mean that the discontent has been largely fanned by men aiming at the subversion of civil order, and *resolved on making government impossible under the Act of Union.*'35

In Belfast support also came on Friday 2 August from the Dungannon Clubs, a militant republican organisation, which had made itself prominent throughout the Belfast strikes by its studious avoidance of any commitment to the struggle of the workers in the city. A statement, given prominence in the *Belfast News-Letter*, included the following:

> Too long, Irishmen have done the dirty work of their English masters for pay, but some of us are finding out that it pays better to be true to Ireland than to sell Ireland. The RIC are finding out at last that they are the sons of Ireland before they are the servants of the English government and that, if they strike, it will not be the heads of their brother Irishmen they'll hit.

Not all Nationalists shared the inspired opportunism of this line; others combined a deeply conservative suspicion of the new trade unionism with purism on matters relating to the police. Thus 'Cill na Tura' writing to the *Irish Independent* on 3 August hoped...

> that our fellow countrymen engaged in the unfortunate strike in the North – which will benefit the English employer and trade unionist alike, and which it is the duty of every lover of his country, both master and workman, to end as quickly as maybe – will make no common cause with the oppressors of their country.

Whatever was to happen on Saturday 3 August, the authorities were more than adequately prepared. The *Constabulary Gazette* described the scene: 'The military have been pouring into the city, and it is no exaggeration to say that in all sections of the population there is a reign of terror.' The *Constabulary Gazette* was, of course, partisan, and gave remarkable support to the rank and file, but that it should openly voice the thought that 'if the police and the military are set in active opposition the result will be hell'[36] shows just how difficult it was to predict the outcome of that weekend.

A huge crowd gathered at the Custom House steps on Saturday afternoon and at 4.00 pm William Barrett appeared to make a speech unique in Irish police history. He said:

> No military can make men work who are dissatisfied with their condition. Down with blacklegs and cheap labour, say I, whether in civilian or constabulary life. All men are entitled to a living wage. Complaints are made that we demand the redress of our grievances at the wrong time. I quite agree that we should have struck out for more pay at the time of the Boer War when there was no military force available in this country.[37]

He described the police as 'victims of a degrading system engineered by the successive governments in the interests of the landlord reactionaries against the masses of the people, by the manufacturers of crime'. He considered that much of the work of the ordinary policeman involved detaining people for offences which only the landlord would consider to be crimes, and believed that the RIC was vastly overloaded with district and county inspectors, and that, in order to justify their existence, they aided and abetted this manufacture of crime.

After the meeting Barrett was chaired by the demonstrators and a crowd of between three and five thousand followed him as they toured the barracks of west Belfast. The procession went via Donegall Street, Upper Library Street and Townsend Street, and then along the Falls Road to the Springfield Road, returning by the Grosvenor Road. The *Belfast News-Letter* reported the events of the march fully, including little details which did not appear in the enthusiastic *Irish News* account. A flute band playing in York Street was carefully avoided, 'for there was certainly a strong Nationalist element in the crowd'. In Upper Library Street, 'the reception was of a particularly cordial nature', there being a continuous chorus of, 'Down with the blacklegs', and 'Home Rule for Ireland'. At one stage the marchers visited Brown Square Barracks and, according to the *Belfast News-Letter*, 'a large crowd gathered on the Shankill Road, and assumed what appeared to be a threatening demeanour'.

The *Belfast Evening Telegraph* headlined the story on the demonstration

NATIONALIST DEMONSTRATION
IGNORED BY CONSTABULARY
BARRETT'S VIOLENT SPEECH

and virtually confirmed the *Belfast News-Letter* account. In truth, Barrett had failed to mobilise the police. Where there had been 500–800 men a week previously, there was now at most a handful. When Barrett and the marchers returned to Custom House Square he could offer no more than the promise that the transferred men would spread the trouble with them – a promise unfulfilled. The mutiny was over.

(*Northern Star*, 10 August 1907)

What were the forces behind the police mutiny? The factual evidence suggests that the movement was non-sectarian and non-political. It is true that the trouble was centred in 'B' division, or Nationalist west Belfast,[38] but of the 208 men transferred 83 were Protestants[39] and we have, for example, the judgment of Councillor F.C. Johnston, a Unionist, who said of the men attending the meeting on Saturday 27 July, 'The gathering was not of a party nature at all, as he saw at the meeting members of the force representing the different religious denominations.'[40] Judgments of police officers or Dublin Castle officials are to an extent suspect. RIC officers in Belfast naturally preferred to blame Nationalist agitation rather than their own administrative incompetence.[41] Dublin Castle, more concerned with the Irish context as a whole, and with Westminster, preferred any explanation other than that Nationalist agitators had infiltrated the RIC,[42] and the lack of repercussions from the Belfast upheaval suggests that Dublin Castle was right. If, indeed, political agitation had been the key to the mutiny, a policy of dispersal would have proved disastrous.

The decimation of the existing force in west Belfast did have immediate and serious consequences. On 6 August a head constable in west Belfast assessed the effect of the deportations in an interview with the *Northern Whig*. He said:

> Ever since the riots of 1898 the aim of the local authorities has been to bring the men into touch with the citizens and make the force to all intents and purposes a local one. It was owing to this fact and to the confidence which exists in the men that no serious collision has taken place between police and people since 1898. The deportation of 300 men undoes the work of the last ten years with the stroke of a pen.

These proved prophetic words. The authorities were aware of the dangers. They recalled the disastrous effects of introducing men from the counties to west Belfast during the 1886 riots. Two precautions were taken: the new men were senior constables from Counties Antrim, Down and Louth. They were nearly all Protestants – an insurance policy against Nationalist agitation, if it was indeed a danger.[43] Secondly, the county men were mainly introduced in areas other than west Belfast. The gaps in the ranks in west Belfast were fully filled by men transferred from other Belfast districts.[44] However, these men were clearly recognised as imports to the district and an *Irish Independent* reporter noted the hostile response to their arrival on 6 August:

> The newcomers as they walked the unfamiliar streets were jeered at and called 'blacklegs' and in some cases mobbed by crowds of mill girls. I saw four of the newly imported men proceeding down the Falls Road last evening followed by a crowd, who boohed and ridiculed the unfortunate men until one felt sorry for them.

An act of internal expediency now put the position of the RIC in the west of the city further at risk. Dublin Castle was now asking pressing questions about how a virtual revolt amongst the RIC in Belfast could have occurred without those in command having any inkling of what was going on. Commissioner Hill offered a scapegoat in the form of the veteran District Inspector Michael Kelly from the west division and it was ordered that he be reprimanded and transferred. Rather than face this disgrace, Kelly resigned the force[45] and, in doing so, further undermined its authority in the testing days to come.

Although the police mutiny was itself of a non-political nature, it was soon clear that it had major consequences as far as the issue of politics and the wider strike movement was concerned. On Sunday 4 August there was an indication of this new influence. For months the Belfast papers had reported the meetings of Arthur Trew and the Belfast Protestant Association at the Custom House steps. Time and again he had required police protection to escape from his platform. Now, it appeared, times were changing. The *Northern Whig* reported, 'He had evidently been recruiting strongly, for his backers were more numerous and determined, and for the first time showed a disposition to retaliate.' At this meeting Trew 'read and commented on the Dungannon Club manifesto', and denounced the police mutiny as a republican plot.[46] The question arises, why should Trew have recruited support now? He had denounced almost every other feature of the strike movement as a republican plot and had been jeered off the streets for his pains.

The police mutiny raised very clearly issues which had been obscured before: questions of government, questions of law and order in Ireland, questions of the interests of the workers of Ireland in relation to the government of Ireland. Any mass labour agitation, even in the loyal north, was bound to raise these questions eventually in a country where large sections of the population were opposed not only to the particular government but also to the form of government.

In 1907 the police mutiny brought these matters to the fore with dramatic intensity. Up to the end of July the strike leaders had maintained the tradition of skilled working-class agitation in Ireland: that politics and trade-union agitation were unrelated. After the police mutiny, that position became increasingly untenable. In Ireland even the most apolitical acts had political consequences if they in any way challenged the authorities.

After the police mutiny Nationalists did seek to make political capital out of the strike movement, and the Government increasingly made a political issue out of it. If the strike leaders denied that politics were involved when they evidently were, they left their followers leaderless when they required guidance. If they retreated from every area in which politics emerged then they abandoned the field of battle to the enemies of the working class who were never afraid of politics.

11
Fight to a finish

The police mutiny raised political issues which confused the strikers, and the coal settlement, with the long-drawn-out revelation of the betrayal involved, demoralised them. Both factors gave the employers new hope that they could divide the strikers between moderates and militants, Protestants and Catholics, or even encourage division between the British trade-union leadership and the Belfast strikers. The Tory press, blessed by the continued lack of new initiatives from the strikers, played on all three themes.

The *Belfast Evening Telegraph* asked workers on 28 July to choose between moderate trade unionism and socialism. Workers had had, it claimed,

> but little opportunities of informing themselves upon the immeasurable difference between socialism and trade unionism proper; they have yet to learn in a large measure that while socialism leads to the complete upbreak of all friendly relations between employer and employee, and introduces that condition of social anarchy and disorder which has prevailed for weeks in our city, the other tends exactly in the opposite direction.

Nomad's Weekly, a middle-class gossip sheet, in its issue of 20 July, summed up just the kind of responsible trade unionism of which Belfast Tories approved, in an article headed, 'Anarchy not Trade Unionism'. This began: 'Mark me well, I do not decry Trades Unions – nor does any employer in Belfast. The Trades Unions have admirable aims in the raising of funds for sickness, accident, out of work, and death. . . against which no-one can say any other than praise.' Thus the Tory press praised 'coffin trade unionism', that is, trade unionism which helped the worker when he was sick or dead. Gee and Mitchell were seen as exponents of this kind of harmless trade unionism and accordingly praised. The *Northern Whig* pointed out on 1 August, 'The delegates who were in Belfast last week were anxious that the parties should be brought together, and they were inclined to adopt a more conciliatory attitude than that which has hitherto been taken by the local leaders of the men.'

The *Belfast Evening Telegraph* also concentrated increasingly on a sectarian interpretation of events. On 26 July it dealt with the general question of the Trades Council which 'has in fact become a mere appendage of the Nationalist Party and has backed the latter's candidates on every occasion. . . the time seems to us not far distant when the whole Labour movement in the city will have to be re-organised in the interest of the workers if it is not to be completely disintegrated'.

In their franker moments, both employers and the Tory press discounted the *Telegraph* conspiracy theory. Gallaher, the most implacable of the employers, said, 'The origin of the whole business is I think due to the uprising of Socialism.'[1] As late as 8 August the *Belfast News-Letter* made a distinction between these labour troubles and the more normal sectarian disputes in Belfast, commenting,

> The active participation of the military in the preservation of peace in the city has in days gone by usually been associated with exigencies which were the outcome of political feeling [the current euphemism for sectarianism] but the clamant demands of Labour socialism have now created a situation demanding equal firmness and promptitude of action.

If scaremongering about Nationalists did not yet count for very much, there were still opportunities for inserting a wedge between the indecisive Belfast leaders and the British GFTU on the issue of violence in the streets. In the earliest stages the strike leaders had insisted that all picketing would be peaceful and that they could maintain law and order in the streets. In the context of such a widespread and bitter strike this hope had proved naive, like so many others. By 25 July the majority of strikers went around armed with staves, with the approval of Larkin,[2] and from the coal settlement of 25 July until the early days of August there were many violent incidents. The strike leaders merely turned a blind eye to all this, but the employers were able to turn to the British trade-union delegates. On 29 July it was reported that 'the English delegates have protested vigorously against the doings in the streets such as the burning of vans and the throwing of lorries into the river. They also indicated that violence and arson must cease.'[3]

There were, in any case, other increasingly serious constraints on such picketing activity: as one striker recalled, 'You were always hearing "so and so's been lifted" – "so and so's being tried in the morning".'[4] Fewer than sixty men were ever actually arrested for picketing offences[5] but for them and their families the consequences could be dire and, even for those who remained free, the strain of maintaining picketing operations after six weeks of constant activity was beginning to tell: 'It got very tough – the men were beginning to get a bit wearied with so long running about.'[6]

The rebuke from the English leaders provided further discouragement, but other tactical reverses, notably the coal settlement, coupled with a new sense of political unease, were more significant, and it was this latter factor which gave a sense of renewed urgency to the efforts of the GFTU to end the strike.

The delegates had left for London on 25 July. Now on 1 August[7] a new delegate, Mr Appleton, of the Amalgamated Society of Lacemakers, hurried to Belfast to be joined two days later by Gee and Mitchell. Appleton had criticised the coal settlement on the grounds that it had weakened the position of the other strikers, but now he too was prepared to make a partial settlement – to withdraw a further wing of the strikers' army by settling the carters' dispute in isolation. His justification was a fear of extended political violence.

> I felt how important it was to negotiate rapidly, because troops numbering between 7,000 and 9,000 had been drafted into the city, and a special contingent of the RIC, numbering nearly 1,000, had been brought into the district, and there was a very serious danger of a conflict between the police and military. I felt that it would be of the greatest use to remove one of the elements of danger, if possible before Saturday [3 August] because then certain steps were to be taken in connection with the dismissal of some of the police.[8]

Appleton was thus prepared to assist the authorities in quelling the police mutineers; indeed he was prepared to sacrifice the interests of other strikers to this end. Appleton was also apparently aware in advance of secret Government plans for dealing with the police mutiny. He was not, of course, aware that the mutiny had merely delayed the use of troops against the strikers; but, above all, Appleton and other labour leaders were not prepared to see any connection between the strikers in the city at large and the police mutineers.

Others too, if for more mundane reasons, were weakening the link between the carters' and the dockers' disputes. It was understandable that Mr Prince, President of the Carters' Association, should wish to extricate his men,[9] but in this he was encouraged by James Sexton of the NUDL who was now in breakneck retreat from the heroic stance of his previous visit. He was soon to explain his attitude, not to a Belfast audience but to the readers of the *Liverpool Weekly Courier*, and, in doing so, to rewrite the history of his earlier intervention.

> The question of the railway companies' recognition of the union was conceded, on my advice, the moment I arrived in Belfast, as I thought it not fair that we should bear the whole brunt of the battle of the railwaymen's movement in the United Kingdom... but we asked, as all the other cross-channel firms in the trade had given the advance of wages asked for, that the railway companies should in fairness do the same.[10]

In writing thus, Sexton was signalling his dissociation from the hopes of Larkin and others on the far left in Britain that the Belfast dockers could lead the way in a wider conflict extending to the mainland. He was also suggesting that the dockers could aspire only to a different and inferior kind of settlement to that open to the carters, and from there it was but a short step to suggesting that the two cases need not be settled simultaneously. Sexton's optimism in suggesting that it was open to the dockers to ask for pay rises, while waiving the question of recognition, was also deliberately misleading in the light of the abject failure of attempts that had already been made to explore this avenue.

As early as 26 July 'a prominent labour leader' had told the *Irish News* that 'the dockers were concerned to go as far in the direction of a compromise as they reasonably could, having regard to their own interests', and, according to the shipping journal *Fair Play*, an approach along these lines was made to the Belfast Steamship Company.

> The strikers, accompanied by the Secretary of the NUDL, waited upon the Chairman of the company with the object of discussing terms of reinstatement. The Chairman, however, declined to receive the men so long as they had with them a union delegate. The delegate then withdrew and the men were

received and informed that, having regard to the congestion caused by the carters' strike, the company had no work for them at present.[11]

Given this experience, it was plain that the position of the dockers would become desperate indeed if the carters secured their own settlement. However, even if this was the route which the English delegates wished to follow, they faced no easy task, for the carters had already rejected terms on two separate occasions. At the end of June they had been offered two shillings a week but had turned it down on the grounds that they would have had to cart to the strike-bound quays. More significantly they had been outraged on 22 July by terms suggested by Gee and Mitchell, who had advocated that they return to work with an offer of arbitration and nothing more.[12] Now, at the beginning of August, they were inevitably suspicious of further proposals coming from the same quarter and they still regarded the position of the dockers as one of the main issues. For the *Belfast News-Letter* on 29 July this remained the 'stumbling block', a point reiterated by Alex Boyd on 2 August when he said 'the difficulty is with the English steamship companies'.[13]

In spite of these problems, Appleton and Prince held preparatory talks with the Lord Mayor on Thursday 1 August, and went some way to allay rank-and-file fears when they insisted that 'Mr Larkin should be a party to the conclave'.[14] Formal negotiations started the following morning and continued almost without interruption until late on Saturday night, by which time no agreement had been reached. However, by the morning of Monday 4 August, it was evident that substantial concessions had been made on the carters' side. For one thing, Larkin had been excluded from the main negotiations and, more tellingly, the *Irish News* now reported, 'It is confidently stated that, should this section of the strikers [the carters] return to work, an immediate settlement of the dockers' question would follow.'[15] The two disputes were therefore no longer to be settled together or, as Lindsay Crawford later put it, 'the dockers had agreed to let the carters blackleg'.[16] Even with the dockers' acquiescence, which can only have been given by Larkin acting under duress from Sexton, the carters were still unwilling to withdraw their solidarity and cart to strike-bound quays, as Appleton was to admit, saying, 'You know how difficult it was to make you agree to that, but eventually and much against your will, you did give in on that point.'[17]

With that obstacle removed, there was a clear prospect of a settlement of the carters' dispute on Monday 4 August. When Alderman Gee departed for England in the evening he left a written agreement requiring no more than the formality of signature by both sides. However, when the representatives reconvened, the union delegates accused the employers of altering the wording, and at the last moment all negotiations broke down irrevocably. It may indeed have been that the employers, sensing that they now had the upper hand, attempted in a provocative fashion to rub the point home. It may also have been that the carters, when it came to the crunch, baulked at signing a deeply unsatisfactory agreement, and that Appleton lost heart in trying to persuade them to do so against their will. Certainly Appleton appears to have been less pliable than the other English delegates in the hands of the employers, and the *Northern Whig* was to comment, 'Apparently what has caused the men to turn their backs on their own agreement and decide to continue the wretched struggle is the departure of Alderman Gee. . . about the only clear headed official acting for them in this matter.'[18]

There was actually little difference of substance between the two sides. The men had agreed to a clause which was to read 'the men to cart to or from any steamer, railway, place or firm', but when the employers added the phrase 'and to work with others, whether union or non-union men' they were, as Appleton put it, using 'insulting words' that proved too much, no matter that the accepted version of the clause allowed for dealings with blacklegs at the strike-bound quays.

Once the break was made it was decisive enough. Alex McDowell declared for the employers that it was now 'a fight to a finish', and Joseph Donnelly, the men's legal representative, stated with equal conviction, 'I shall take no further part in negotiations.'[19] The strikers had, in fact, bought little breathing space by scrambling out of a miserable settlement. For, although the employers had for the moment lost their chance at the negotiating table, conditions had greatly changed between the first such attempt in late July and the current situation on 5 August. The police mutiny had come and gone and yet 6,000 troops remained in the city. The employers now looked in that direction.

From the point at which the police had broken under the strains of providing additional protection, a rising tide of demands from the city's employers had poured into Dublin Castle, starting on 25 July with a threat from the Shipping Federation to raise its own police force. The Federation's letter addressed to the Chief Secretary, ran in part:

> My executive are driven to the conclusion that, as the resources of the Government seem to be unequal to the provision of protection for men who desire lawfully to carry on their work, the only course left open to them is to organise a force of their own for this purpose. They realise the gravity of this step which they have under consideration and they feel strongly that the protection of their workers from physical violence is a duty which should not be cast upon the employers in a civilised community, and a burden with which no industry should be saddled.[20]

Four days later the Chamber of Commerce followed up with demands for martial law in all but name, and they could rely on effective representation because it was none other than Lord Shaftesbury who, in his capacity as President of their Council, rather than Lord Mayor, passed their views on to Dublin Castle.[21] On 30 July further demands flooded in from ratepayers,[22] and from Thomas Gallaher who added a new political nuance to the invective, saying, 'There is no government in this country now. The authorities want to make us out as bad as they are in the South and West. There is now a spirit of lawlessness in the city, and it is entirely caused by the laxity of the authorities in dealing with the strikers and their sympathisers.'[23]

These were views stridently supported by the local Tory press. Thus the *Belfast News-Letter*, returning to the original Shipping Federation theme, argued that 'if the Government cannot give the trade of Belfast protection from the lawless tyranny that has held the streets for the last six weeks, then the traders must organise a force of their own'.[24] In the following days the Grain and Flour Merchants Association, the Master Carriers, and the Coal Merchants[25] added their voices, and on 6 August the Harbour Commissioners, a body widely representative of business interests, spoke of 'intimidation, attacks and serious assaults on the part of the crowds of lawless men, generally armed with weapons'.[26]

From the moment at which troops began to pour into the city to deal with the police mutiny, these pressures from the business community were being applied in new and advantageous circumstances. The Dublin Castle administration, which up to that point had tended to be complacent about the plight of the Belfast employers, now perceived the Belfast situation as a threat to law and order on a wider front and, in any case, had no sympathy for trade-union agitation. It seems likely that, even before the police mutiny had finally been quashed, the decisive Assistant Inspector General Gambell was considering alternative uses for the soldiers. On 1 August he requested a sixth regiment because five were 'insufficient for the work to be done', that is 'for policing the city by military'.[27] Certainly on 4 August, immediately following the weekend when Barrett's last stand failed, Gambell submitted to Dublin Castle detailed plans, which he had drawn up with Brigadier General Dawson, for securing all the city-centre streets against the civilian strikers, with a massive blanket of troops.

He explained, 'The General and I think that for the good of the city and for the purposes of showing the turbulent classes how easily we can cover the city with military pickets it would be very advisable to put this scheme into operation as soon as it receives government approval.'[28]

Even without the implementation of such measures, the Government was already under pressure at Westminster from the Labour Party over the use of troops in the city, and on 6 August Pete Curran again angrily raised the issue. In his reply Richard Cherry, Birrell's Parliamentary Under Secretary, maintained the fiction that the disposition of troops in Belfast was purely a matter for the civil authority, saying, 'The troops were not sent to Belfast by the Government at all, they were requisitioned by the Lord Mayor of Belfast.'[29]

Such questions did little to interfere with Gambell's plan, which was put into operation the following morning with dramatic effect, as recorded by the *Northern Whig*:

> The city has for military purposes been divided into five districts, and pickets are placed at every dangerous point in the area inside which the bulk of the heavy carting is done. The centre of the city and adjoining districts such as Bedford St., and Grosvenor Road, where the majority of the linen houses are situated, York St., and Corporation St., Shankill Rd., Falls Rd., Newtownards Rd., are all held in force.

Significantly, it was felt that trouble was equally likely in both Catholic and Protestant working-class areas and the scheme of coverage was accordingly elaborate – 'detachments of 20 or 30 infantrymen under an officer constitute the different posts, all of which are linked to one another by an elaborate system of military and constabulary patrols, while signallers and buglers are at hand in case of emergency to convey orders to outlying forces'.[30]

It was only after these steps were taken that serious doubts about their legality arose within the administration. Birrell at Westminster faced a fresh flurry of angry Labour questioning, and queries arose about the precise sequence of events which had led to the escalating deployment of troops. Sir Anthony MacDonnell in Dublin now wired Gambell in Belfast and received a decidedly disquieting message in reply:

> The Lord Mayor telephoned me just now; he refers to Mr Cherry's answer last night in the House stating that the troops were sent here on the requisition of the Lord Mayor, and [that] the Government have nothing to do with it, and he asked me if the troops have been requisitioned by me and for what purpose.

Nor did Gambell's more general reply provide any comfort, for he pointed out that 'all through these whole proceedings from first to last it was I who moved as regards to troops and not the Lord Mayor'. Gambell, too, was anxious to ensure that he could not be made a scapegoat for over-precipitate action and reminded his superiors that 'even before I applied for troops on Monday 29th [July] a message reached me from headquarters telling me to consider the question of troops in the city'.[31]

While such exchanges established that the Government's reply at Westminster on 6 August was entirely untruthful, and that the requisitioning of troops and their use on the streets on 7 August was not carried out according to the due legal process (that is by the request of the civil authority, represented by the Lord Mayor), this was not a state of affairs destined to become public. Lord Shaftesbury's protest to Gambell arose because he was suspicious of Liberal motives in making him the sole potential scapegoat for anything that might occur. He was also, no doubt, discomfited by the failure of police and military adequately to consult with him, but he did not actually oppose the measures that had been taken. Accordingly, while MacDonnell had to relay the Lord Mayor's displeasure to Birrell, he was able to report that agreement had been reached with him on a new and bland formula for describing the requisitioning process, one which referred to the 'concurrent recommendation of the Lord Mayor, the General Commanding, and the Police Authorities'.[32] Birrell was able to put this device to good use in fending off more Labour questions on 8 August. He was careful not to mention the Lord Mayor and yet still distanced himself and the Government from the actions taken, saying, 'I decline to make myself responsible for the chief authorities at Belfast' and adding, 'I have no power to remove the military from Belfast if the civil authorities wish them to remain there.'[33]

If Birrell was at pains to confuse the issue, he in turn was never fully informed of the sequence of events. As late as September Sir Anthony MacDonnell was still disguising part of the record. When he instructed District Inspector Clayton to draw up a history of the Belfast strikes, he wanted the police mutiny mentioned only 'very briefly' in order that 'enough should be said to show that it was necessary to call in extra troops', an emphasis designed to obscure Gambell's concurrent plans to use them against civilian strikers.[34]

So it was that an ambitious police officer, with the active support of an Under Secretary at Dublin Castle, determined the largest concentration of troops on the streets of Belfast in the entire period up to 1914, while the Liberal Government disclaimed responsibility, indeed was not fully responsible. It was a situation facilitated by a not unfamiliar theme of disharmony and suspicion between the authorities in Belfast, Dublin and London, and compounded by the complacency of Augustine Birrell. In these circumstances, the formula eventually devised for presentation to the public left opponents without a clear target for attack, and ensured that blame would be difficult to apportion if anything went wrong. As so often, it was on the streets of Belfast that the fruits were to be gathered of decisions obscured elsewhere by a deliberate process of disinformation.

Strikers rapidly came into contact with the new military presence, jeering the Rifle Brigade as it arrived at Bridge End,[35] but it was soon clear that the soldiers had the upper hand. On 8 August, in particular, strikers making numerous attempts to stop carts faced military intervention, and on occasions were forced to reload vans they had upset.[36]

Gambell was soon convinced that his scheme had worked and, after the first day's operations, wired Dublin to say 'everything worked admirably today, everyone highly pleased'.[37] Soon statements were issued confirming that, at least as far as the business community was concerned, this was true. Thus on 7 August the Grain and Flour Merchants Association acknowledged 'with great satisfaction the greater facilities existing today for cartage in the city'.[38] The Conservative press too noted the changing situation by 10 August, with the *Belfast News-Letter* observing that 'the freedom afforded to cross-channel companies and merchants generally, in regard to the protection given to them to freely remove merchandise from the quays, has resulted in a very satisfactory decrease of the congestion which for weeks past has existed at the Donegall Quay'; while the *Belfast Evening Telegraph* commented that 'each day witnesses a large increase in the amount of carting that is being conducted under military protection, and the streets fairly swarmed this forenoon with heavily laden lorries'. There were other indications too that the strikers' grip on the situation was slipping. The Barrow boat was able to resume its normal berth after an absence of more than two months,[39] and Combe Barbour's iron foundry, the largest of several concerns closed by shortage of supplies, was now able to reopen.[40]

Far from being content with these signs of progress, the employers encouraged other insidious rumours; thus it was anticipated that more traction engines were on the way. The *Belfast News-Letter* was quick to hammer home the significance of this, saying, 'The strike may have very far reaching consequences so far as the men are concerned and it may be that they will be permanently debarred from plying their avocations as carters, their places being taken by power driven machines.'[41]

Against this background, both sides watched anxiously for any signs of a break in the carters' ranks. As early as 7 August a dozen carts belonging to Messrs Cullen Allen and to Wordies were on the streets and there were reports that the men employed by four other firms were suing for peace. By Friday 9 August carts belonging to Cowans were out, and at least thirty belonging to Cullen Allen and to Wordies were on the road, although it was said that all these were 'being manned by the clerical and indoor staff'.[42] However, Messrs Gregg, a firm of timber merchants, issued details of a settlement they had reached with their men,[43] and a day later carts belonging to Messrs Mercier were on the road, in spite of a denial from the men.[44]

It was a period in which activists had to admit that 'there was firms doing things on the quiet and getting stuff taken to the quays' and that 'some of the men in the firms would have went back'. Those who were 'hard and fast' faced insuperable odds in trying to circumvent

(*Nomad's Weekly*, 10 August 1907)

the overwhelming military presence, and even for them there was often an ambivalence in their thinking when faced by troops. One at least saw it thus, 'We didn't insult them because we knowed they was doing their duty – most of us was soldiers ourselves.'⁴⁵ Boer war experience may have accounted for this, but there was the added Belfast factor that, at least amongst Protestant workers, dislike of the RIC had been deeply ingrained since the 1886 riots. Troops were far more welcome, and in 1898, the replacement of the RIC by the military in Protestant areas had brought an immediate end to serious rioting.⁴⁶

Nonetheless, the introduction of troops on the streets was now the major issue facing the strike leadership and here too there was an ambivalence. As early as July the Trades Council had passed a resolution dealing with the first intervention of the military, and this had shown a strange set of priorities, the use of troops being seen firstly as 'discouraging to enlistment' and only then as 'a direct incentive to employers to oppress the underpaid workers of the country'.[47]

Those who penned such a resolution saw themselves as members of a great imperial family, indeed as natural supporters of the armed forces and of law and order. It was in those circumstances that they had avoided taking advantage of the police mutiny, and had in effect assisted the authorities in dealing with it. True, they were appalled that the troops had now been turned loose in their own narrow arena of a labour dispute, but that in no sense meant that their minds turned to thoughts of insurrection. Their initial reaction was to attempt to persuade the Government to rectify what they saw as a terrible mistake, one which they half hoped was not seriously intended. Larkin and William Walker rushed to London on 7 August to make precisely this case, only to be refused a meeting with Birrell.[48] Their protests could do no more than form the basis of parliamentary questions by Labour the following day, and Birrell's subsequent stonewalling merely provided further discouragement.

Following this reverse, strike rhetoric became more strident, a reflection of frustration, even desperation, rather than of any specific intent. Larkin told the men that 'he was not a believer in bombs, but if a bomb could settle the whole matter he would not hesitate'[49] and that 'it was a scandalous thing that they should disgrace a broken bottle by using it on an officer of the British army'.[50] Others too weighed in, with Alex Boyd arguing that 'they would not be intimidated by either military or police and were determined to win if one stone was not left upon another in Belfast. Should the soldiers walk over the dead bodies of the strike leaders there would be no surrender until the men came out on top.'[51] Meanwhile Joseph Harris complained, 'it was not fair that they should stand up and see the peace broken by the military and the police without moving a hand to prevent it. If they roused the people by these tactics were they [the strikers] to be blamed if riots resulted?' and in a final cry of helpless outrage he added, 'let them not be afraid of the soldiers. They dare not fire upon them and once they did so the British Constitution would fall and shatter.'[52] From all of this, little that was positive emerged, typical being the suggestion of W.J. Murray on 9 August to an audience of some 10,000 workers at the Custom House steps that they could get a petition signed by 50,000 calling on the Government to withdraw the troops.[53]

For more advanced socialists, the new clarity of the situation certainly presented organisational opportunities. A branch of the ILP had at last been set up formally in the city in May,[54] and by August, with reports of thirty dozen copies of *Labour Leader* selling each weekend,[55] the National Executive was sufficiently excited to send over W. Stewart as an organiser.[56] Meanwhile, the Belfast Socialist Society, the early nucleus of self-proclaimed left-wingers in the city, gained great kudos from its role in organising the often massive Sunday meetings at the Customs House steps. Comrades from afar could measure their progress in paper sales, with fifteen dozen of the Social Democratic Federation's *Justice* and ten dozen of Glasgow's *Forward* selling in a weekend.[57] More encouraging still, a new branch of the Socialist Society was established in Ballymacarrett.[58]

This did not necessarily imply that the now more numerous radicals had any effective answer to the presence of troops, and nor did the increasing number of prominent British socialists who now flocked to the city, aware at least that the struggle there was potentially one of great significance. John MacLean, one of the formative figures of Scottish socialist republicanism, was in the city from 6 to 9 August as a guest of the Socialist Society and stayed with Larkin. He concluded, 'Never have we had a better chance to expose the Liberals who have done in Belfast what the Tories did in South Africa' but he could offer little more than a euphoric account for British readers of the mood of the time – one in which 'the workers have gone mad on trade unionism, and are rushing up to all the prominent men in the strike, wanting to join a union – any union. They are flocking into the Co-operative Society. They are rolling up in tens of thousands to the Custom House steps on the Sundays to listen to the revolutionary gospel of socialism.' His decidedly optimistic view extended as far as the oft-expressed hope, usually proclaimed as fact by socialists of left and right, that 'religious riots are a thing of the past'.[59]

MacLean's visit overlapped with that of Victor Grayson, the newly elected MP for Colne Valley and much to the fore in pressing questions on the Belfast situation at Westminster. On 8 August he raised the question of violence at a packed meeting in St Mary's Hall, arguing that 'if it came to the dirty means of brutal warfare, if it came to war, he was satisfied that the people who suffered oppression would render a good account of themselves'.[60] Four days later he was to achieve notoriety in Huddersfield by expressing the same view in more colourful terms, suggesting that 'if the people had not shrapnel to shoot they had broken bottles to throw'.[61] Yet he had expressed no more than the commonplaces of current Belfast rhetoric, and had shared his platform in St Mary's Hall with William Walker — evidence that in Belfast both militants and moderates were finding themselves driven into the same corner.

Nor did radicals in Belfast reject more conventional tactics. In spite of earlier parliamentary failures, there was unanimous support within the strike movement for the next initiative of the leadership — the organisation of a mass rally on 10 August, centred round the parliamentary representatives for the city. It was doubly ironical that this essentially moderate stratagem was to play a significant role in a major escalation of the crisis.

The invitation to the MPs was based on the entirely viable assumption that the two Ulster Unionist MPs would not attend, but that Joe Devlin and Tom Sloan, the two MPs with any working-class credentials, and representative of both sides of the sectarian divide, would do so. As it turned out, this expectation took insufficient account of the unbounded opportunism of Tom Sloan, who at the last minute cried off.[62] This in itself was significant, for Sloan, as a follower rather than a leader of Orange working-class opinion, was reflecting fears about the implications of the police mutiny, doubts about condemnation of the troops, and fears for the ultimate fate of the strike movement. More seriously, it left the meeting dangerously unbalanced with Devlin, a Nationalist, the only MP appearing, and, although Lindsay Crawford soon replaced Sloan as a spokesman for Protestant radicalism, his eloquence could not fully compensate for the absence of an MP at what had been billed as a mobilisation of the city's parliamentary forces.

This failing did nothing to diminish attendance at the meeting, with well over 10,000 present[63] and when Crawford, still Grand Master of the Independent Orange Order, spoke, he proved himself more radical on the question of troops than were many of the labour leaders. He asked the Government, 'Would they expect after this to get recruits from the citizens of Belfast? If that sort of thing went on, men like himself who had always been loyal to the Government, loyal to the King and constitution, would have to start an anti-enlisting campaign.' He also noted quite correctly that the Government 'did not bring Irish troops into the City of Belfast, because they knew that Irish troops would not long stand the work they would have to do. It was a shame and a scandal that the soldiers should have to turn their guns upon the men from whose class they sprang.'

Alex Boyd, the main Labour speaker, chose to follow the parliamentary theme which had formed the original basis for the meeting. In this, he could merely recount the failures to secure effective intervention at Westminster, and argue that nothing would be right 'until they sent men of their own into the House of Commons'. The emptiness of this message merely increased interest in the next speaker, Joe Devlin, now making his first intervention in the strike, and certainly press attention was largely concentrated on him.

Devlin, excusing his failure to appear on strike platforms before, was at least accurate enough in his assessment of the effect of his belated appearance. He had 'practically held aloof from any expression of opinion on the issue, in favour of one side or another' for fear that 'the capitalistic press' would use his appearance for sectarian ends. He was, even now, a study in moderation in his references to the strike, explaining, 'I stood to the one side in the hope that good influences, a kindlier feeling and the due recognition of mutual responsibility would guide the masters and the men to a common agreement for the advantage of both sides.' It was only when he spoke of the police mutiny and the role of the military that he turned on the fire, attacking the Lord Mayor as 'the Czar of Belfast'.

Why indeed did Devlin appear at the rally? His paper, the *Northern Star,* was sectarian and anti-socialist; his later behaviour was to show that he had little sympathy with 'Larkinism'. The truth was that, just as Sloan was confused and alarmed by the police mutiny and the use of troops, so Devlin was attracted by these issues. Nationalism had very little to say about the agitation of the urban working classes, but it had a lot to say about the police and military, the instruments of British rule in Ireland. After the events of late July and early August, Devlin was prepared to use a strike platform, with which he had little sympathy, to play upon issues which he, as a Nationalist, considered crucial.

The labour leaders gave Devlin this opportunity because of his status as an MP, because he was an influential leader of one section of the community, and because he was considered progressive on labour matters. The myth that the strike was above politics, and the confusion between socialism and populism, lived on and gave Devlin his chance.

As Devlin's rhetoric roused the crowds in Belfast, Larkin was speaking at a safe distance in Dublin where there was no need for fiery militancy, and he expressed the stark fears of many of the Belfast strike committee members when he said, 'The only danger was that the men might lose their head and attack the military. That must be stopped by any and every means. Their men could not fight against bullets and bayonets.'[64] Alas, warnings from Dublin could not restrain embittered workers excited by the oratory of Devlin and left in the lurch by the equivocation of many other speakers.

12
Bullets and bayonets

Devlin's appearance on a strike platform coincided with an increase in tension in the Lower Falls area, his own power base. The deep-sea dockers, mainly Catholics, had not initially been involved in the strikes, but by now had almost all been laid off. The earlier impact of the strike movement on Protestant working-class areas now extended to the Catholic ghetto. Larkin too was active there as part of the campaign to maximise working-class support. On 8 August he urged mill workers either to strike or to support the existing strikers, and the work force in at least one mill followed his lead.[1] This heightened enthusiasm for the strike movement coincided with the decision by the military on Friday 9 August to extend protection for blacklegs to the Falls. These measures met with a stormy reception from 'men throwing stones', but the angry crowd included some 500 women and children, many of whom were evidently mill workers, as they were 'using the tin cans which they usually carry to and from the mills' while other 'women were seen tearing paving stones out of the streets and using pokers for the purpose'. That evening, for the first time, military reinforcements were sent to the area.[2]

The following day, Saturday 10 August, more serious trouble occurred. At noon, just as workers were knocking off for the weekend, three carts left Hughes Dickson's mill. Strikers and mill workers made a concerted attack. One carter and one officer were injured and other escorting soldiers heavily stoned. Crowds stretched from the Model School to Mill Street and Castle Lane, and the carts were under attack all the way to High Street. Disorders did not stop until troops were withdrawn at 2 pm.[3]

The authorities were by now aware that the introduction of blacklegs to the Lower Falls presented a particular problem. Sir Anthony MacDonnell informed Mr Birrell, 'It was apprehended that difficulty would be experienced in connection with the transport of goods through the Falls Road district in which the Grosvenor Road is situated and measures were being concerted between police and military for the special treatment of this.'[4] It was against this background that Joe Devlin made his speech at the strikers' rally on the afternoon of Saturday 10 August. The combination of his oratory and the events of the previous week meant that it did not require further military intervention to spark off trouble.

Rioting erupted in the Lower Falls area at about 5 pm on Sunday 11 August, sparked off by a minor and farcical incident. Two drunks were fighting in Leeson Street and were arrested by the police. This was sufficient. A crowd gathered and tried to free the men. The police were stoned and retreated with their prisoners to Springfield Road barracks. A police van then set off down Grosvenor Road, carrying the prisoners to the Central Police Office. A large crowd ambushed the van from McDonnell Street. In the desperate struggle which ensued, all in the pouring rain, twenty policemen were injured, and the crowd of rioters grew to 2,000. The police van finally escaped but the fighting went on unabated.

Police reinforcements arrived and the rioters retreated to the top of Grosvenor Road. The *Belfast News-Letter* described the scene:

> The mob withdrew to the side streets and directed upon the police a constant fusillade of brickbats, stones and road metal. A number of women joined the fray, and assisted the men by supplying material for the fight. The result was that the constabulary were frequently driven back by the rabble and in many cases had to seek shelter in the doorways to escape the showers of missiles that were falling in all directions. It seemed in fact as if the mob was in absolute possession of the locality, and that the forces of law and order were for the time being compelled to retreat before the determined attack. Even the barracks in Roden Street was surrounded by a threatening crowd, and there appeared every likelihood of its being wrecked.

Two thousand six hundred soldiers, eighty cavalry and five hundred police were ordered to the area at 7 pm.[5] The troops included elements of the Royal Essex Regiment, the Cameron Highlanders, the Sussex Regiment and the 3rd Dragoon Guards. Their arrival was watched by huge crowds which gathered in Grosvenor Road right down to Great Victoria Street.

The first bayonet charge was made at 8 pm, and cavalry charges soon followed. The troops were unfamiliar with the area and so were most of the police, for the majority of the latter had been drafted in after the police mutiny. Descriptions of the fighting in the *Northern Whig* and *Belfast News-Letter* made clear the tactical advantages the rioters had. The *News-Letter* described a cavalry charge: 'In one of the bye streets a squadron of cavalry were subjected to a terrific storm of paviors, which were rained on them from the upper windows, and the men to save their faces had to lie down on their saddles.'[6]

The *Northern Whig* described similar scenes:

> There were some wildly dramatic moments, the most sensational of which were the combined charges of all arms. At a given signal the dragoons took the lead; behind them were massed the foot soldiers, and behind them again the black columns of the police. The force would double off along McDonnell St., or Cullingtree Rd., the cavalry horses spoiling the alignment as they shied at the volley of stones that never failed to meet them, and the infantry behind hoping that at last they would get a fair chance. The crowd as always would scatter and run, but from adjoining streets stones poured in a ceaseless stream on the heads of the assaulting column. A few prisoners would be scooped in, and then the men would return, and in a quarter of an hour the game would have to begin all over again.

The main fighting took place in the small streets between Leeson Street and McDonnell Street, but the Albert Street end of Cullingtree Road had to be defended against crowds attempting to attack Cullingtree Road Barracks. The Falls Road itself was quiet all night. Efforts made by the local priests, Father Convery and Father Healey, to stop the fighting failed.

> It was now pitch dark and the rain still descending in torrents. The street lamps are small and dim in this district, and the conditions were altogether favourable to the kind of guerilla warfare a stone-throwing mob pursues... the maze of streets where the rioters were sheltering from pursuit resembles a rabbit warren, which while the rioters knew every hole, the forces of the law were hopelessly ignorant of the ramifications.[7]

It was only by 11 pm that fighting began to die down, and not until midnight was all quiet.

In subsequent court cases soldiers admitted that they had smashed windows and doors in many streets[8] on the pretext that they were following rioters. Even if the claim was true in some cases, this was a form of rough justice which increased the bitterness of the community and helped stoke the fires for the following night.

The *Belfast Evening Telegraph* gave strong hints that the authorities had decided to occupy the Falls in force on Monday night, and that they intended to use any means necessary to suppress disorder. The paper said, 'It is stated that, should there be a repetition of last night's fierce stone-throwing, the Riot Act will be read', and 'it is ominous that large numbers of residents in the Cullingtree Road district have been warned to keep their children indoors, as the authorities will not be answerable for the consequences'.[9]

There were no disturbances during Monday, but piles of stones lay around from the riots of the previous night. The troops were withdrawn at 5 pm from their carting duties, but, confirming the forecast of the *Belfast Evening Telegraph*, it was decided to bring out detachments from the Victoria Barracks to garrison the area during the evening. The Gordon Highlanders were marched across Crumlin Road and Shankill Road to the Falls, and their appearance there set ablaze the fire that had been smouldering all day.[10] These soldiers marched under a constant fusillade of stones to the top of Grosvenor Road. They then wheeled down Grosvenor Road, taking up position in front of the Royal Victoria Hospital. Here they were pinned under an intense bombardment from the bottom of Springfield Road and Dunville Park.

Police and military reinforcements then cleared Dunville Park and had it locked, and the trouble died down in that quarter. The crowds ran down to Cullingtree Barracks and, after heavy bombardment, the police and military inside charged out and began to attempt to clear the area. A desperate battle went on there until after 7 pm.

Soon after 6 pm trouble began, independently of this battle, on the Falls Road. The fighting there started immediately after the arrival of 150 soldiers. Major Martin Thackeray, RM, later gave evidence that he reconnoitred the road at 6 pm and all was peaceful.[11]

This did not last long. John McKeown, son of the NUDL branch Secretary, Michael McKeown, saw the initial phase of the fighting on this front, near the Falls Road Baths:

> From the side streets women were delivering loads of stone paviors to some dozen or so strikers, or rioters in favour of the strikers, while hundreds lined the side walk. . . the paviors bounced round the soldiers who had to duck sometimes to save their heads. The corporal in charge maintained a steady stoical stance but eventually winced when struck by a stone. He ordered and led a charge on the rioters. The leader of the rioters was a well known character, 'Covey' Cochrane, who was well fortified. He never flinched as the soldiers came for him at the double, the leader well ahead of his troops. Cochrane advanced staggering to meet him and flung a heavy pavior that caught the plucky corporal in the midriff.[12]

With the arrival of cavalry at 6.30 pm the fighting intensified as the soldiers attempted to move up the Falls, clearing the road as they went. It was soon evident that they were in a tactically weak position, being attacked both frontally and from sidestreets. As they went further up the road, they had to leave more and more men to cover sidestreets already passed. The result was that fewer were left to carry on the battle to the fore. Soon the soldiers themselves resorted to stone-throwing: as the *Northern Whig* reported, 'The singular sight was witnessed of the Tommies digging up kidneys for all they were worth. In some cases a regular stone-throwing duel resulted. An infantryman in marching order, however, was no match at this game for the Falls Road rowdy, very little encumbered with clothing, and the military were driven back.'[13]

Several times troops and police were forced to retreat. Of the picket of twelve soldiers at the front – faced by a crowd variously estimated at between fifty and five hundred – four were injured. At this juncture, as Thackeray later described it, 'I held up my stick in my hand and shook it at the crowd' and then at approximately 7.25 pm, near the end of Peel Street, he attempted to read the Riot Act, but he had to admit that he was quite inaudible – 'it was impossible to give any intimation to the people that we were going to fire'.[14] Moments later, seven men in the picket, under the command of Major Edgar Greene, fired up the Falls Road. The firing caused immediate panic amongst those to the fore in the riot, but further back many could not believe that live ammunition had been used, as John McKeown recalled:

> My pals and I ran up the road to get out of the danger zone. As

we passed, a man named 'Sinn Fein' Nolan standing on the kerb shouted, 'Yellow bellies – running from British blank shot.' 'You stay then,' said one of our boys, 'We're for Conway Street, they haven't made bullets yet to go round corners.'[15]

One of those killed in the fusillade, twenty-three-year-old Maggie Lennon, in fact lived in Conway Street – she had gone out to look for a child. A second victim, Charles McMullan, died as he made his way home from work. No suggestion was ever made that those killed were other than innocent victims.[16]

The fighting slackened for a few moments and was then redoubled in fury. Until well after midnight rioters pelted troops from the relative safety of sidestreets. All lights were put out, cables were stretched across roads to upset the cavalry, boiling water was poured from upstairs windows,[17] but at last the fighting died down as the military penetrated deep into the area.

The following day, Tuesday 13 August, a deputation of clergy and laity from the Lower Falls visited the Lord Mayor to urge the withdrawal of the military from the area, and offered to maintain the peace themselves.[18] The Lord Mayor acceded to their request, a decision which implied a recognition either that the previous policy of garrisoning in force had been disastrous, or that it had served its political purpose, namely to isolate Nationalist areas from other working-class areas in the city and, in so doing, to insert a wedge into the strike movement.

Certainly there was no immediate reason to believe that the Falls had been effectively pacified, for piles of dug-up kidney stones still lay in the street. One labour commentator, H.R. Stockman, was later to suggest that there was every possibility of more far-reaching disturbances, describing how 'all day on the Tuesday men went around collecting rifles and revolvers and laying in a supply of vitriol' and how that night 'vast crowds from the reputedly loyal districts of the city poured into the Nationalist quarter, and, had they received the slightest provocation from military or police, the riot of Sunday and Monday would have become a revolution'.[19]

While Stockman's account of the tensions of that Tuesday night may have had some degree of accuracy, his 'revolutionary' perspective was a decided gloss on the realities of the situation, which may have enthralled the English readers of *Labour Leader* but was not reflected by any other local commentator. True, there were others, like Roger Casement, prepared to engage in heroics from afar. Casement told his cousin, Gertrude Bannister, 'I go up there tomorrow and please God I'll take a gun and if it comes to shooting I know who I'll shoot',[20] but there is no evidence that he arrived. The reality on that Tuesday night was very different, with all influential parties, including priests, Catholic magistrates, and 'many local trade union officials',[21] seeking to maintain the peace. The main threat to this came not from some fancied workers' insurrection but from an Orange gathering which proceeded from the Shankill Road down Northumberland Street intent on sectarian affray on the Falls. The previous night the same phenomenon had occurred on a smaller scale when a group from the Shankill had thrown stones from Northumberland Street in the direction of Albert Street, hitting soldiers and Catholic rioters indiscriminately.[22] Now, on the Tuesday night, the larger grouping with similar intent represented the major threat to a fragile peace, as the *Northern Whig* recorded:

> Grouped at the extreme end of Northumberland Street they saluted the grimly silent crowd who stood well within stone-throwing range and who had an inexhaustible supply of missiles at hand, with such appropriate ditties as 'Derry's Walls', 'Kick the Pope', 'The Lily O', and 'The Protestant Boys'. As one Falls Road man said, 'It would try the temper of a saint', but though there were low growls, the crowds, with almost superhuman restraint, never made a movement. It was an exhibition that would be rare in any city, but was absolutely unparalleled in Belfast, and was all the more wonderful when one considers what is the temper of the crowds after Monday night's fighting.[23]

In spite of such provocation, the last major threat of trouble passed that night, and for the rest of the week the groups of civilians who kept the peace patrolled often empty streets.

The disinclination of Falls Road people to get involved in a sectarian battle bore out the *Belfast News-Letter*'s assessment of the riots on 12 August: 'The riot was not a fight between Protestants and Roman Catholics, or between strikers and non-strikers, it was a fight between Nationalists and police.' This was not the whole truth; the tensions in the area definitely arose from the strike situation, but there is no doubt that the reaction in Nationalist areas to the arrival on the scene of large numbers of troops was very different from that in Protestant areas. All over the city, workers resented the appearance of the British Army as a strike-breaking force, but otherwise viewed it with very conflicting emotions. Only in Nationalist areas was it viewed clearly as a foreign army of occupation. The inflammatory intervention of Joe Devlin helped to spark off the riots but, worse still, convinced Protestant workers that the riots on the Falls represented a self-interested piece of Catholic Nationalist opportunism, taking advantage of the troubled state of the city, and, indeed, there is no evidence that those engaged in the riots had any wider concept of working-class struggle. As a result, the Falls fought alone and the battle merely served to alarm other sections of the working class.

Attempts were made by the representatives of the deceased to raise more general issues at the inquests. They suggested that the Lord Mayor had personally ordered troops into the Falls in order to promote sectarianism. The representative of the Crown argued that troops were sent into the Falls on Sunday 11 August only after serious rioting, and that after the events of that night it was reasonable to garrison the area on the Monday. In any case, attempts to have the Lord Mayor called as a witness were of no avail. The magistrate explained, 'I cannot produce him, I think he has been very badly treated. I think he is a perfect gentleman.'

As for the actual shooting, the Crown case was that Major Thackeray and his soldiers were in such a desperate situation that they had to open fire. The relevant section of King's Regulations read:

> Firing on a mob can only be excused by the necessity of self-protection, or by the circumstances of the force at the disposal of the authorities being so small that the committing of some felonious outrage. . . such as the burning of a mill, or the breaking open of a prison, or the attacking of a barrack, cannot otherwise be prevented.

No attempt was being made to attack property, therefore justification rested on the self-defence argument. The crucial point here was that at no stage was Thackeray's retreat cut off. He may have faced frontal attack by an overwhelming crowd, but his retreat down Divis Street was protected by pickets of soldiers he had left at each sidestreet on the way up. He was reduced to twelve men but there were fifty more close at hand between Peel Street and Albert Street. He was asked at the inquest, 'Could you not have retired down the road?' to which he replied, 'I could have', but when asked if he had considered retiring, he merely replied, 'I never ordered them to retire.' The jury ultimately disagreed on a verdict, a likely outcome in a case of this kind in which both Nationalists and Unionists were represented on the jury. However, in this case there does seem to have been a valid reason to doubt the necessity of the shooting.[24]

This was not to be the end of the argument over the wider issues involved. During September the British Labour Party and the TUC called for a parliamentary enquiry into the use of troops in Belfast.[25] The Liberal Government, disquieted by the publicity in England and alarmed at the way events had escalated in Belfast, with damaging effects on its relations with the Irish Party in the House of Commons, agreed to a parliamentary enquiry on the use of the military in civil disturbances, and this duly took place in 1908.

R.B. Haldane, Minister for War, giving evidence to the enquiry, never revealed that it was, in fact, the Government, rather than the Lord Mayor, who ordered troops to Belfast. He steered the enquiry in the direction of what was in 1907 a purely hypothetical question, namely, did an officer have to obey the instructions of the Lord Mayor? Here Haldane made an apparent concession. He told the enquiry that he intended to amend King's Regulations, 'to make it plain that an officer in command of troops is fully entitled to exercise his discretion as to complying with the requisition [from the civil power] when from knowledge or reliable information he has reason to believe that it has been unnecessarily made'. Haldane cited, as an example, disturbances in Winchester in 1908 when an army officer had refused to help the civil authorities because he felt it was unnecessary and would provoke trouble. Haldane praised the officer's action.[26]

Haldane did not mention circumstances where the Government took the decisions and then pushed the responsibility onto the shoulders of the civil authority, and his blind was successful. Implied criticism fell on the Lord Mayor of Belfast rather than the Government. Specific criticism of what had occurred in Belfast came from peculiar quarters. Thus, Major-General George Browne CB, DSO, when asked about the 'duty of the civil authority to exhaust every possible means of preserving the peace' before calling in the army, replied, 'I do not find that this has been done in the cases I have gone into... it was not done in Belfast or Winchester.'[27] However, this parliamentary enquiry had no bearing on the situation in mid-August

1907 when the Belfast strikers faced the legacy of that fierce battle between Catholic workers and the British Army.

Whatever the legal argument, the Tory press was very clear on the lessons to be learnt from the riots. The combination of the great Devlin rally and the subsequent riots on the Falls provided ready ammunition. The *Belfast News-Letter* saw these events as proof that the strike was a Nationalist conspiracy to 'inflict a blow on the Unionist and Protestant cause and on the prosperity of the city'.[28] The *Northern Whig* described Devlin's appearance as 'the most natural thing in the world'.[29] The *Belfast Evening Telegraph* was reminded of the 'religious war' of 1798 when Protestants suffered 'in the burning of Scullabogue and the bloody massacre of Wexford Bridge'.[30]

At least one Unionist, Fred Crawford, later to achieve fame as the organiser of the Larne gun-running in 1914, had few such blood-stained fears, positively celebrating what had happened: 'What a blessing all the rioting took place in the Catholic quarter of the city. This branded the whole thing as a Nationalist movement.' For Crawford, branding was the key point, for even he had to admit 'the serious part of the business is that they have a lot of Protestants who call themselves Independent Orangemen'.[31]

Thomas Sloan was an obvious candidate to fall prey to these territorial imperatives, as he made clear in a House of Commons speech on 15 August, saying, 'all the disorder had been confined to one particular division... Only those who lived in Belfast could understand that the disorder was occasioned, not by the men who had a legitimate claim to have carried on the picketing', but had been led by 'won't works' who had brought 'disgrace and suspicion' upon the strikers.[32]

From the moment at which rioting had broken out, this was precisely the kind of interpretation that the labour leaders in Belfast had feared. Accordingly, from an early stage, they had sought to stop the riots and, above all, to prevent any sectarian disturbances. On the Sunday during the riots they held a meeting in Distillery Street, the area in which mixed crowds of up to 5,000 people were watching the riots, but were jeered by those angry about the rioting and ignored by others who joined the fray.[33]

At the Custom House Square meeting on Monday 12 August, Larkin gave the strike committee's view of the riots:

The Lord Mayor invoked the aid of the military with the deliberate intention of sowing seeds of dissension among the dockers. The masters rejoiced at the rioting, because it gave them the opportunity of asserting that this was a party struggle. But the cause they were fighting was the cause of the workers against the employers, and Protestants and Catholics were banded together regardless of religion or politics. Had he [Larkin] been in the city on Sunday he would have done all in his power to avoid any disturbance, because he realised that the people who would suffer were the workers. . . drink was at the bottom of all that had occurred and he urged the strikers and those that were friendly to them to abstain from all excesses during the present crisis and to show that they were anxious to maintain law and order.[34]

On the same night, posters were put up all over the city by the strikers, giving a clear statement of their position:

Men of Belfast – don't be misled. The employers of Belfast and the authorities are trying to make the present disturbances in Belfast a party matter, for they know that if they can get the Protestants and Catholics to fight they can beat the workers. This is not a fight between Protestant and Catholic but between the employers, backed by the authorities, and the workers. Let no party cry be raised or paid attention to, not as Catholic or Protestant, as Nationalist or Unionist, but as Belfast men and workers stand together and don't be misled by the employers' game of dividing Catholic and Protestant.[35]

The *Belfast News-Letter* praised the peace-keeping efforts of the Labour men on the Tuesday night – 'Credit is due to Mr William Walker, Mr Alex Boyd, Mr Joseph Murphy and several others' – and again on the night of 14 August when 'the help which was given by several of the Labour leaders was most acceptable'.[36] The Labour leaders did their best to use their role to recement the general alliance created by the strike between workers of all religions. Thus, on Sunday 18 August William Walker, speaking at the Custom House steps, explained:

The riots of last week were not Nationalist ones. On Tuesday evening he had gone down to the Queen's Island when the men were coming out of work, and he had got 350 Protestant volunteers to assist the priests, Catholic magistrates and other volunteer constables on the Falls Road, and during all the evening there was not a party cry heard on the road except for a few irresponsibles in Northumberland Street.[37]

Walker went on to claim that these events, and particularly the effectiveness of Labour peace-keeping efforts, 'spelt the downfall of capitalism and the dawn of a new era for the working men of Belfast'.[38] This was a very different form of revolution from that hinted at by H.R. Stockman earlier, but if Walker at least based his claims on the realities of the Labour role in the aftermath of the riots, they were nonetheless exaggerated. As H.R. Stockman himself was to point out, Labour did not get widespread credit for its peace-keeping role.

That this was so may have reflected the undoubted interest of the Unionist press in maximising the damage that the riots did to the labour movement, and nor were Nationalist sources necessarily any more sympathetic. The Falls Road was not natural Labour territory and, while on the Tuesday following the riots Larkin could obtain 'the homage of a cheer from the very roughest section of the crowd',[39] there were others intent from the beginning on restricting the role of Labour. On the same day, the *Belfast News-Letter* saw fit to comment on the relationship between the Catholic clergy and the Labour men, noting that:

> Since the dissemination of Socialist literature in greater volume than heretofore, together with the propaganda in connection with the present labour troubles, there has been a noticeable feeling of less willingness to allow Roman Catholic clergymen to wield so much power as they formerly exercised, but at the same time they can assert a powerful influence, and last evening they successfully urged the people to refrain from violence.[40]

In the following days it was to be the clergy who reasserted their authority in traditional fashion, most notably when on 18 August Father Convery delivered a thunderous and widely-publicised sermon at St Paul's. Rarely can the material interests of the church and the preservation of 'law and order' have been so explicitly connected. He said:

> It was a scandal and a shame that the police should have been attacked in such an outrageous way. They were responsible for

law and order, and for the preservation of life and property. They must come back in peace, and be allowed to perform their duties in peace. This he insisted upon. They were the best Catholics in the city; they were steady, respectable and sober men; they were their own kith and kin, and Irishmen, every one of them. When he was in financial difficulties in regard to the completion of the church the men in Cullingtree Road and Roden Street Barracks had responded nobly. These men must not be attacked and, if forced to it, he would see that they were not attacked in the future.[41]

Assistant Inspector General Gambell wired Dublin the following morning to say, 'I think these sermons will have a good effect.'[42] Father Convery was prepared to back words with action. On 15 August a soldier became isolated from his patrol. A mob gathered and he was chased into a house in Divis Street. Rescue was at hand – 'Very Rev. P. Convery, Rev. J. Healey, Rev. J. Doyle and other Roman Catholic priests came quickly to the spot and, with fists, umbrellas and peremptory commands, drove the rowdies back from the door.'[43]

The basic reason for friction between the clergy and the Labour men was the bitter opposition of the Catholic Church to socialism or any form of radicalism. This was well illustrated in a sermon by Cardinal Logue at the inauguration of a new Bishop of Derry on 29 September. Cardinal Logue told the faithful that he was not. . .

> prepared to sacrifice the faith, to sacrifice Catholic principle, even for Home Rule, and he was sure he spoke the minds of Catholics and laity in Derry, when he said they were not prepared to make this sacrifice. Hence I think it is a very ominous thing when we find the politicians of this country entering into an alliance with secularism and socialism under the pretence of securing Home Rule for Ireland. Socialism as it is preached on the continent, and as it has commenced to be preached in these countries, is simply irreligion and atheism.[44]

Now, in August, Labour men faced attitudes of an equally reactionary nature when they sought to make their influence felt in the Falls area, and here also they faced the consequences of past neglect – at no time had Labour as a political organisation sought seriously to make an impact in the area. If they were now reduced, in a period of acute tension, to fire-brigade actions of doubtful impact it was because in the past their message had principally been one designed for an Orange and Protestant audience elsewhere.

If there was one arena in which the Belfast Labour leaders might well have hoped for a helpful response in the aftermath of the riots it was that of the wider British Labour movement. Certainly, the riots placed the issue of Belfast centre stage and provoked an immediate response from comrades across the water. In East London George Lansbury led 10,000 marchers from East India Dock to Victoria Park, carrying drapes of black crepe and led by a band playing the 'Dead March'. The procession was headed by a banner reading 'In memory of and sympathy with our comrades in Belfast killed in the interests of capitalism. Workers remember Trafalgar Square 1887; Featherstone 1893; Belfast 1907.'[45]

In Liverpool a similar demonstration was held, although there the Trades Council saw differences between the English situation and that in Ireland, arguing that 'the men of Belfast need no apologists, they were goaded into deeds which could not be possible in other towns in the United Kingdom'.[46] Elsewhere, many other Trades and Labour Councils sent protests to Birrell,[47] a course that John MacLean, who concluded that the Government were 'murderers',[48] can hardly have thought worthwhile.

This was the predictable response from one wing of the labour movement but it was by no means the only one. Philip Snowden, a future Labour Chancellor of the Exchequer, was quick to respond to MacLean, calling him 'a fool of the most colossal dimensions', and he had a rather different perception of the non-English characteristics of these Irish disturbances, condemning 'that portion of the Belfast population which is almost as much accustomed to rioting as a savage tribe is to constant warfare'. Snowden, however, admitted that there had been errors of judgment by the authorities in Belfast where 'the military were called out in obedience to the requests of the terror stricken shipowners and traders who anticipated riots and not because the state of things... require[d] the military. The inevitable effect... was to precipitate the need for their services.'[49]

Robert Blatchford, writing in the *Clarion*, was not even prepared to go this far. For him a 'howling' mob, organised by the strikers, had attacked a 'few good natured Tommies',[50] but for both Snowden and Blatchford the moral was the same. As Blatchford put it, 'The effect of a volley of bricks and stones: what is that? But the effect of the return of two hundred declared Socialists to the House of Commons:

imagine that!' Snowden argued rather more pragmatically that this was now an era in which Labour was 'being recognised as worthy to be entrusted with the responsibility of administration'. In either case, the events in Belfast were viewed as an embarrassment and, because they were not comprehended, were dealt with in language often applied to native peoples on more far-flung islands.

At Westminster Labour's response was muted indeed. At Question Time on 13 August Conservative MPs immediately raised Victor Grayson's 'broken bottle' speech, with the implication that Labour had incited the riots. Following a statement from R.B. Haldane, Minister of War, Pete Curran, earlier a most strident critic of Government policy in Belfast, limited himself to a purely defensive question, asking, 'Is the Right Honourable Gentleman aware that my colleagues, including myself, on the Labour benches have counselled peaceful behaviour during the strike?'[51] The Government, which might well have anticipated a more damaging attack, was happy to concede the point and end the discussion in unexpected amity.

While the Labour Party did, in the long term, help to secure the later enquiry into the use of the military in civilian disturbances, this was safe ground and of no immediate relevance to the situation in Belfast, where the cautious balance of the Labour position at Westminster merely added to new weaknesses in the strikers' position.

13
Dockers isolated

The riots created a new atmosphere. There had been no actual sectarian fighting, but sectarian fears and suspicions had been aroused. Working-class Protestants had been first surprised by the police mutiny, then alarmed by the rioting on the Falls. They had seen Nationalists, like Devlin, or more militant republicans, like Bulmer Hobson, make all the propaganda on these issues while the labour leaders remained largely silent. Working-class Catholics, on the other hand, felt they had been betrayed because they had fought alone. There were fewer Catholics involved directly in the dock strike than Protestants, and the people of the Falls did not understand the belated arrival of labour leaders on the scene to tell them to stop rioting.

This division, this change of atmosphere, was a critical blow to the strike movement. Before this, whatever tactical blunders had been made, strike leaders had been able to rely on huge non-sectarian crowds at every meeting. There might have been failures, little might have been done, but while that atmosphere had prevailed there had always been the feeling that so many opposed the employers that success had to come in the end. Now all that was past. In the sullen days of mid-August it rapidly became a question of who could get back to work first and where.

For Larkin one hope remained – that the disturbances would persuade the Government to intervene more actively in the industrial disputes. Arbitration with Government backing was now virtually the only avenue that offered a chance for both carters and dockers. Accordingly on 13 August, as the riots were still proceeding, Larkin sent a telegram to Augustine Birrell, saying, 'We would agree to leave ourselves entirely for a fair settlement of the dispute in the hands of the Rt. Hon Carlisle... the largest employer of labour... and one who has fought and worked with tradesmen for so long.' If Carlisle, the manager of Harland & Wolff and considered a dangerous maverick by other employers in Belfast, proved too controversial, Larkin was prepared to accept the verdict of Sir Anthony MacDonnell in the same role.[1]

KICKED!

By late August the employers sensed victory. The hope that they might expel Larkin as far as Liverpool was to prove wishful thinking. (*Nomad's Weekly*, 24 August 1907)

It was a telegram which Birrell was glad to misuse for his own purposes at Westminster in deflecting any Labour criticism of the Government's handling of the situation in Belfast. He now announced, 'I have just heard – I think somewhat authoritatively – from the representatives of the trade unionist party in Ireland and from the trade unions that they are perfectly willing to refer this matter to arbitration.'[2] This was hardly a new discovery, as Birrell implied, for all along the Belfast strike leaders had emphasised their willingness to accept arbitration and it had been the employers who had refused. Larkin in his telegram had made clear that this was one of the major difficulties, arguing that 'the dispute can be closed in a few hours if same is accepted by the employers'.

Larkin's telegram contained an added note of desperation when he complained of the efforts of the press 'to make it a political or religious dispute and thereby carry away the outside public from the real issue, namely trade-unionism'. Unfortunately, the issues were now wider but Larkin was, at least, realistic at a very early stage in recognising the damaging impact of the riots on the strike movement. From Birrell's point of view, this change of atmosphere in Belfast made Government intervention, quite apart from its useful cosmetic effect in the aftermath of the riots, a more plausible proposition in itself. It was not that the Government was any more inclined than before to compel the employers to accept arbitration, but it was felt that, if conditions had altered in their favour, even Belfast employers might find such intervention acceptable.

Sir Anthony MacDonnell explored this territory in meetings on 14 August and soon established that the employers were indeed prepared to engage in talks. Meanwhile Isaac Mitchell, now a Board of Trade official rather than a GFTU representative, and G.R. Askwith, later to establish a reputation as the Board's most formidable expert on industrial relations, were sent posthaste from London. Askwith, who soon after his arrival was given a tour of the troubled areas by Thomas Johnston,[3] was much impressed by the gravity of the situation:

> This was no half-genial dispute, with latest details interesting to the readers of the evening newspapers, orderly arbitration with grave attempt to settle the right lines for the future development and peace of an industry; but the city of Belfast held up by a state of civil turmoil, guards at the railway stations, double sentries with loaded rifles at alternate lamp-posts of Royal Avenue, a very few lorries, with constabulary sitting on the bales and soldiers on either side, proceeding to guarded, congested but lifeless docks, and 10,000 soldiers in and around the city.[4]

It is also to Askwith that we owe one graphic account of the negotiations, given many years later in his autobiography. According to this, he and possibly Mitchell sought out Larkin who 'was very surprised to see us, but after intimating that the British Government and all connected with it might go to hell, launched into a long exhortation on the woes of the carters and dockers and denunciation of the blood-thirsty employers'. Askwith then relates how he weathered the storm and discovered a weakness, in that 'Mr Larkin could not tell exactly what the carters wanted'. In Askwith's recollections, matters then proceeded with almost childlike simplicity as 'it was suggested that some of them [the carters] should be got' and 'this idea interested him and it was done'. This provided further colourful excitement because 'so great was Mr Larkin's zest on this new tack, and so angry did he get at the carters' differences of opinion and changing proposals, that he did most of the talking – and gave them lectures which no employer would dare to utter'.[5]

In minor respects Askwith's account rings true – even Larkin's own men admitted that Larkin was 'a bit rough in his speaking'[6] and that his style of negotiation was often 'to hit the table and make it bounce'.[7] However it is inconceivable that Larkin was unaware of the detailed aspects of the carters' position, all of which had been considered exhaustively in the abortive negotiations at the beginning of August. Most misleading in Askwith's account is the, perhaps self-serving, impression given that any talks he may have had with Larkin were central to the negotiations. Instead it was a tribute to Larkin's prowess as a negotiator that the employers, while now willing to negotiate, still refused to do so if Larkin was present.

In the event, the sole representative of the strikers at the main negotiations was Alderman Gee, still a representative of the GFTU, a principal architect of the disastrous coal settlement, and the man who had left the city on 3 August convinced that he had settled the carters' dispute on terms which involved their working with non-union men and carting to the still strike-bound quays. He was now determined to wrap up matters on the basis of his earlier abortive proposals and in this he had vital off-stage support from James Sexton. True, Sexton was not at the talks, which may have led Askwith to suggest that he was 'practically ignored',[8] but, as General Secretary of the NUDL, Sexton was bound to be a vital element in ensuring that any agreement at the talks was accepted elsewhere. He was not slow to state his views on this aspect of the situation, saying, 'It was the same settlement he offered in Belfast three weeks ago, when he fully recognised that it was practically impossible to get the railway companies who were affected to agree to recognition of the union and he consented to waive that point.'[9]

In the light of these attitudes, Askwith was certainly correct when he said, 'Nothing would or could be done as regards the dockers until they returned to work... the carting employers might be willing to settle if a fair tariff could be arranged.'[10] Indeed, with the main points conceded by the strikers' principal representative at the outset, the talks began so favourably that it became clear that recourse to arbitration would not be necessary and that matters could be settled by direct negotiation. Askwith, as the Board of Trade's principal arbitrator, may therefore have been less central to affairs than he later chose to relate.

The public at large and the strikers did not have long to wait for indications of the way matters were going. On Wednesday 14 August, as the main talks were getting under way, the *Northern Whig* was able to comment, 'There is considerable surprise among some of the Labour people that the carters' dispute is being discussed and dealt with separately, as it has been declared by Larkin and some of the others that the dockers', the coal heavers', and the carters' troubles would now have to be settled simultaneously.' At the same time, the comment of Alex McDowell, reported in the *Irish News*, to the effect that there was 'no hope of a settlement of the dockers' dispute', added to the atmosphere of gloom.

The main negotiations lasted two full days, concluding at 6 pm on Thursday 15 August. Delay was not caused by any major differences of principle, rather by the detailed work on the tariffs now to apply to the carters. However, the business of putting the terms to a subsequent mass meeting of the men in St Mary's Hall was an altogether more tense affair, and here the main burden fell on Sexton, for, significantly, Larkin did not speak on this occasion. Sexton did not undertake his responsibilities lightly, and afterwards Askwith and others 'chaffed Mr Sexton, a small man, for having taken the additional precaution of putting two revolvers in his pocket'.[11] It was not to be the last occasion on which Sexton felt the need to go armed in the face of Irish dockers. In his autobiography he was to describe a journey to Cork two years later, in order to give evidence against Larkin in a court case, when 'literally I carried my life in one hand... and took good care to keep that hand in my pocket where it clutched the butt of a revolver'.[12] As it turned out, Sexton's armoury was not required, but there was 'some delay' before the men in St Mary's Hall gave in.[13]

In Askwith's view, the response to the settlement was ecstatic: women 'knelt in the mud to pray, others seized my hands, some kissed me, and others clapped my back' and he was followed by 'two or three thousand shouting women, dockers and carters' as he hurried to the City Hall to report the outcome of the meeting.[14] Again it is a memory coloured perhaps by the passage of time, for

William McMullen, veteran and historian of the period, could find no confirmation of either the mood or the events described by Askwith.[15]

Relief may have been felt by many, but jubilation hardly. As far as the carters themselves were concerned, they were not even guaranteed re-employment, nor did they achieve union recognition. They did, however, achieve pay increases, and wages, previously between nineteen shillings and twenty-two shillings, now rose to between twenty-two shillings and sixpence and twenty-six shillings, with the exception of youths driving light vans who were to receive sixteen to eighteen shillings. The *Belfast News-Letter* fairly summarised the situation when it said, 'As there was no general scale before the strike, no comparison can be made, but there is no doubt that a considerable advance in wages has been conceded.'[16] However, this was far less impressive when it was borne in mind that as early as the end of June the carters had been offered an increase of two shillings a week.

The strike leaders did not make any attempt this time to pretend that a great victory had been won. At a mass meeting in Custom House Square following the settlement, W.J. Murray virtually conceded that the outcome was, in significant respects, a failure:

> The terms of the settlement were not all that they desired. There were three points on which the dispute committee and the carters had given way, but they only did that for the time being in the interests of the men themselves and the trade of the city. A considerable amount of discussion took place over one matter... the consent of those on whose behalf the negotiations were conducted to work along with non-union men – a voice, 'It is not good enough' – but he believed that before twelve months had passed away all the carters would belong to the society. At the moment Mr Larkin and the other leaders, including Mr Walker and Mr Boyd, were in St Mary's Hall giving the men directions what to do in order to bring about the object without the necessity of coming out again.[17]

More and more, the speakers were leaving present harsh realities aside and focusing attention on future and intangible prospects. Suffice it to say that Larkin's new plans were not made public.

Although the strike leaders appeared to have been cowed, workers, including new groups, still showed signs of unrest and militancy. On 13 August dockers at the Ulster Steamship Company came out because the firm was using blackleg carters.[18] On 14 August two large flour mills which had just reopened, thanks to the work of blackleg carters escorted by troops, had to close again because the employees refused to handle material brought in by blacklegs.[19] On 16 August sailors on the cross-channel steamers came out on strike, after threatening to do so for more than a month.[20] However, these gestures were either futile, in the light of the carters' settlement, or crushed in their own right, as in the case of the sailors who were intimidated by the call-up of the Naval Reserve to take their places if necessary.

As the carters returned to work, the last hope for the dockers was that the Board of Trade would now deal with their problem. Indeed, the *Irish News* expected such intervention 'without delay'.[21] However, the Board of Trade could intervene only if both parties to the dispute were prepared to accept arbitration, and the employers were not prepared to talk about the dockers. Sir Anthony MacDonnell described the actual state of affairs on 22 August in a memorandum to Birrell, saying, 'The reinstatement of the dockers depends entirely on the goodwill of the London and North Western Railway, the Lancashire and Yorkshire, and the Midland Railways,' and urged Birrell to see personally Sir Richard Harrison, manager of the London and North Western Railway, to see if, as an act of grace, he could be persuaded to make any concessions.[22] The railway companies would not talk about the dockers but they were not against all negotiations at this stage. They were quite prepared to settle other problem areas, particularly the coal quays, in order finally to isolate the dockers.

The labour leaders had first to be persuaded to talk about the residual problems on the coal quays while ignoring the dockers, and a little new pressure soon removed any unwillingness on their part. On 14 August the Flax Spinners' Association once again threatened mass lockouts, citing the trouble at the coal quays as the reason. The lockout notices were due to take effect on 28 August,[23] but by 21 August talks about the coal quays alone had begun, with Alderman Gee once again representing the workers.[24]

If the failure to deal with the problem of the dockers revealed the impotence of the Board of Trade faced by the intransigence of the employers, the coal negotiations and their sequel revealed the basic prejudices of the Government, even in those areas where negotiation was possible. For once, the talks were protracted and did not end in agreement, but when they concluded on 26 August the arbitrators nonetheless published their judgment. They recommended that the employers should be free to employ non-union men and that union officials should have no right of access to the men at work. In their preamble to the proposals, the arbitrators made it clear they had rejected the union case on one crucial point, security of employment for known union men, and here the arbitrators commented:

> While we consider that on principle and in theory such a declaration is admissible and such a safeguard reasonable, in our opinion the insertion of such safeguards in these documents is quite unnecessary. It has also been contended that the tariff scale should be expressly stated to be an agreement between the NUDL and the several employers, and that it be so headed. We consider this also unnecessary.[25]

The wages recommended by the arbitrators were equally unsatisfactory for the men. They were to be at a level won at Kelly's yard as early as 11 May, but there was an unpleasant catch even to that. A new flexibility in methods of payment, altogether advantageous to the employers, was to be introduced. The arbitrators recommended that the employers should be allowed to choose whether to pay weekly or tonnage rates, giving a week's notice of any change. This meant that employers could pay a tonnage rate when business was slack and a weekly rate when the men might have benefited by a tonnage rate.

As Sir Anthony MacDonnell put it, the employers' position was 'amply provided for' in the arbitrators' document,[26] and it did not much matter that the workers did not agree to it. The coal employers simply posted up the terms and announced that they would employ only men who accepted them.[27] Michael McKeown of the NUDL protested to Dublin Castle without result, and, indeed, when it came to the putting into effect of agreements it soon became clear that Government arbitrators were either hopelessly naive or prejudiced in favour of the employers.

When Michael McKeown complained about the victimisation of carters, in spite of the carters' agreement, Sir Anthony MacDonnell made no attempt to check the details independently, but wrote to Alex McDowell, the employers' representative, asking for clarification, and then adopted McDowell's comments as the basis for his reply to NUDL allegations.[28]

The final success of the employers in isolating the dockers soon began to have effect. As early as 20 August carters directly employed by the Midland Railway Company surrendered. These carters were in the same position as the dockers because the Midland Railway Company had refused to have anything to do with the carters' agreement.[29] At the Belfast Steamship Company quays the process took longer. On 24 August Gallaher made an offer to the strikers, but he was not prepared to take back those who had first come out. The men met on 26 August,[30] and decided to delay a decision. Gallaher met them again on 2 September, encouraged by reports of disillusion in the ranks, but his proposals met with uproar.[31] Gallaher then announced his departure for America for six weeks and, in the face of that threat, the men finally had to surrender on 6 September. Those who were allowed to return did so on terms no better than those in force when they came out.[32]

As to the other quays: on 30 August the Midland Railway Company made an undisclosed offer to its men;[33] on 13 September the Heysham steamers took back twenty men but continued to employ twenty cross-channel blacklegs;[34] the Fleetwood steamers never took back their regular men, and engaged only a few spellsmen. As late as 30 October Larkin had to remind the Trades Council that the dock strike was not over, because some of the men were still locked out.[35] For many of the men who had borne the brunt of the battle throughout, the results were bitter. As one who worked at the docks at the time put it, 'I felt a pity about the fate of the men I knew — they were never again employed by the shipping company.'[36]

14
A last stand

By mid-September the employers had every reason to think that their main troubles were over. All the strikers were back at work, except for those whom the employers themselves had chosen to leave on the streets. The union organisations appeared exhausted by the battle and, what was more, there were signs that discontent at the meagre fruits of the long struggle had led to new divisions in the ranks of the workers.

From July onward, the *Belfast Evening Telegraph*, in particular, had made persistent efforts to divide skilled workers from unskilled, moderates from socialists, and Catholics from Protestants. These attempts had not at the time carried much weight, but in the bitter atmosphere of defeat they found new support. Particularly serious were more specific allegations of sectarianism made by the *Belfast Evening Telegraph* against the NUDL.

On 1 August the *Telegraph* referred to a rumour 'in circulation amongst the men that Roman Catholic strikers had received strike allowance of 10s. 0d. weekly while Protestants received only four or five shillings'. The same rumour was repeated on 2 August. The paper reserved its main offensive for the coal quay workers who, perhaps of all the workers, had the most reason to feel let down by the strike leaders. On 5 August the *Telegraph* reported:

> Complaints are loud and deep too amongst the coal heavers that it is the Protestant workers who have had to walk about the streets on miserable strike pay, while firms that employ mainly Roman Catholics have been permitted to go ahead all through without difficulty. The opinion seems to constantly gather adherents that politics and religion have much more to do with the strike movement than the leaders are willing to admit.

On 13 August, in the midst of the Falls riots, the *Telegraph* returned to the subject with redoubled fury. The whole course of conduct of the strike leaders. . .

had been influenced by a malignant sectarian spirit which has been exercised for the benefit of one section of employed and employers to the distinct detriment of the other section which differs from them in creed and politics. We emphasise the fact that the proprietors are of the same faith as some of the leaders as being a most singular coincidence. We call the heavers themselves as witnesses of the fact that the leaders have become practically agents on behalf of these firms, and have made the singularly audacious demand upon importers that they must drop Protestant stevedores for RCs. . . No more men will be admitted to the Coal Heavers' Union, and the Union is already packed with RCs. . . it is high time for Protestants to resort to some measures to protect their interests.

All this came somewhat ill from a paper which opposed all the strikes, supported the coal settlement of 25 July, and bitterly opposed any proposals for widening the strike to ensure a better settlement for the men. But when Protestant strikers showed signs of discontent at their settlement the *Telegraph* was not over-concerned with consistency in making use of the issue. Amidst the welter of rumour, there was only one specific incident reported. On 12 August union men came out on yet another unofficial strike at Alexander King's coal yard where they refused to work with a non-union man. The *Belfast Evening Telegraph* commented on 13 August: 'The man in question was a Protestant. How long will the Protestant labouring classes of Belfast stand this tyranny?'

The *Telegraph* then refused to publish the strikers' reply which appeared in the *Irish News* and *Northern Whig* on 14 August. The coal men wished to 'flatly contradict' the *Telegraph* allegations:

There are usually between 30 and 40 men employed by the firm in question, and out of this number there were about 3 RCs on the day referred to, showing that this is not a matter of religion at all. At no time was there ever any reference shown to any person either at Messrs Kings or anywhere else on account of his political or religious beliefs.

The letter was signed by 'J. Burns (asst. Secretary), John Davidson (delegate), Sam Munn (C'tte)'.

The allegations were sufficiently dangerous to require a more general reply and on 19 August Larkin himself wrote to the *Northern Whig*, referring to 'the case of Mr King and the so-called dis-

Larkin, here characterised as a bomb-throwing anarchist, in propaganda designed to divide a labour movement now in retreat (*Nomad's Weekly*, 14 September 1907)

crimination between Protestant and Catholic employers'. His position was, 'that I challenge honest enquiry in this as in all allegations of a similar nature'.

The Trades Council took an equally serious view of the matter and on 5 September took up Larkin's suggestion of forming a committee, 'to investigate certain claims of sectarian favouritism in the administration of the Dockers' and Carters' strikes'. Larkin spoke in defence of the union and read a signed denial by one of the alleged victims of the partial administration. He was quite prepared to submit the matter 'to a jury of three Protestants'.[1]

A further special Trades Council meeting was held on 12 September, and at this a resolution was passed calling on Councillor Gageby and the editor of the *Belfast Evening Telegraph*. . .

to form a court of enquiry into the alleged charges against the carters' and dockers' trades. Those charges are that more dispute money was paid to RC members than to their Protestant fellow members and that the officials of the Dockers' Union wanted to get the RC members to fill all the situations at the Belfast Docks so as to make it a close borough.

One Trades Council member, John Keown, consistently attacked Larkin both at this meeting and at a third meeting on 21 September; Keown was, however, the most unregenerate enthusiast for sectarian controversy within the Trades Council ranks.[2] In the angry row that ensued Larkin could rely on the passionate support of a Mr Mitchell who stated, 'he had charge of the books since the strike began, and of the 190 Liverpool men, 170 were Protestants, and they got from 10 to 18 shillings per week',[3] and of a Mr Farrell who said,

> The joint committee of the strike, of which he was a member, was now under a cloud that was setting one portion of the community against another. He, as an Orangeman and a Protestant, said the Joint Committee was entirely or almost entirely Protestant and, that being the case, they could not hear of a Protestant being ousted by a Roman Catholic... he refused to allow the editors of any newspapers to sit in judgment upon them.[4]

The controversy over these specific allegations was allied to other proposals from Unionist quarters, which combined the objective of eliminating militancy from union organisation with that of securing safe Protestant control; thus a Mr Aspdell, speaking at the General Committee meeting of Shankill Conservative Association on 6 September, argued that 'the day had come when a Protestant Trades Council should be started which would be run on respectable lines, and win the respect of the citizens'.[5]

In this climate the Trades Council could not let the matter rest and on 3 October, following the refusal of the editor of the *Belfast Evening Telegraph* to take part in an enquiry, passed the following resolution:

> That this council having formally offered the publishers of certain charges against the Dockers' Union as to sectarian favouritism in the payments of strike money, and that after being refused for reasons best known to the parties concerned,

> we desire to place on record our strong condemnation of the systematic distraction indulged in by the *Ulster Echo* and *Evening Telegraph* and we believe the charges made to be utterly incapable of proof.[6]

This was, in fact, the last major business transacted by the Trades Council in relation to the 1907 dock strike. The dispute had in effect been dead for more than a month, but the allegations of discrimination against Protestants were a lie that had to be nailed: they affected more than Larkin's reputation, they also threatened the political base of other labour leaders, and it was to politics as before that William Walker now wished to return.

He showed no more confidence in the prospects in Belfast now than he had in early 1907, and at the beginning of September, before the dock strike was decently dead, was in active contention for the Labour nomination in the Liverpool Kirkdale by-election, indeed was favoured by the executive of Liverpool LRC. Their proposal was, however, overruled, possibly as a result of pressure from the National Executive.[7] Nonetheless, both Walker and Alex Boyd campaigned actively for John Hill, the candidate selected.[8] Why Walker's interest in Kirkdale? The constituency was almost unique on the mainland for its similarity to narrow ground nearer home – as Philip Snowden put it, it was 'a constituency where Protestantism of the most militant kind is very assertive'.[9] Although Walker lost the candidacy, controversy was still to surround the campaign, causing the *Labour Leader* to condemn the 'pusillanimous' tactics of those working 'with the object of compelling Mr Hill to pose as a Protestant candidate, and subordinate his distinctively Labour principles to the prejudices of a certain section of the electorate'.[10]

If the foray to Liverpool illustrated that Walker and Boyd were still essentially interested in a Protestant constituency, whether in Belfast or elsewhere, the first major public meeting held by Labour in Belfast following the dock strike illustrated that Walker was intent on putting the events of the summer behind him. Speaking in the YMCA Hall on 16 October, he made no mention of the strikes but spoke instead on 'speedy evolution', the provision of old-age pensions and the nationalisation of railways. The *Belfast News-Letter* was suitably contemptuous, suggesting that 'Mr Walker and his friends have evidently no great faith so far in the Belfast working man'.[11] It was clear that, as far as the Tory press was concerned, the threat of the summer had indeed receded. Yet Walker was by no means exceptional in wishing to return to 'normal' Labour politics. As early as 30 August the more radical Hugh Stockman had expressed the view that the strikes of the summer were disruptive of vital organisational work, noting that 'naturally the exciting events of the last few weeks have considerably upset the work of the newly formed branch of the ILP'.

Unlike Labour leaders, the employers considered that they still had unfinished business to complete, and as early as 12 September Larkin told the Trades Council that 'a man, who was a Trades Unionist, had been paid to form a bogus Trade Union, but the men would have none of it. A meeting was called, but the men did not turn up, and these people slunk back to the holes they came from.'[12] On Saturday 14 September the *Belfast Evening Telegraph* gave prominence to these attempts to start an 'Amalgamated Coalmen and Carters' Union'. The organisers denied that it was sectarian: they claimed that it would be better for carters and coal heavers to be separated organisationally from the dockers, and they were opposed to Larkin's militancy. They had organised a meeting in Whitehall Buildings for Tuesday 10 September, but...

> when the committee arrived they found the room full of men armed with sticks, some of which were concealed, evidently with the intention of causing a disturbance. The Committee, on seeing the hostile attitude of the assemblage, immediately withdrew to the street... it afterwards transpired that the crowd which had prevented the meeting belonged to the NUDL.[13]

This reverse did not snuff out the new body and by mid-November NUDL members felt compelled to take action. Between 14 and 16 November 300 coal heavers, working for six firms, came out on strike. The main issue involved was recruitment by the new organisation, now described as the Belfast Coalworkers and Carters Benefit Society. At a meeting held in the rooms of the Municipal Employees Association on 15 November Michael McKeown explained that the NUDL men had been willing to stand by the earlier agreement with the employers but an entirely new situation had arisen because 'the employers had formed and organised an organisation amongst the men for the purpose of disintegrating the Union'. Larkin explained that, apart from this, the coal employers had not stuck to the financial details of the earlier settlement. The Board of Trade had been approached but had done nothing, in spite of Larkin's warning that 'if the Board of Trade official did not interfere as was promised they would take the matter into their own hands'.[14]

Even the *Belfast Evening Telegraph* had to admit, on the issue of the new union, that 'there is not the slightest doubt that the men feel very strongly on this point',[15] and in its 'Labour World' column of Friday 22 November it confirmed the NUDL view of the new union: 'The present dispute is really a trial of strength between the new union, backed by the masters concerned, and the body with whom the settlement was made only three months ago.' The solidarity and determined action of the NUDL men at this late stage, in spite of their isolated position and the immediate effect of the strike, proved that the vast majority of the coal men remained loyal to the NUDL. The NUDL issued figures on the religious affiliation of members of their committees in Belfast to refute allegations that they now merely represented Catholics in the deep-sea docks. On the local committee nine out of ten were Protestants; the cross-channel committee was all Protestant; on the carters' committee five out of seven were Protestant, and on the general dockers' committee seven out of twelve were Protestant.[16]

The employers reacted quickly to the new threat. On Saturday 10 November men paraded the city with wheelboards reading:

> Strike! Strike!
> At John Kelly's, Coal Merchant
> Because he employed a man who was not one of Mr Larkin's lambs.
> Men apply at once.
> Good wages!   Good conditions!

On the same day the Employers' Protection Association met and feeling was in favour of a general lockout if the strikers succeeded in causing more than a few days' dislocation. Mill-owners, in particular, favoured this course because they were planning to go on short time on 25 November in any case.[17]

First blood, however, went to the coal men. On 16 November cranemen at Kelly's yard refused to do the work of coal men. They were suspended by the Harbour Commissioners, their employers, and dismissed after the Harbour Commissioners' meeting on 19 November. All fifty cranemen in the port, members of the British United Engine and Crane Men's Trade Union, promptly came out on strike under threat of dismissal.[18]

Elsewhere, thirty carters in three firms came out in sympathy with the coal men, and coal ships were blacked in Newry, Derry, Drogheda and Dundalk. Coal men struck at other firms where they themselves had no dispute with the employers, but where the Harbour Commissioners had sacked striking cranemen, and by 20 November nine coal firms and 700 men were affected.[19]

However, the employers managed to recruit blacklegs locally or could rely on members of the new organisation. Thus on 20 November members of the new union cleared the SS *Balmarino* at Kelly's yard and on 22 November the *Belfast Evening Telegraph* was able to report:

> In every one of the firms affected there has been a very decided increase in the number of men who began work this morning, and almost without exception every yard is now fully manned. Speaking generally not a great many of the men who went out on strike have resumed, but their places have been filled by other workers, so that from this point of view the strike has been rather calamitous for the men who came out.

Meanwhile, the Harbour Commissioners had imported two cranemen from London, and more were on their way. However, only a few cranes were working in the port.[20] The situation was still serious enough for the army to have to do its own little bit of blacklegging – 'The Army Service Corps this morning sent half a dozen of their own service carts and a body of men to convey coal from the quays to the Victoria Barracks. The rather unusual sight of military coal carters attracted considerable notice.'[21]

On 20 November 400 strikers met at Scrabo Street and, marching down Queen's Quay, were met by the RIC and members of the Harbour Police. When incidents developed round a coal cart the strikers were driven back down the quays with batons. The following day the Chamber of Commerce passed a unanimous resolution:

> That, in the opinion of this meeting, it is desirable that a deputation should be appointed forthwith to wait upon the Commissioner of Police to urge upon him the necessity of taking prompt action to put an end to the attempted recrudescence at present prevailing at the coal quay of intimidation against men willing peaceably to follow their lawful employment.[22]

The success of the blacklegging, the failure of the NUDL members to prevent it, the lack of significant support from the rest of the labour movement, and hence the lack of other sympathetic action, all contributed to the first major blow suffered by the strikers. The cranemen capitulated on 25 November, addressing a humble petition to the Harbour Commissioners:

> Sir... we, your late cranemen and enginemen, frankly acknowledge we have made a mistake in ceasing work, as we did so not understanding our position accurately; we unreservedly place ourselves in the hands of the commissioners, and we humbly pray that no man shall suffer for the action we have taken in the unfortunate dispute.

Coal men, in consequence, returned to the two firms where the sole issue was their support for the cranemen.[23]

It was at this point that cross-channel union leaders once again took a hand. On 26 November it became known that James Sexton, National Secretary of the NUDL, would visit Belfast. The *Irish News* commented, 'We hope the visit of an experienced and level-headed leader of labour like Mr Sexton will be the signal for a cessation of hostilities.'[24]

Sexton's visit was indeed a lightning one. He arrived on the morning of 26 November and departed the same evening on the Liverpool boat. He did meet Larkin and the local NUDL delegates but the meeting was almost certainly stormy. It may well have been on this occasion that, as Isaac Clarke recalled, 'The men insisted and Larkin insisted that he [Larkin] would go into the shipping offices along with Sexton, but, whatever transpired, Sexton wouldn't hear of Larkin going in with him.'[25] Sexton duly visited Alex McDowell and appears to have been less interested in resolving the dispute on satisfactory terms than in disclaiming responsibility for it; thus he 'deplored what had happened in connection with the Belfast section; it was not due to anything in connection with headquarters but was a troublesome sectional dispute'.[26] Sexton was later to repeat this view more publicly, arguing that Larkin had 'tried to undo all our good work by publicly repudiating a settlement made in his [Larkin's] absence'.[27] The revelation of such divisions within the NUDL ensured that McDowell could respond to any actual requests made by Sexton from a position of absolute strength. Sexton did ask if McDowell 'could make arrangements for the restoration of the men' but the latter replied that 'a large number of additional men had been employed, and I could not make any arrangement at all'.[28]

Yet that evening, before his departure, Sexton told a mass meeting of the men that they should return to work and that 'no advantage would be taken of any man. All was to be plain sailing.' True, there were some who 'demurred at the idea of going back unless some definite agreement was arrived at', but Sexton's further suggestion that 'arbitration by the Board of Trade would follow' was enough to secure acceptance of his proposals.[29]

Why indeed should Sexton have given such a fundamentally misleading account of the situation? The only plausible explanation is that his behaviour stemmed from an almost complete breakdown in his relations with Larkin. In January 1909 he was to describe how far these had deteriorated in this the latter part of 1907:

> When the negotiations for a settlement of the Belfast dispute were in progress Larkin did not consult him although he was the chief officer of the union. Because of the treatment he had received he felt humiliated when he arrived in Belfast during the dispute. Larkin repudiated him and refused to recognise his authority until he wired the Executive Committee of the union. Even then Larkin did not consult him, and he had stood on platforms in the city and bit his lips when he heard Larkin tell the crowd he recognised no boss but himself.[30]

This was an attack made with the benefit of hindsight and perhaps coloured by subsequent events elsewhere, but, although the specific incidents referred to are not identifiable, they clearly occurred prior to November 1907. From Larkin's point of view, disenchantment was also setting in as Sexton retreated from his first expression of euphoric support for the Belfast struggle to a position where he readily abandoned all hope for the dockers, and now opposed any further dispute.

Whatever the cause, it appears clear that in November 1907 Sexton's prime interest on his flying visit to Belfast was to stop Larkin in his tracks, if necessary at the expense of the coal quay workers. Certainly they now had to pay the price for what was the most disastrous intervention by a British trade-union leader during the entire 1907 dispute.

When the men attempted to return on 27 November the majority were informed that their places had been filled. Meanwhile, the employers were still advertising for a large number of hands to whom they could guarantee 'constant employment all the year round'. At some firms men were told that they would have to give up their union cards and badges and leave 'Larkin's Union' before they could be re-engaged. At others they were offered places only at rates of pay below those agreed after the earlier strikes. By 29 November the position was no better. Rural blacklegs, well satisfied with £1 a week, had been drafted into the city and were still filling most of the coal men's places. The employers were pleased with their victory. The NUDL organisation had been seriously damaged and, in circumstances such as these, Sexton's promise of further Board of Trade intervention proved to be mere fantasy.[31]

If Larkin had cause to be bitter with Sexton, he had equal grounds for anger at the lack of support he received locally. Perhaps others felt that they had given their all during the dispute in the summer, perhaps they felt that the renewed strike at the coal quays was from the start a lost cause, but the fact remains that the Belfast NUDL members engaged in this contest virtually alone and lost heavily. Soon after, Larkin left for Dublin, and some, no doubt, must have felt that his departure removed a source of embarrassment. Yet almost all involved in the events of the summer were to find that their own fortunes were more closely tied to Larkin's movement and its defeat in the city than they cared to imagine.

The strikes during the summer had been the first in Belfast to enlist the wholehearted support of unskilled workers and, in particular, unskilled Protestant workers. Hopes had been high, great sacrifices had been made and yet all had turned to dust and ashes. For all that the Trades Council had formally refuted allegations of underhand dealing with strikers, the mood was still a bitter one in which, in the absence of any positive rallying cry, many were prepared to find scapegoats in all those involved in the leadership of the dock strike.

For the moment, Labour activists remained oblivious to these dangers and concentrated on an apparently formidable organisational build-up. Thus, by 22 November, Harry Stockman was able to report the formation of at least five ILP branches based in the North, South, and East divisions of the city, with the West still a significant omission. Apart from branches at constituency level, another was located in Duncairn and a further branch was designated Central; and the Belfast Socialist Society was still functioning.[32]

On the basis of this strength, Stockman was hopeful about the January 1908 council elections, predicting that 'in a few weeks time the ILP will be represented on the Belfast City Council'.[33] A rude awakening followed when all the Labour candidates, including Alex Boyd, lost heavily and there were 'not even enough men to man the polling booths'.[34]

Alex Boyd of the Municipal Employees Association suffered particularly in losing his seat in St George's Ward which he had previously held as an independent. The connection with the strikes in the previous summer was a clear one. Robert McElborough, an MEA member in the gasworks, recalled, 'All the help we had given to the dockers and the destruction of food by the strikers and the loss of thousands of pounds by the city was cast against him during this election.' The loss of the seat weakened Boyd's position as organiser of the MEA because his members now had 'no representative on the council if you were dismissed' and as a result 'a large number left the union'.[35]

Boyd was also particularly affected by the collapse of his previous Independent Orange support, one of the other wings of the 'clover leaf' which had provided backing for the strike movement. Tom Sloan had distanced himself from the cause as early as August and, desperate to save his South Belfast seat, used a rally on 17 December in the Ulster Hall as an opportunity to adopt a position of studied impartiality on labour issues – 'He would never vote against the working class, but he would never wilfully injure capital' – but at the same time he damned those who had allowed the Falls Road to be placed 'in the hands of a few clerics' and thus, by implication, those who had supported the strike.[36] Lindsay Crawford still held his ground, convinced more than ever by the strike experience that the Protestant section of the working class could not achieve its own industrial emancipation unless it was prepared to consider political emancipation for the Irish people as a whole, but he, like Boyd, was now on a losing wicket.

If Sloan could justly be accused of being a dangerous fair-weather friend to any Protestant radical, none of those involved in the events of the summer of 1907 reneged as comprehensively as Joseph Devlin who, like Sloan, used the Ulster Hall to launch his recantation, but in this case as early as 28 October:

> He knew nothing whatever about the strike in its inception. He knew nothing whatever about the strike in its progress. He

did not think he knew even at the present moment what the results of the strike were. He had only spoken to Mr Larkin in his life once and that was for barely two minutes. He had never received a communication from Mr Larkin or anyone connected with the strike during its progress, before it commenced or after it ended. He had never received a single communication from any of Mr Larkin's associates in that strike.[37]

Devlin may have been aware, more than the Independent Orangemen or Labour supporters, of Larkin's rapid progress elsewhere, and, in his denunciation by disassociation, was merely anticipating subsequent, more virulent Nationalist attacks. For the moment others, even with their rapidly declining political fortunes, felt safer without Larkin and little dreamt that his activities would lead to a new crisis in Belfast, this time within the trade-union movement.

15
Divided we fall

Even as Larkin faced final defeat on the coal quays in Belfast, the first direct evidence that his message had taken firm root elsewhere came in the form of sympathetic strike action in Newry. On 19 November dockers there blacked a coal ship, an action that was soon to develop into a fully-fledged strike, and was to far outlast the dying embers of the Belfast dispute. It was a bitter contest, led with militant fervour by James Fearon, but by January 1908 the Newry men had been starved into defeat.[1]

Elsewhere, however, dramatic progress had been made which was ultimately to be of greater significance. As early as July 1907 Larkin had visited Dublin in the hope of raising funds for the Belfast dispute, and found the prospects there so encouraging that, instead of spending the crucial weekend of 11 and 12 August in Belfast, he chose to attend the inauguration of a new Dublin branch of the NUDL. His confidence in the situation there was well founded and 2,000 members had been recruited by September 1907.[2]

Following the defeat in Belfast, the focus of Larkin's attention shifted south, indeed after November 1907 he was only a rare visitor to the northern city, but his strategic outlook initially remained unchanged. He was still very much the organiser of an English-based union; his family remained in Liverpool; he retained responsibility for British seaports and fulfilled other responsibilities on the mainland. Thus for much of March 1908 he was in London giving evidence to a Government enquiry on the regulation of dock wages, and in April attended the British Labour Party Conference. This was no mere matter of duty for as early as October 1907 he had helped form a Dublin branch of the ILP.

Viewed from Belfast, Larkin's role in this period presented no problem. Indeed the labour movement in the city, although in desperate straits itself, could take pride in the feeling that it had helped to give birth to a movement now apparently extending throughout Ireland, and within the established concepts of trade-union and political organisation. Indeed, when Larkin visited Belfast in July 1908 to be presented with an illuminated address by the No. 13 Branch of the NUDL, Alex Boyd was on hand to declare that 'if the same struggle were to be fought over again tomorrow, he would take up his stand alongside Larkin and the dockers as he had done last year'.[3]

While it was still possible to cast a benign and reminiscent glow over past battles, the future was fraught with danger. On 10 July 1908 the Dublin employers made a concerted attempt to smash the union with a series of lockouts. Partly because Larkin, perhaps learning from the experiences of Belfast and Newry, had avoided premature action and had consolidated the strength of the union, it was soon possible to win arbitration and have the lockouts called off. By comparison with what had occurred in Belfast, this was a victory, but it was one from which James Sexton was to snatch defeat. He it was who represented the dockers at the negotiations and who, amongst other concessions, agreed that, in contravention of NUDL rules, members would not wear their union badges at work. It was also clear that Sexton and the employers were as one in agreeing that Larkin's role should be circumscribed almost to vanishing point. Any major disputes in the future were to be the subject of arbitration at national level between the employers and Sexton. Larkin's baleful silence as the outcome of these negotiations was announced presaged a more far-reaching conflict but it was not yet entirely clear what form it would take.

It was on Sexton's instructions that Larkin proceeded to Cork. There too the organisation flourished, but when in early November 1908 a dispute broke out Sexton denied the new branch any support. Larkin was now under increasingly onerous restrictions from headquarters – despite his evident commitment there, he had twice been refused permission to travel to Cork. In mid-November he was in Londonderry under instructions to travel to Aberdeen when a strike by Dublin carters broke out – and he chose instead to travel there. When he requested support from Sexton he was told to 'stew in your own juice'.[4] Although Larkin, without assistance, was able to achieve a not unsatisfactory arbitrated settlement, the NUDL Executive proceeded to pass a resolution 'strongly condemning' him for 'acting contrary to instructions' and in addition Sexton was given power to suspend Larkin at his own discretion.[5]

Larkin now, in spite of his remarkably successful record in the previous year, faced the almost inevitable prospect of being cast into outer darkness as far as the existing trade-union movement was concerned. Defection to another British union was hardly open to him because no such union would have risked an inter-union dispute with the NUDL on a United Kingdom basis over one organiser easily portrayed as a maverick. There was one other option open to Larkin, one which he had certainly discounted and possibly actively discouraged as recently as March 1908. At that time Joseph Harris, one of those active in Belfast in 1907 and now in Dublin, had suggested the formation of a new Irish-based union for unskilled workers, but without Larkin's support the idea initially came to nothing.[6] It was only now that Larkin, faced with a complete impasse in every other direction, chose to reconsider it. With Sexton's threats hanging over him, he gave public voice to the possibilities, but, in doing so, he spoke not with the voice of the theoretician who sees the course of events as predetermined and the outcome self-evident. He spoke rather in tones of indecision, and in the terms of one forced at the eleventh hour to make unpalatable choices:

> He had always believed in the solidarity of Labour the world over but it might be that the best way to bring Irish workers into line with the workers of the world was to organise them on Irish lines first. He couldn't say yet whether he would put his hand to the plough – but if he did he would not turn back.[7]

Sexton soon made Larkin's decision for him by suspending him on 7 December.[8] Larkin now had to determine the platform from which he would fight and here he had to consider opponents other than Sexton, for he had been denounced equally by Arthur Griffith of Sinn Fein as 'an English organiser' of a 'foreign labour union'.[9] But, while his position *vis-à-vis* the English-based unions was irrevocably an isolated one, his 'Irish Ireland' opponents could be disarmed. Just as Larkin had made masterful use of populist rhetoric as a means to organisation in the Protestant Belfast of 1907, so too it was in the practical interests of his new union, the Irish Transport and General Workers Union, founded on 28 December 1908,[10] that he now spoke with a distinctively Irish flavour. This in turn was reflected in the first rule book of the new organisation where Larkin asked rhetorically, 'Are we going to continue the policy of grafting ourselves on the English Trades Union movement, losing our own identity as a nation in the great world of organised labour?' and replied to his own question, 'We say, emphatically, no. Ireland has politically reached her manhood.'[11] In arguing thus, it is almost certain that Larkin hardly considered the possible effects in Belfast where the battle-scarred remnant of the dockers' organisation was no longer the crucial prize in the immediate battle.

If Larkin's new departure – one of the most significant in Irish labour history – was forced on him for largely pragmatic reasons, what of James Sexton, the unwitting architect of the development? Beyond his undoubted personal antipathy to, and jealousy of, Larkin, he was later to express the reasons for the conflict in the patronising terms of an English trade unionist oblivious to Irish needs, arguing that in 'Newry and Dundalk and every other port that could be influenced by Messrs Larkin and Fearon, men were called out on strike and without the slightest consultation with us in Liverpool, the only place where the money of the union exists to any extent'. He continued even more contemptuously to imply that Larkin's position was that any 'Tom, Dick or Harry in Ireland may call a strike on his own and ask us to supply the money'.[12] After the breakaway of the ITGWU both Larkin and Sexton required broader justifications of their actions, but in Sexton's case these appear to have been based on a travesty of the actual facts. As late as May 1908 the annual report of the NUDL had praised the way 'the organisation all through Ireland has grown to a remarkable extent' and by the end of the year, with the addition of a large branch in Cork and substantial developments in other centres such as Waterford, that position was more than maintained. Nationally the NUDL in 1908 achieved both an increase in membership and an improvement in its finances, and accordingly Sexton's vision of irresponsible Irish actions destroying the more responsible mainland sections of the union was quite unfounded. Nonetheless it was to constitute the basis for his ideological offensive which reinforced the Irish emphasis within the ITGWU.

It was now Belfast's misfortune to become the cockpit for the first major battle between the new union and the old. Dublin hardly featured in the contest, for there Sexton effectively conceded defeat without a fight, but in Belfast he was well aware that there were divisions that might be worked on, and that the Irish emphasis of the ITGWU, which was proving an effective weapon in the south, might backfire and provide the basis for a successful rearguard action by the NUDL.

The northern Labour movement was singularly ill prepared to deal with this new and potentially divisive dispute, for while throughout 1908 Larkin's campaign to organise the unskilled in the rest of Ireland had gathered pace, the fortunes of Labour in Belfast had deteriorated steadily. By the summer of 1908 the rash of ILP branches formed in late 1907 was but a memory; in August, in the hope of rallying those still involved, an English organiser was appointed for one month, but in order to pay his salary it was necessary to stop bringing over speakers from England.[13] There is no evidence that either the arrival of an English organiser or the halt in the supply of English speakers had the slightest effect on the situation. At the same time the response of most activists to this collapse in organisation and support was to shy away still further from all areas of potential political controversy. This had become evident at Easter 1908, when representatives of the Belfast labour organisations were invited to Dublin to discuss the formation of a United Labour Party in Ireland. The majority in Belfast favoured calling the new organisation 'The Irish Co-op League' on the grounds that this name would prove less controversial than anything to do with Labour or socialism. A left-wing group walked out and, finally, with a minimum of enthusiasm, the Belfast delegates agreed to press for their old policy of extending the British Labour organisation throughout Ireland. Hardly surprisingly, the talks in Dublin proved abortive.[14]

The real flavour of fear, suspicion, indeed witch hunt, characteristic of the time was, however, more directly evident in the Independent Orange wing of the radical alliance active in the 1907 dispute. Matters here centred around Lindsay Crawford who, even in the aftermath of defeat, did not retract one word of his support for the strikers, and elsewhere continued to show an increasing tendency to support some form of Irish self-government. At the height of the strike movement Crawford had been able with ease to beat off any critics of his stand, but, with the reaction that set in following defeat, his critics, led by Thomas Sloan, soon gathered strength.

They made their move against him in May 1908 when he was expelled from the Independent Order by the Belfast County Grand Lodge. Here Crawford was denied even the comfort of a respectable departure – called to explain his views on Home Rule, he was expelled for disorderly conduct.[15] In June his appeal was considered by the Grand Lodge of Ireland and, according to Crawford, his reinstatement was approved by twenty votes to thirteen,[16] yet it appears that this did not take place. Instead in the following weeks others among Crawford's supporters resigned from the Order. On an individual basis these included rank-and-file members like Thomas Carnduff from Sandy Row,[17] but the resignation of at least seven entire lodges, including the Manifesto Lodge from Ballycarry[18] and the Magheramorne Lodge which 'cordially endorsed his public utterances on the Irish question',[19] suggests that even at this late stage Crawford retained considerable support, although he and those who agreed with him were now cast out or marched of their own accord into the political wilderness.

Another barometer of Crawford's fortunes was his relationship with the Ulster Liberals. Because of his role in the Independents and his skills as a journalist, the Liberals, in opportunist fashion, had appointed him editor of the *Ulster Guardian,* and hoped that he would act as an effective conveyor-belt mechanism which would carry Protestant workers in the direction of the Liberals. Their first doubts had arisen at the height of the 1907 strikes when Crawford's vitriolic attacks on employers were too close to the mark for some big Liberal industrialists. Accordingly at that time he received two written instructions, the first ordering him 'to confine all Labour matters to the column "Labour World" and to insert at the top of the column a notice disclaiming any responsibility for what appeared therein', and the second instructing him 'to discontinue all articles relating to the '98 movement'.[20]

In the climate of 1907 Crawford had been able to weather this storm. Indeed for the Liberals, in spite of Crawford's tendency to overstep the mark, he still had significant pulling power, but with his expulsion from the Independents that asset disappeared. It was no accident that fresh moves against him from the Liberal leadership coincided with his difficulties with the Independents. In early June he announced his resignation from the editorship of the *Ulster Guardian* in the face of an ultimatum from the directors 'that the paper must not be used to advocate directly or indirectly, either Home Rule or devolution in any form'. Crawford defended his right to discuss such matters and also launched a blistering attack on what he viewed as Liberal hypocrisy on social issues, arguing that 'to denounce landlord rights as tenant wrongs is a cheap passport to political fame for some Liberal employers of labour who own no land, but these same men if linen merchants have a different code of ethics in their relations with the flax grower and worker'. He went on to offer what he viewed as a suitable epitaph for both Liberals and

Sloanites as 'weaklings who, having screwed up their courage to achieve something, forthwith shrink from the shadow of their deed and march to the rear'.[21]

Others too in the labour movement were marching to the rear, and here the more dramatic events within the Independent Order were not without influence. The fortunes of both movements were closely tied up in the events of the 1907 strike, and allegiances were often overlapping, most notably in the case of Alex Boyd. The fate of Lindsay Crawford within the Independent organisation now only served to reinforce the tendency within the labour movement to retreat to safe ground, indeed to repel those proposing new adventures.

The formation of the ITGWU descended as a bolt from the blue on the Belfast scene, one where labour organisation was already to a large extent demoralised. Although the causes of Larkin's breakaway were inherent in many of the problems that had occurred in Belfast in 1907, subsequent events had taken place elsewhere, and even then at no point had the wider issues involved in the dispute between Sexton and Larkin been spelt out by either party.

Larkin's delay to the last moment in taking steps to form a breakaway union meant, in any case, that organisational arrangements were hurried and confused, and in preparing the ground in Belfast he had been able to do no more than involve his faithful lieutenant Michael McKeown who, in large measure, took it upon himself to declare Belfast for Larkin. McKeown was subsequently to describe how 'a meeting of the Irish Executive of the National Union had been called in Dublin for Boxing Day'. It was this non-existent body within the NUDL[22] which was to establish the ITGWU, and here McKeown asserted that he had a Belfast mandate, albeit one of supreme vagueness, because 'at a previous branch meeting in Belfast a resolution had been passed appointing delegates who were authorised to act in what way they thought fit on behalf of the members of the branch'. No matter that there were other delegates appointed, McKeown was in the end the only one able to exercise the mandate because 'the Dublin meeting was postponed to the following Monday [28 December] and he was consequently the only Belfast delegate who attended, and according to his powers, had thrown in his lot with the new union'.[23] McKeown, thus, for the second time played a historic role in the history of dockers' organisation in Ireland. In 1892 he had first established the NUDL in the country; now in 1908 he became one of the founders of the ITGWU.

McKeown must have hoped that his authority as a veteran, and as Belfast Branch Secretary of the NUDL with control of NUDL records and premises, would be sufficient to carry the day in a complete defection to the ITGWU. It was, however, soon to become clear that he had underestimated the fears among the mainly Protestant cross-channel dockers of any Irish-based organisation, and the capacity of both local labour leaders and James Sexton to play on these tensions and their sectarian undertones.

The ITGWU was formally established in Dublin on 4 January 1909[24] and two days later a meeting opposing the development was held in Belfast, organised by Alex Boyd.[25] He was never one to limit his involvement in the affairs of the dockers, in spite of his own actual position as organiser of the Municipal Employees, but on this occasion was acting on the direct authority of James Sexton.[26] Boyd now established the guiding principles of the NUDL counter-offensive, arguing that the ITGWU was 'a Sinn Fein organisation that not even a decent Nationalist in Belfast would have anything to do with'.[27] This was suitable polemic in a Belfast context even if it bore little relation to Larkin's actual standing with Sinn Fein – on 23 January Arthur Griffith was to say of Larkin and the ITGWU that 'the first essential of such a body is that those connected with it are not suspended or dismissed officials of the English union which they formerly lauded as the one and only union to which Irishmen should belong'.[28] Larkin's actual dilemma, assailed on the one hand by James Sexton, and on the other by Sinn Fein, was therefore one that Boyd either did not comprehend or chose to ignore and the meeting addressed by him duly passed a resolution protesting at the break-away from the NUDL and 'pledging the members to remain loyal to that union'.[29]

Larkin's supporters responded by calling a meeting on 8 January which was attended by 400 dockers, mainly deep-sea men, with a Protestant, James Flanagan, in the chair. Here a resolution was passed renewing 'confidence in Mr Larkin' and concluding, 'We one and all join the ITGWU and will have no other union but this one.'[30]

There were still those who hoped that these disastrous divisions could be resolved in more pragmatic fashion. Thus, in decided contrast to the role played by Alex Boyd, W.J. Murray, President of the Trades Council, proposed that a committee should be established, consisting of two dockers from each side with a neutral chairman, to see if the dispute could be patched up.[31] It was an offer entirely in the Trades Council tradition of favouring arbitration in all circumstances however unfavourable; but, while it can be argued that Murray was simply turning a blind eye to the country-wide nature of the schism and was accordingly engaging in hopeless optimism, the language in which Larkin still described the split offered some hope that it might yet be resolved. At the meeting on 8 January Larkin argued that he was not validly suspended as NUDL organiser, a stance supported by Andrew Quinn who claimed to be a Belfast delegate to the NUDL Executive.[32] Later still, Larkin was to challenge Sexton to 'resign his position as General Secretary of the union', and to argue that 'if he did, he [Larkin] would stand against him for the post, and he could guarantee that out of 20,000 members Mr Sexton would only get 3,000 votes'.[33]

This may have been rhetoric reflecting back to the anguished months in which Larkin's differences with Sexton were still being fought out within the NUDL; or it may have been a claim designed to establish a quasi-legitimate background to the ITGWU breakaway, when constitutional legitimacy was one argument powerfully wielded on the NUDL side. Either way, Larkin can have been under few illusions that the break was in fact final, and the speed of events in Belfast was soon to destroy the hopes of any potential peacemakers.

The new ITGWU branch began formally to enrol members on 12 January 1909,[34] and by mischance Sexton chose that night to appear in person, in an attempt to reassert his authority, at a meeting chaired by Alex Boyd.[35] The majority who attended soon made it evident that they were amongst those who had enrolled in the ITGWU in the morning and, what is more, that they had spent much of the day celebrating their new allegiance. Sexton, 'a picture of pallor and evidently suffering from extreme nervous tension', was well prepared, with 'a bundle of typewritten documents and a little book which turned out to be the rules of the society', but 'not a word could he utter'.

As the meeting threatened to break up in utter chaos there was one last plea for moderation from James Flanagan, chairman of the first pro-ITGWU meeting but now speaking from the floor. He appealed to those present 'as sober men and dockers to suspend judgment and wait and see if they could arrange to get Mr Sexton and Mr Larkin together', but, in the event, only one further piece of business was transacted when John Quinn, seconded by Edward McGhee, proposed that the men no longer recognise the NUDL so long as Sexton remained General Secretary. Soon after, Boyd and Sexton were forced to retreat from the platform under a hail of discarded NUDL badges and at least one bottle.

The following day the ITGWU sought to maintain the illusion that a debate on the issues between the main protagonists was possible, and placards were circulated announcing that 'Jim Larkin, in accordance with challenge, will meet James Sexton, General Secretary NUDL, and Alex Boyd'. The challenge appears to have been one entirely devised by the ITGWU. In the event neither Sexton nor Boyd rose to the bait, and that night the ITGWU supporters met in relative calm.[36]

Boyd and Sexton returned to the fray on their own account on 14 January and this time the ground was prepared carefully. The York Street Hall was packed with NUDL supporters and, as a double precaution, the presence of 'a large body of police' had been arranged. In the face of a now sympathetic audience, Sexton rejected any possibility of a meeting with Larkin 'because it was a waste of time to deal with a man who was not even a good liar'. Nor was he prepared to accept any criticism of his position, for when one or two ITGWU supporters made their presence known Sexton was soon on his feet 'shouting excitedly "Put him out, put him out"' and expulsions were roughly effected.[37]

The two rival meetings on the successive nights of 13 and 14 January reflected the now almost total separation in the ranks of the formerly united dockers. Squalid public notice of the schism was given on 15 January when the NUDL commenced court action to repossess the union headquarters and books from Michael McKeown and the ITGWU, an action to which the supporters of the new union eventually had to give way.[38]

Such was the inevitable outcome of bitter fratricidal strife; but in the course of the dispute more far-reaching issues were raised, and these were no longer limited to Alex Boyd's simplistic condemnation of Irish-based organisation. The most critical difference became clear when both sides sought to justify their actions in relation to the 1907 dispute. Here Larkin was unrepentant, indeed made excessive claims for what had occurred, saying 'the strike had been referred to all over the universe as the greatest fight between capital and labour for forty years',[39] and if it had not been a complete success, then he blamed Sexton, for 'he [Larkin] had always repudiated the last settlement in Belfast'.[40] Sexton, by contrast, blamed the hardships suffered by the men on Larkin's rashness and indiscipline.[41]

These differences of interpretation tended to exacerbate the divisions in the dockers' ranks because deep-sea dockers and cross-channel dockers had had different levels of experience in 1907. The latter had borne the brunt of the dispute and had in the end suffered defeat, and were now naturally sceptical of militant rhetoric, while the deep-sea dockers, who had suffered no more than long lay-offs in 1907, felt that militant tactics had never been properly tried on their behalf.

This was not a purely abstract division in the conditions of early 1909. While the dockers' organisation was being split asunder, a fresh attempt by the employers to weaken union organisation generally was under way. In late 1908 they had established a Labour Bureau, ostensibly with the objectives of providing sickness and accident benefit for dockers,[42] but it bore an uncanny resemblance to previous employer-backed labour organisations, such as the Amalgamated Coalmen and Carters' Union which had been used as a direct instrument against the NUDL in October and November 1907.

Arguments about the conduct of the 1907 dispute now became enmeshed with the question of the proper response to the new Labour Bureau. The *Northern Whig* noted the tensions over this as early as 13 January 1909, commenting, 'The Labour Bureau, established a few months ago on Donegall Quay and patronised by a number of the cross-channel firms, has, it seems, been a grievance with the union men, and some of the cross-channel workers appear to apprehend that Larkin intends instituting an aggressive policy against the Bureau.' The issue of the Bureau may indeed have been a local bone of contention between Larkin and McKeown on the one side and Sexton on the other. Certainly the NUDL now did little to dissuade those who remained loyal to the old union from collaborating with the employers' organisation, and on 14 January the *Northern Whig* noted that this was now being joined by 'the better class labourers'.

Larkin was quick to denounce NUDL ambivalence on the issue, arguing that 'the Belfast Union of Dock Labourers consisted of about 60 men of whom 40 were now in the Free Labour Bureau as scabs and blacklegs'.[43] This, however, was a gross underestimation of the extent of continued support for the NUDL, and here the *Northern Whig* was again perceptive with regard to the social factors involved, observing that 'Larkin's new society seems to have captured most of the "spell men", while the majority of the cross-channel men remain with the old union'.[44] The majority of regularly employed, and therefore higher-status, dockers worked at the cross-channel quays, but the fact that spellsmen there also appear to have supported the NUDL, leaving the ITGWU dominant only at the deep-sea docks, suggests that the division was principally a sectarian one of Protestant cross-channel quays against the Catholic deep-sea docks, albeit that this was a division to a considerable extent mirrored by the social distinction between casual and regular dockers.

It was not likely that this position would remain stable, with each union still anxious to consolidate its position at the expense of the other and with the employers waiting gleefully in the wings. Indeed it was the employers who made the next move — one carefully aimed at the ITGWU, which, as the most evidently militant of the two unions, was a necessary first target. The instrument of their new offensive was the Labour Bureau whose operations were extended to the Head Line, normally served by ITGWU dockers. On 8 February men were refused employment discharging the *Bengore Head* unless they were members of the Labour Bureau, something which the ITGWU men were not prepared to entertain. Now, 'as the Bureau men passed through the shed... they were made the subjects of a hostile demonstration by a large body of dockers assembled in the vicinity'.[45]

As Michael McKeown protested, the ITGWU had in effect been locked out, and in the following days it was systematically excluded throughout the York Dock. The ITGWU men were reduced to impotent demonstrations on the perimeter of the quays, and more determined attacks on straying Bureau men were rewarded with severe prison sentences.[46] An attempt was made to enlist the solidarity of the NUDL but was immediately scorned by Hugh Reid, now acting as NUDL organiser in the city, who stated, 'The display on the present occasion of placards bracketing the National Union and the Transport Workers Union together is totally unauthorised, as the members are in no way co-operating.' This indeed was an understatement, for by this stage, according to the *Northern Whig*, the Labour Bureau was 'composed jointly of men of the NUDL and those not belonging to any union', a collaboration confirmed by Hugh Reid who confidently asserted that 'there is no trouble between the employers and the members of that body [the NUDL]'.[47]

The last hope for the ITGWU men in these circumstances was to seek outside assistance, and on 13 February McKeown wrote to the Parliamentary Committee of the ITUC, complaining of 'blacklegging' by the NUDL.[48] However legitimate the protest, the ITGWU was, at this early stage, not even affiliated to the ITUC, and hence the complaint were merely referred to Belfast Trades Council which took no action.

Within a matter of weeks, the ITGWU branch in Belfast had collapsed, leaving Sexton to dance on its grave, claiming that 'the Augean Stables had been cleaned as a result of the recent struggle', and that, 'had the ITGWU survived, it would have been an Ishmael in the international trade-union movement'.[49] Far, however, from being a moment of supreme triumph, it was one possible only at a time of deep demoralisation, reflected in the recantation of James Flanagan, who now, in a 'candid confession', admitted that 'the recent strike [1907] was a big mistake' and that 'he believed that the last possible remedy was a strike'.[50]

For the NUDL itself it was no more than a pyrrhic victory. In May, while NUDL delegates from Londonderry and Drogheda attended the ITUC, none came from Belfast,[51] and if the branch survived there it did so in semi-moribund form. Perhaps in Sexton's scheme of things it was sufficient that the ITGWU has been repulsed in Belfast, ironic though it was that his union, smashed there in 1892 because of its Nationalist associations, had now seen fit to play the Orange card. Nor did those, like Boyd, who had backed him ensure a stable alternative to Larkinism – they merely played a part in ensuring that unskilled organisation in the city would be dogged by sectarianism in the future. Even that problem was only to re-emerge later for, as James Clarke, a veteran docker, was to recall, the years 1908–11 were to be 'three of the terriblest years' when 'none of the two unions was employed' and only those connected with the 'Masters' Bureau' could get a start.[52]

16
Conclusion

The Belfast strike movement of 1907 failed to achieve most of its immediate objectives, and the hopes of those involved who had wider aspirations were soon dashed, at least in a Belfast context. That in no way detracts from the importance of the events of the summer of 1907 as a turning point in the fortunes of the northern working class and of the Irish labour movement as a whole.

In limited circles a perception of the significance of the experience survived. Late in life, Thomas Johnston was to argue that the events of the entire period 1914–21 'can be connected directly with the strikes on the docks in Belfast in 1907 and the military intervention at that time',[1] while his contemporary, William McMullen, was to spend his old age writing a history of the 1907 dispute rather than reflecting on his own subsequent successes as a Labour MP at Stormont, Dáil Senator, and President of the ITGWU.

Was this the mere reminiscent pleading of labour activists of the time? Do the events of 1907 matter, given that, whatever the hopes of that summer, the years leading up to 1914 were those in which the final battle lines between Unionism and Nationalism were drawn, or in which, as some have suggested, the conflict of the 'two nations'[2] within Ireland became fully fledged, and in the process the cause of labour, at least in the north, was almost obliterated?

The explosive sequence of events in 1907 reflected quite other divisions in northern society; underlying the apparent identity between the northern industrial economy and that of the British mainland lay a very Irish, indeed quasi-colonial, economy of cheap unskilled labour, and in that twilight world there was deep and pervasive discontent. The struggle of the unskilled for emancipation was not, of course, a phenomenon unique to Ireland. James Sexton initially welcomed events in Belfast because he saw in them a precise analogy with his own formative experiences on the Liverpool docks in 1889, but nearly twenty years had elapsed and by 1907 it was open to him and others like him to seek accommodation within a more inherently stable British social framework. It was in 'British'

Belfast in 1907 that it first became apparent that no such easy avenue was open to Irish unskilled workers north or south, and in this sense the struggle there set in motion a course of events that was to lead to the great 1913–14 Dublin lockout and beyond.

Considered purely as an industrial dispute, the Belfast dock strike, while of pioneering importance, never directly involved more than 3,500 workers.[3] Its impact stemmed rather from the largely spontaneous and non-sectarian mobilisation associated with it, whether measured numerically, in terms of the daily attendances of 5,000–10,000 at strike meetings and the 100,000 or more who marched on the Trades Council demonstration on 26 July, or measured in terms of action on the quays and elsewhere with its cumulatively dramatic consequences.

The largely uncontrolled escalation of events also reflected the weakness of pre-existing organisation amongst those who now played a crucial part. This was self-evident in the field of trade-union organisation where until 1907 the unskilled were, with few exceptions, unorganised, but it was also true in the wider political sense. The electoral decline of Labour and the relative stagnation in the fortunes of the Independent Orange Order in the immediately preceding years had given few indications of what was to follow,[4] and indeed the revolt of the unskilled began independently of any existing leadership. Once it was under way, established labour leaders were to play a critical part and for them in turn the mass mobilisation of 1907 was to prove the decisive testing ground in the entire pre-First-World-War era.

To this unexpected battleground northern Labour brought preconceptions developed in the confined world of skilled labour and fine-tuned in William Walker's three electoral contests for North Belfast. For them labour issues were simply an extension of identical problems in, say, Birmingham or Manchester, and in seeking to resolve them they had implicit faith in the institutions of British social democracy – its trade-union movement, its parliament, even its army. All of these aspects of belief were to leave them singularly ill equipped to provide effective leadership in a new and unprecedented situation.

They were, however, called upon to respond to a situation sparked off by a man who, by all initial appearances, seemed to be cast in quite a different mould – James Larkin. In so far as there is a heroic and revolutionary mythology associated with the events of 1907, it quite legitimately revolves around him. His revolutionary instinct, made all the more potent because it was combined with exceptional talents as a populist orator and enthuser of men, had an immediate and profound impact and ignited tinder where others had failed for years past. His reputation as militant of unprecedented proportions, or bogeyman to the employers, was enhanced by his willing extension of the strike movement, first to embrace all the cross-channel dockers and then the carters. These steps can be interpreted in a millenarian sense, as an application of syndicalist tactics before syndicalism had a general currency on the left of the British labour movement.[5] Certainly Larkin referred rhetorically to strikes in England and America, and more specifically may have hoped to pull British dockers and railwaymen into a general confrontation with the great railway companies. However, his actions can equally be interpreted in the light of the previous history of the NUDL. One historian writing of that formative Liverpool strike of 1889 has commented on the 'desperate attempts to enrol new members... and, once the strike had commenced, to encourage sympathetic action by other workers'.[6] Can it be said that Larkin in the Belfast of 1907 went further than this? Certainly his own advocacy of fair arbitration, one shared with other Belfast labour leaders, and later enshrined in the first rule book of the ITGWU, ran quite counter to any more romantic revolutionary vision.[7]

In other respects too, Larkin's outlook was readily recognisable by Belfast labour leaders and not necessarily diametrically opposed to theirs. He, like them, separated the sphere of industrial action from that of political activity; he, like them, saw the best form of political expression in the election of Labour MPs to Westminster; he was first arrested while campaigning for William Walker, and was to remain an enthusiastic supporter of the politics of the ILP long after he left Belfast.

The critical distinction between Larkin and others in 1907 lay not in points of policy but in the way he welcomed the discovery that his approach, that of an English trade-union militant, had revolutionary implications in an Irish context. He accordingly had an acute feel for the popular momentum of the strike movement and sought to make maximum use of it, as opposed to those who saw in the phenomenon increasing cause for alarm. It was this tension which, in large measure, led to the leadership crisis at the beginning of June, a forerunner of later and more fundamental divisions in the Irish labour movement. However, in 1907, still Larkin's Irish apprenticeship, the difficulties were largely, albeit temporarily, resolved; indeed, in the increasingly desperate circumstances, all shades of opinion were thrown together in the shared responsibilities of collective leadership. Within this context, Larkin had no more answer than the other labour leaders to the acute dilemmas posed by the police mutiny, the introduction of the army onto the streets or the August rioting.

How indeed was the strike movement first stopped in its tracks and then largely crushed? It was certainly the misfortune of Belfast's unskilled that their sudden and unexpected achievements were ones calculated to galvanise their opponents in a way not normally experienced in a mainland British context, and also to render fainthearted or fickle those who might have been counted upon as allies in that more stable arena. This, in turn, reflected the awareness of Unionist employers, the Liberal Government and the British labour movement of the Irish context in which events were taking place, an aspect of affairs from which northern Labour, to its detriment, was all too willing to shy away.

For Belfast employers, economic interest and the politics of Unionism were inextricably linked, and they accordingly saw in any major economic agitation — something serious enough in itself — a more fundamentally destabilising threat. In these circumstances, they were quite willing to condone deliberate attempts to raise sectarian tension as a method of working on the potential divisions within the ranks of labour. It was a strategy given fullest public expression in newspapers such as the *Belfast Evening Telegraph* and the *Ulster Echo,* and voiced in private by men like Fred Crawford. In the declining phases of the dispute employers such as Sam Kelly felt able to intervene more openly in the creation of bogus and sectarian employees' organisations. For Crawford, Kelly, and others, like Alex McDowell, the employers' legal representative, or George Clark who defeated Walker in the 1907 North Belfast by-election, such tactics were necessary to secure the defeat of the 1907 labour upsurge and to prepare the way for their own counter-revolution in 1912–14. All were to serve then on the secret inner committee of the Ulster Unionist Council, responsible for procuring arms, and, in doing so, they were to reveal a willingness to operate quite outside the British democratic tradition in which Belfast's labour leaders placed such faith.[8]

The Liberal Government was an unnatural ally for the Belfast employers who, as Unionists, were determined opponents of Liberal policies in Ireland. The long-running distaste of each for the other was evident in the lack of assistance given by the Irish administration to the authorities in Belfast in the early stages of the 1907 dispute, but not for the last time an avowedly 'radical' British Government was in the end moved to action by the 'viceregal' priorities of law and order in Ireland. Thus it was that, following the police mutiny, the Liberal Government assisted, beyond the wildest expectations of the Belfast employers, in the smashing of the strike movement with the use of overwhelming military force. It was a familiar and slippery slope in which military actions took on a momentum all of their own. This was aided by a decision-making process blurred by governmental remoteness from the situation and, in any case, deliberately concealed from the public. In acting thus, a Liberal Government helped destroy those who might later have proved effective allies: in so doing they unwittingly played into the hands of Unionist employers who were nonetheless to remain their inveterate opponents.

These very Irish considerations also fatally weakened support from the one quarter from which Belfast labour had the most reason to expect it – the British labour movement. If Liberal Ministers dealt with circumstances in Belfast with patrician disdain, there were those within the British labour movement who spoke of Irish disturbances with a more garrulous, and specifically English, chauvinism. More insidiously, the British trade-union movement of 1907 was not attuned to events on the scale of those in Belfast, although these foreshadowed more widespread industrial agitation on the mainland in the following years. The Irish locale of events gave both trade-union and Labour leaders an additional excuse for distancing themselves from circumstances which they increasingly viewed with alarm. Early expressions of solidarity soon gave way to a safer emphasis on parliamentary bi-partisanship with the Liberal Government, mirrored by the 'impartial' approach of British trade-union negotiators. While British labour could consequently claim credit in British terms for its responsible approach to the Belfast crisis, this was at the expense of effective solidarity with those involved in the dispute.

Such betrayals and external assaults created formidable problems for the strike movement, but cannot obscure the extent to which its collapse occurred from within. Precisely those events which concentrated the minds of the strikers' opponents and impelled them to resolute action had the reverse effect on the strike movement itself for which the hour of crisis coincided fatally with the onset of acute ideological confusion and consequent indecision.

Larkin and the other local labour leaders, whatever their other differences, had consistently argued that a struggle, even on the scale of that in which they were involved, could be waged in a purely economic sphere. Developments now confounded this firmly-held belief and lent weight to the allegations of the Unionist press that the strikers had always conspired otherwise. A more credible scapegoat in this respect was Joseph Devlin who engaged in shameless Nationalist opportunism, but he only did so in the aftermath of the police mutiny, that is when wider issues were already clearly on the agenda. In truth it was Protestant workers themselves, those most dismayed by the turn in events, who, by the simple act of engaging in militant struggle for very basic rights, created the conditions of crisis and, given their pivotal role in the northern citadel, it was inevitable that this should be so.

If, then, the 1907 dispute revealed in full array the capacity of Protestant workers to provide a formidable vanguard in industrial agitation it also illustrated the limitations of such agitation, as the powerful impact of the workers' actions raised issues which threatened other compelling supremacist imperatives. In recoiling from this discovery they hastened their own defeat. The experience of 1907 was to prove a classic illustration of a more enduring dilemma for this forgotten majority, in which opportunities for real social advance, albeit with attendant political risks, were lost, and they remained trapped instead in a barren oscillation between the twin poles of proletarianism and sectarianism.[9]

In 1907 the euphoria of the first phase of the process was to be matched by the bitterness of the reaction. In any circumstances men who suffer defeat in a long-drawn-out struggle are prey to demoralisation – in this respect Belfast was no different than elsewhere – but in Belfast rearoused sectarian fears added a dangerous dimension to the aftermath. Features of the strike movement which had been necessary strengths at the time, its non-sectarian nature, its militancy, were now readily viewed as evidence of far-reaching conspiracy.

In such a perilous climate the response of the labour movement to defeat remained of crucial importance. Far from addressing the issues raised by the strike, William Walker, and even the avowed radicals within the local movement, retreated thankfully to what they viewed as the safer ground of the conventional labour politics of the previous era. Increasingly abstract theorising on the supposed benefits of aspects of British labour policy was, however, of dangerous irrelevance to the conditions now surrounding them, and did little to protect them from the backlash of popular opinion, particularly within their own chosen constituency of the Protestant working class.

By contrast, Larkin's commitment to the central importance of militant industrial agitation was strengthened by the Belfast experience. Regardless of any reverse suffered there, he recognised the explosive nature of the response sparked off in the city by his message, and the potential for similar, and hopefully more successful, struggles elsewhere.

Accordingly, he soon departed from Belfast, borne by instinct and his own tendency to perpetual and restless movement rather than by any theoretical certainty about future developments elsewhere. Perhaps also his early leavetaking owed something to a disinclination to dwell on defeat. Certainly the manner of his going provided little more succour for the men who had supported him than that offered by the other Belfast labour leaders. True, he left a union organisation still in some measure intact, although sadly diminished in strength, but he left behind him no coherent body of opinion either to defend his own interests or to pose alternatives to the increasingly disastrous strategies of the rest of the labour movement in the city; nor could he, given his own lack of any longer-term or more theoretical perspective.

Preoccupation with the crisis of the moment was, equally, the hallmark of the period leading up to the formation of the ITGWU in 1909. This crucial breakaway owed at least as much to Larkin's immediate need to foil James Sexton's efforts to disrupt his work as to any broader or more coherent vision. Justification in broader terms only followed the act. Failure in Belfast to spell out the lessons of 1907, or to build on the experience, was now compounded by the venture of the ITGWU which, accordingly, could all too readily be viewed as a fruit of Larkin's personal opportunism, and as a surrender to Nationalism, rather than as a step vital to unskilled labour organisation in Ireland.

If Larkin is thus open to the criticism that, in Belfast, his transient successes on the battlefield were in the end matched by a damaging failure to instill a broader vision, it is a criticism made with the benefit of hindsight, and in the knowledge that no other labour leader in the period 1907–9 foresaw with any greater clarity the outcome of events stemming from the Belfast strike, and none was involved in activities of equal significance. Other activists in Belfast were no less instinctive in their reaction to developments but theirs were now narrowing horizons, in which confident assumptions about their pre-eminence and ideological dominance in a relatively quiescent Irish trade-union movement were replaced by fears of disruptive militancy in a specifically Irish context. With the formation of the ITGWU in Belfast, they were forced to take sides, and the sordid episode in which the new union was smashed in the city, with the help of blacklegging and collaboration with employers, was testimony enough to the choice made at parochial level. This was also reflected in the increasingly negative role played by Belfast labour leaders within the ITUC where William Walker and others engaged increasingly in unholy tactical alliances with the most conservative Nationalist elements, in the hope of halting the progress of the new forces in the Irish trade-union movement represented by Larkin and later Connolly. If instinct – that is, a gut fear of breaking the link between Protestant populism and Belfast labour – played a part in this response, Walker at least was to attempt a wider justification in his controversy with Connolly in the columns of *Forward* in 1911.[10] Walker's argument, however, no longer bore much relation either to the harsh realities of the situation in Belfast or to his own remaining commitment there. In the January 1910 General Election he finally achieved his ambition of contesting a mainland seat, Leith Burghs.[11] Ironically, Walker's failure in Leith owed much to the votes of hostile Irish immigrants, but defeat there left him free to make one final foray in Belfast politics where he chose to stand for the council as a 'People's Candidate'[12] rather than as a Labour candidate, a final expression of his increasing tendency to populist, rather than socialist, politics. In 1912 he retired from active politics on his appointment as a commissioner under the new National Insurance Act.[13]

In the years following 1907 Larkinism was successfully repelled in Belfast, a negative victory for opponents of radical change, won at the dreadful price of exacerbating sectarian frictions amongst the unskilled, and adding that burden to the existing and unaltered sectarian exclusiveness of the skilled unions. However, the fate of Walker, Gageby and Alex Boyd, who appears to have been driven from his post as organiser of the Municipal Employees by 1912,[14] indicates that, in the process, they did not even retain the support of their own limited and primarily Protestant constituency. Many, indeed, of Walker's arguments provided ample, if unconscious, justification for the now mobilising forces of Ulster Unionism. In fairness, Walker would have disclaimed any such connection, just as he discounted any fatal threat to Labour from that quarter.

The unrealism of this benign assumption became evident in the pogroms of 1912 when, alongside 2,400 Catholics, some 600 'rotten Prods', many of them Walkerites, were driven from their jobs.[15] If Labour's most significant leaders in the preceding years had adopted different strategies it would not have guaranteed the safety of the movement, but what is evident is that Walker's own contribution to Protestant working-class ideology did not do so, and in other respects had disastrous consequences for the labour cause in Ireland.

The rejection by Walker and others of developments elsewhere in the Irish labour movement had one further far-reaching consequence. When James Connolly arrived in Belfast in 1910 to attempt to re-establish the ITGWU[16] he found an environment as hostile as Larkin had found it favourable in 1907, and it was impossible for him to make substantial headway in the face of the bitter sectarian tensions of the time.

Larkin, 'snarling' from the safe distance of Dublin, was hardly helpful, 'drawing comparisons between what he accomplished in Belfast in 1907, and what I [Connolly] have done'. Connolly knew that conditions were now different and jumped to the ready conclusion that Larkin was 'conveniently ignoring the fact that he was then the Secretary of an *English* organisation, and that as soon as he started an Irish one his union fell to pieces, and he had to leave his members to their fate'.[17] If Larkin had been honest with Connolly he would have admitted his own failure in Belfast, but could truthfully have dated it well prior to the formation of the ITGWU – the actual defeat of the dockers in 1907 was the point at which reaction set in, albeit that the ITGWU breakaway provided the moment for a final twist to the agony.

Connolly's oversimplified, but quite understandable, view of the demise of Larkin's endeavour in the city was confirmed for him by the outright hostility of Walkerites and most Belfast trade unionists to those developments which Connolly, like Larkin, viewed as essential in the struggle for the emancipation of the Irish working class as a whole. Denial of such support, or even of understanding, in what was the major industrial city in the country may well have been one factor which led Connolly to ally the cause of revolutionary labour in the south, lacking as it did adequate strength in its own right, with that of Nationalist revolutionaries. Whatever the later shortcomings of that strategy, northern critics would do well to consider its possible northern origins.

If such was the legacy of 1907 for the labour movement in Belfast and further afield, it was one which also affected its erstwhile allies. Of these the most significant had been the Independent Orange Order, itself a reflection of the wide-ranging discontent amongst the Protestant section of the working class.

Lindsay Crawford, as we have seen, had been expelled from the Order in 1908, testimony perhaps to the impossibility of transforming an organisation which, if in no malign sense, had an avowedly sectarian constitution into a vehicle for a wider non-sectarian ideology. In the year in which he remained in Ireland, before unemployment drove him to America, he failed to find any secure base, although a frequent speaker at a wide range of political meetings. In February 1909 he told the Young Ireland Branch of the United Ireland League in Dublin 'that there is no party to which the Protestants in Ulster tended more than to the party of Sinn Fein'.[18] On the face of it this was a statement of supreme unrealism, but it reflected his awareness of the role of young Protestant idealists in the formation of Sinn Fein, and his recognition that its early politics were non-sectarian when set beside the worst aspects of the clerical Nationalism with which the Liberal Government preferred to collaborate. By the time of Crawford's arrival in America in 1910 his own commitment to Nationalism was clear: he wrote to the veteran Fenian, John Devoy, offering to write on 'The Rise and Fall of the Independent Orange Movement in Ireland' and signing himself 'Yours in the cause'.[19] Subsequently he was to become leader of the Irish Self-Determination League in Canada, and in 1922 first Free State trade representative in New York.[20] Crawford was not the only Independent leader to cross the political spectrum; Richard Braithwaite, the Belfast Protestant Association stalwart and the man who secured William Walker's sectarian answers to the BPA questionnaire in the North Belfast by-election of 1905, was to be found by James Connolly's side at the meeting held in Belfast in April

1914 to protest at the exclusion of Ulster from Home Rule, and was later to join the Irish Citizen Army under the pseudonym Brannigan.[21]

Both were, however, no more than isolated refugees from the cause of Independent Orangeism, and they served to feed the growing appetite of more traditional Orangeism for the discovery of traitors. Crawford at least can enjoy the posthumous satisfaction that the eloquence with which he pinpointed many of the dilemmas of the Protestant situation still echoes uncannily down the years. Nor was his fate any worse than that of Thomas Sloan, the principal architect of his downfall. Sloan lost his South Belfast seat in 1910 when his growing reputation as something of a dandy did not help his cause, leading Unionists to celebrate in verse how they 'buried him openly. . . with his fur coat wrapped around him', but his real offence, according to the versifiers, was that he was a 'wobbler'.[22] Although his electoral defeat effectively finished his career, this was a crime for which more than poetic interment was required and during the 1912 pogroms his house was wrecked by an Orange mob as he lay ill inside.

The leading figures of the Independent movement, regardless of the perspectives adopted by them in 1907 and its aftermath, accordingly suffered the same eclipse that befell all wings of the labour movement. This reflected their common roots within an inherently fickle Protestant working-class constituency which soon recoiled from the 1907 assertion of proletarian independence and its consequences.

By contrast, no such penalties were paid within the Catholic community. Joseph Devlin, who ranked with Sloan in his opportunistic response to the events of 1907, was to remain pre-eminent in Catholic ghetto politics until his death in 1934. In the circumstances of a beleaguered minority, in which there was little scope for friction between the working class and those who constituted the nucleus of a future Catholic bourgeoisie, it was easy for him to recement a pan-Catholic alliance, representative of the ghetto, regardless of his adventurism in the 1907 dispute and his subsequent backtracking. Although, in following years, the Catholic community was to be subject to assault from outside, this merely served to confirm the durability of its own institutions and politicians. Internally the community was immune from the upheavals that affected the Protestant majority, and thus it was that Protestant radicals, driven from their jobs in the pogroms of 1912, found themselves partially dependent on Father Convery and the Catholic social structures which they had briefly hoped to supplant in 1907.[23]

To thus conclude an account of the events of 1907 with the bitter sequel of the pogroms of 1912 establishes a direct link with the present day when the fortunes of the northern Labour movement are at their nadir. The analogy goes further in that the evident decline of Labour well in advance of the pogroms of 1912 bears comparison with similar difficulties faced by the movement prior to the outbreak of the present troubles in 1969.

Earlier in the 1960s those gathering in the Labour Club in Waring Street, beneath the portrait of William Walker, had higher hopes. Against the background of a mounting recession in Ulster's traditional industries, Labour won four seats in the Northern Ireland parliament, largely on the basis of Protestant working-class support won on a narrow economic basis. Yet, even in a period of relative communal peace, Labour was disastrously vulnerable to sectarian pressures, a weakness highlighted in 1966 when the Labour group on Belfast Corporation split on the issue of opening swings in city parks on Sundays, and Labour councillors cast the votes which ensured that they remained locked.[24] It was an issue farcical in any other context, but in Belfast deeply symptomatic of communal loyalties, and for Labour indicative that the consciousness of the movement had advanced little from the point when, in 1889, the sabbatarian issue had destroyed the first attempt to form a trade-union organisation for the whole of Ireland.

It was, in the event, the Northern Ireland Labour Party's last failure in the attempt to establish the validity of a tradition of labour democracy coexistent with a Protestant ethos which was primarily concerned with dominance. The party was to be one of the first casualties of the revolt of the Catholic community in 1968–9, for civil rights and ultimately against the Unionist state itself, a revolt which was to focus attention on the inability of a society, with democratic pretensions, to accommodate its minority. This focus ignored an equally significant failure of the preceding era, stretching back before partition and very directly to 1907 – that of the Protestant community to encompass an effective and functioning democracy even for itself.

REFERENCES

Where abbreviated references are given, full details can be found under author in bibliography.

Key to abbreviations

B   Bodleian Library, Oxford
BLPES British Library of Political and Economic Science
BPL   Central Library, Belfast
ITGWU Irish Transport and General Workers Union
LHL   Linen Hall Library
LP   Labour Party, London
LPL   Liverpool Public Library
NLI   National Library of Ireland
PRO   Public Record Office, London
PRONI Public Record Office of Northern Ireland, Belfast
SPO   State Paper Office, Dublin

CHAPTER I

1 *Belfast and Province of Ulster Directory* (1907), p.69
2 Ibid.
3 *The Forgotten Conference,* pp.3–4
4 SPO CSORP 1908 20333, District Inspector Clayton, 'Report on Belfast strike', par.8
5 PRONI D3358/1, David Bleakley and Sam Hanna Bell, transcripts of interviews with strike veterans (1957–58), Joseph Cooper and James Clarke
6 E.W. Stewart, *The History of Larkinism in Ireland,* p.1
7 For Larkin's early career see E. Taplin, 'James Larkin and the National Union of Dock Labourers: the Apprenticeship of a Revolutionary', and Emmet Larkin, *James Larkin,* pp.3–24
8 For Sexton see his autobiography, *Sir James Sexton: Agitator*
9 National Union of Dock Labourers. Executive Report for the year ending 31 December 1905
10 James Henderson, *A Record Year in my Existence as Lord Mayor of Belfast in 1898,* p.200
11 *Ulster Guardian* 3 August 1907
12 C.E.B. Brett, *Buildings of Belfast,* p.56
13 Ian Budge and Cornelius O'Leary, *Belfast: Approach to Crisis,* p.28
14 *Belfast and Province of Ulster Directory* (1887), p.14 (1907) and p.64
15 Jonathan Bardon, *Belfast,* p.156
16 Samuel Smiles, *Men of Invention,* pp.288–323
17 Edward G. Maguire, *The Sirocco Story*
18 *The Industries of Ireland. Part I: Belfast and Towns of the North,* p.96
19 *Belfast and Province of Ulster Directory* (1907), pp.72–73
20 Sybil Gribbon, *Edwardian Belfast,* p.51
21 See Lord Dufferin quoted in Sir Alfred Lyall, *The Life of the Marquis of Dufferin and Ava,* vol.2, p.162
22 Henry Patterson, *Class Conflict and Sectarianism,* p.29
23 Report of an enquiry by the Board of Trade into Working Class Rents, Housing, Retail Prices and Standard Rate of Wages in the United Kingdom (1908, Cd.3864, cvii), p.xxxix
24 Report of an Enquiry by the Board of Trade into the Earnings and Hours of Labour of Workpeople of the United Kingdom, Part I, 'The Textile Trades in 1906', (1909, Cd.4545, lxxx), p.xlix

25. Gribbon, *Edwardian Belfast*, p.17, suggests 26 per cent, basing her figures on the 1911 census returns.
26. See D.L. Armstrong, 'Social and Economic Conditions in the Belfast Linen Industry 1850–1900', p.265
27. Alistair Reid, 'Skilled Workers in the Shipbuilding Industry', p.127
28. *Irish News* 8 August 1892
29. *12th Abstract of Labour Statistics* (1908, Cd. 4413, xcviii), p. lxxxxviii
30. Sir George Askwith, *Industrial Problems and Disputes*, p.114
31. Quoted in *Ulster Guardian* 3 August 1907
32. UK average wages in 1906 for labourers in shipbuilding were 20s 11d for those paid on time rates, compared with 15s 0d to 18s 0d in Belfast. *Report of an Enquiry by the Board of Trade into the Earnings and Hours of Labour of Workpeople of the United Kingdom* Part VI, 'Metal Engineering and Shipbuilding Trades in 1906' (1911, Cd. 5814, lxxxviii), p.107
33. *Report of an enquiry by the Board of Trade into Working Class Rents, Housing, Retail Prices and Standard Rate of Wages in the United Kingdom* (1908, Cd. 3864, cvii) p.xxxix
34. See also W.E. Coe, *The Engineering Industry of the North of Ireland*, p.178
35. SPO CSORP 1908 20333, Clayton Report, par. 5
36. Gribbon, 'An Irish city', p.215
37. *Irish News* 6 June 1907
38. PRONI D3358/1, Joseph Cooper
39. Illegal deductions were the subject of an early meeting of the NUDL men. (*Forward*, 9 March 1907)
40. PRONI D3358/1, James Clarke and Joseph Cooper
41. Connolly's negotiations with the shipping companies in August 1913 include reference to a diminishing proportion of permanent men (NLI, William Smith O'Brien Papers, MS 13,934).
42. The dockers' case never went to arbitration and the variety of employers also confuses the issue. Alex Boyd, at the British Trades Union Congress in September 1907, claimed that permanent men earned 20s 0d to 23s 0d for a seventy-two to seventy-nine hour week. *Forward* 1 June 1907 claimed 25s 0d for sixty-seven hours, a figure confirmed by the Belfast Steamship Company (*Belfast Evening Telegraph* 17 May 1907).
43. Austen Morgan, 'Politics, the Labour Movement and the Working Class in Belfast, 1905–1923', p.65
44. *Belfast News-Letter* 16 August 1907
45. PRONI D3358/1, John Orr
46. James Henderson, p.200
47. *Report of an enquiry by the Board of Trade into Working Class Rents, Housing, Retail Prices and Standard Rate of Wages in the United Kingdom* (1908, Cd. 3864, cvii), p.564
48. Seebohm Rowntree, *Poverty: A Study of Town Life*
49. *Ulster Guardian*, 24 August 1907. That this account remained influential is confirmed by the use made of it by Thomas Johnson in arguing for an increase in municipal labourers' wages in March 1913 (J. Anthony Gaughan, *Thomas Johnston*, pp. 22–23).
50. A.C. Hepburn and B. Collins, 'Industrial Society: the Structure of Belfast in 1901', p.210
51. Gribbon, *Edwardian Belfast*, p.16
52. Report of Miss Martindale, a factory inspector, quoted in *Ulster Guardian* 27 July, 3 and 10 August 1907
53. *Report of an Enquiry by the Board of Trade into the Earnings and Hours of Labour of Workpeople of the United Kingdom*, Part I, 'The Textile Trades in 1906', (1909, Cd.4545, lxxx), pp. xlix and 3
54. Miss Martindale in *Ulster Guardian* 27 July, 3 and 10 August 1907
55. *Report on the Health of the County Borough of Belfast*, 1907, p.106
56. *Ulster Guardian* 27 July 1907

57 *Report on the Health of the County Borough of Belfast*, 1907, p.107
58 A.C. Hepburn and B. Collins, pp. 217–218
59 John Gray, 'Thomas Carnduff', p.36
60 Ibid. p.35
61 Ibid. p.39
62 James Connolly, *Labour in Ireland*, p.217
63 Patterson, 'Industrial Labour and the Labour Movement, 1820–1914', p.170
64 *Belfast Health Commission: Report to the Local Government Board for Ireland* (1908, Cd. 4128, xxxi), p.13
65 Ibid. pp. 31–37
66 A. Malcolm, *Sanitary State of Belfast*, pp.12–13
67 *Reports of the Inspector of Factories upon the conditions of Work in Flax Mills and Linen Factories, and upon the Mortality amongst Textile Operatives, &c, in the United Kingdom* (1893–4, C.7287, xvii), pp.6–7
68 Ibid. p.7
69 Ibid. p.5
70 *Belfast Health Commission: Report to the Local Government Board for Ireland* (1908, Cd.4128, xxxi), pp.96 and 102
71 *City of Belfast, Minutes of Evidence taken before the Special Committee... to Consider and Report on the present high Death Rate of Belfast*
72 Dr Anderson in *Belfast Evening Telegraph* 21 October 1896
73 *City of Belfast... high Death Rate*, p.28
74 Ibid. p.174
75 Ibid. pp.70–71
76 Ibid. pp.9–10
77 John Byers, *Public Health Problems*, p.24
78 Ibid. p.112
79 Sybil E. Baker, 'Orange and Green: Belfast, 1832–1912', p.805
80 Gribbon, *Edwardian Belfast*, p.42
81 *Belfast and Province of Ulster Directory*, (1907), p.53
82 See Henry McCormac, *An Appeal on Behalf of the Poor*, p.5, for an account of the consequences.
83 *Belfast Town Relief Fund, Report of Committee; Winter 1878–9*, pp.7–8
84 Patterson, 'Industrial Labour and the Labour Movement', p.171
85 *Belfast Labour Chronicle* October 1904
86 PRONI Belfast Trades Council Minutes, 2 July 1908
87 Gribbon, *Edwardian Belfast* p.37
88 Henry Pelling, *A History of British Trade Unionism*, p.131
89 Gribbon, *Edwardian Belfast*, p.35
90 Henry McCormac, p.7
91 Gray, 'Thomas Carnduff', p.35
92 C. Desmond Greaves, *The Irish Transport and General Workers Union*, p.11
93 William McMullen, typescript history of 1907 strike, ch. 1, p.13. (ITGWU)
94 PRONI D3358/1, Bob Getgood
95 Gray, 'Thomas Carnduff', p.38

CHAPTER 2

1 *The Forgotten Conference*, p.vi
2 Budge and O'Leary, p.89
3 *Belfast Police Manual*, 2nd ed., 1898
4 Gray, 'Thomas Carnduff', p.34. See also Thomas Carnduff, 'I Remember', p.278, and J.W. Boyle, 'The Belfast Protestant Association', p.120
5 *Report of the Belfast Riots Commission, with Evidence and Appendices* (1887, C.4925, xviii), map facing p.564
6 Street directories which give the occupation of head of household, provide a rough and ready but nonetheless emphatic basis for these conclusions.
7 Fred Heatley, *The Story of St Patrick's Belfast*, p.50. See also Joseph Nugent, 'Pawnbroking in Belfast', pp.34–35
8 Heatley, *St Joseph's Centenary 1872–1972*
9 Morgan, 'Politics, the Labour Movement and the Working Class', pp. 284–285. See also Joseph Connolly quoted in Gaughan, pp. 404–7
10 Baker, 'Orange and Green', p.807
11 Ruddick Millar, 'Grand Opera House Memories', *Irish News* 10 January 1933. Carnduff, 'I Remember', p.280 recalls an almost identical riot.

12 *Census of Ireland, 1901,* Vol III, 'Province of Ulster City of Belfast' (1902, 1123a, cxxvi), pp.15–32

13 Rev. A. Hume, *Results of the Irish Census of 1861*, pp. 57–60

14 *Report of the Commissioners of enquiry respecting the Magisterial and Police Jurisdiction, arrangement and establishment of the borough of Belfast* (1865, 3466, xxviii), par.2475

15 Quoted in Patterson, *Class Conflict and Sectarianism*, p.29

16 Rules of the Catholic Representation Association quoted in Morgan, 'Politics, the Labour Movement and the Working Class', p.413

17 *Christian Brothers, Hardinge Street Belfast Trades Preparatory School Prospectus,* 1912. The comparison of skilled and unskilled wages was repeated five times!

18 Reid, p.119

19 *Report of an Enquiry by the Board of Trade into the Earnings and Hours of Labour of Workpeople of the United Kingdom,* Part VI, 'Metal Engineering and Shipbuilding Trades in 1906' (1911, Cd. 5814, lxxxvii) p.xxxiv

20 PRONI D3358/1, William Hunter

21 See for example pro-Unionist political postcards showing the City Hall in ruins etc. under Home Rule. For more on these see John Killen, *John Bull's Famous Circus.*

22 W.J. Pirrie, *Speeches*, pp.330–331

23 Ibid. p.187

24 *Belfast and Province of Ulster Directory,* (1907), p.72

25 Edward G. Maguire, *The Sirocco Story.* See also W.E. Coe, *The Engineering Industry of the North of Ireland*, pp.117–118, 121–122

26 Gribbon, 'An Irish City', p.208

27 See, for example, a Union Jack Committee rally at the Ulster Hall reported in the *Northern Whig* 3 February 1909. James Craig, the main speaker, provided a gloss of patriotic rhetoric, but the first resolution at the meeting, a protest about a proposed Catholic Disabilities Bill, was of more parochial and sectarian significance.

28 Gribbon, *Edwardian Belfast*, p.14

29 Pirrie, p.622. Pirrie also cultivated the Ancient Order of Foresters (p.26).

30 *Northern Whig* 26 June 1907

31 *Report of the Belfast Riots Commission, with Evidence and Appendices* (1887, c. 4925, xviii) par.494. Ewart's Mill, which in normal times employed a minority of Catholics, was not prepared to do so in a period of tension.

32 *Census of Ireland, 1901. . . Belfast* (1902, 1123a, cxxvi), p.25

33 Ibid. pp.21–22

34 Gray, 'Thomas Carnduff', p.38

35 John McKeown, typescript memoir, pp.103–105

36 *National Union of Dock Labourers, Report of the Executive to 30 June 1891 and for the Year ending 1892.* See also *Belfast United Trades Council, Reports and Balance Sheet for the Years ending 1889, 90, 91*

37 For both see *Dictionary of Labour Biography*, vol. 7, pp.152–159

38 E.L. Taplin, *Liverpool Dockers and Seamen 1870–1890*, pp.76–78

39 McKeown, p.105. Dockers were notoriously difficult to organise. Sexton described the problem of caste combined with sectarianism in Liverpool where 'the coal heavers had one society at the North end, another at the South. The leader of one was a North of Ireland Orangeman, the leader of the other was an equally perfervid Irish Home Rule Catholic. . . the only point on which they were united was a mutual objection to mere cargo hands handling coal' (*Sir James Sexton: Agitator*, pp.109–110).

CHAPTER 3

1 J.W. Boyle, 'The Rise of the Irish Labour Movement 1880–1907', Ph.D. thesis, Trinity College Dublin, 1963, p.228

2 *Belfast United Trades Council, Reports. . . 1889, 90, 91*

3 *Irish Trades Union Congress, Seventh Annual Report*
4 J.D. Clarkson, *Labour and Nationalism in Ireland*, p.348
5 Ibid. pp.192–195
6 Ibid. p.350
7 *Belfast United Trades Council, Reports... 1892–3*
8 Patterson, *Class Conflict and Sectarianism*, p.31
9 For Walker's early career see 'William Walker – a character sketch' in *Belfast Labour Chronicle* 1 September 1905. Walker's father was a boilermaker, and at the age of fifteen Walker began his apprenticeship as a joiner in the shipyards. As a youth he helped form the Mariners' Young Men's Debating Society. In 1891 he was elected as a delegate to the Trades Council. He helped to form the Belfast branch of the Tyneside and National Labour Union amongst shipyard platers helpers (afterwards the National Amalgamated Union of Labour) and was later first organising secretary of the Irish Textile Operatives Union. In 1897, with Alex Bowman, he helped form the Municipal Employees Association, in 1898 he became Assistant Secretary, and in 1899 Secretary of the Trades Council, a post he was to hold until 1903. In that year he became Organising Delegate for the Belfast District of the Amalgamated Society of Carpenters and Joiners, and also served as Trades Council President. In 1899 he was elected to the Poor Law Board and in 1904 to Belfast Corporation.
10 Employment by the Corporation was one field in which Catholics regularly alleged discrimination. The loyalist complexion of the workforce almost destroyed the first attempt by Will Thorne, of the gasworkers, to organise them. He appeared at a meeting in Ormeau Park wearing the green sash of his union and it was with the utmost difficulty that a riot was prevented (Robert McElborough, *Autobiography of a Working Man*, p.12).
11 Patterson, *Class Conflict and Sectarianism*, p.33
12 Ibid. pp.34–36
13 Ibid. p.35
14 Pirrie, p.521–2
15 PRONI Belfast Trades Council Minutes, 3 August 1906
16 PRONI Belfast Trades Council Minutes reveal that in 1902 the Council had twenty-one officers of whom seven came from engineering, three from textiles and eleven from other unions. In 1907 there were twenty-six officers of whom six came from engineering, three from textiles and no less than seventeen from other unions.
17 *Belfast United Trades Council, Reports... 1899–1900*
18 PRONI Belfast Trades Council Minutes, 3 August 1905
19 Ibid. 5 July 1906
20 Ibid. 19 September 1903
21 Ibid. 2 June or 7 June 1906 (date illegible)
22 J.F. Harbinson, 'A History of the Northern Ireland Labour Party', Ph.D. thesis, Queen's University Belfast, 1966, pp.12–13
23 J.W. Boyle, 'Rise of the Irish Labour Movement', pp.218–221
24 Ibid. pp.239–40
25 PRONI Belfast Trades Council Minutes, 7 August 1902
26 Ibid. 13 January 1906
27 J.W. Boyle, 'Rise of the Irish Labour Movement', p.175
28 Morgan, 'Politics, the Labour Movement and the Working Class', pp.284–5
29 Ibid. p.286. Trew appears to have been something of an industrial militant on behalf of the linen lappers.
30 *The Forgotten Conference*, p.vi
31 Morgan, 'Politics, the Labour Movement and the Working Class', p.702
32 Patterson, *Class Conflict and*

Sectarianism, pp.52–53. Given Walker's subsequent role, his espousal of Pete Curran was surprising, as Curran had entered politics via the Irish Land League in Glasgow (*Dictionary of Labour Biography*, vol.4 pp.65–69).

33 J.W. Boyle, 'Rise of the Irish Labour Movement', p.319
34 Patterson, *Class Conflict and Sectarianism*, pp.52–53
35 *Labour Leader* 10 May 1907
36 PRONI Belfast Trades Council Minutes, 20 December 1902
37 Ibid. 2 or 6 June 1906 (date illegible)
38 *Forward* 3 June 1911
39 Ibid. 11 January 1908. The fate of the 1898 'six' served to re-emphasise the weakness of Labour representation. Of the six, McInnes went mad and died, Davis died, Liddell fled the country suspected of embezzling union funds, Taylor resigned to manage a newsagency, and Alex Bowman resigned to become Superintendent of Falls Road Baths. Only Gageby remained active.
40 David Bleakley, 'Trade Union Beginnings in Belfast', M.A., Queen's University Belfast, 1955, p.94
41 Morgan, 'Politics, the Labour Movement and the Working Class', p.291
42 The Citizens' Association was founded in 1905. Up to 1907 membership was confined to householders of £20 valuation. The minimum annual subscription was 5s. 0d., later reduced to 2s. 6d, although anyone standing for the committee was expected to subscribe £1. Out of eighty officials thirty were estimated to be connected with the linen trade. Employers who backed it included Gallaher of Gallaher's Tobacco and the Belfast Steamship Company, and Davidson of Sirocco. (*Forward*, 4 January 1908)
43 *Belfast Labour Chronicle* June 1905
44 *Northern Whig* 16 April 1907
45 A series of 'Hammer' leaflets was produced. No. 1 described Walker as 'a sound Unionist' and added that 'the Labour Representation Committee declines to hand over itself body and soul to the radical party.' Leaflet no. 3 in the series emphasised Walker's priorities urging electors to 'VOTE FOR WALKER AND SHOW THE ENGLISH WORKMEN that besides being UNIONISTS you are also in favour of SOCIAL REFORMS' (NLI, William O'Brien Collection).
46 Patterson, *Class Conflict and Sectarianism*, p.60
47 *Northern Whig* 11 September 1905. The questionnaire was presented to Walker by Richard Braithwaite, then prominent in the Belfast Protestant Association and the Independent Orange Order.
48 Geoffrey Bell, *Troublesome Business*, p.19
49 Usually considered as Unionist black propaganda, but an album, apparently connected with the printer Hugh Quinn (BPL), suggests that he was a Catholic Nationalist. He later printed leaflets for the Catholic Defence Association. This, however, was backed by Unionists against Devlin so perhaps the issue remains obscure.
50 Predictably the *Belfast Labour Chronicle* took this line in its issues of 23 September and 21 October 1905, but so also did *Labour Leader* on 1 September 1905.
51 BLPES Labour Representation Committee Minutes, 4 October 1905
52 Patterson, *Class Conflict and Sectarianism*, p.63
53 J.W. Boyle, 'Rise of the Irish Labour Movement', p.364
54 *Labour Leader* 8 February 1907
55 LP LPGC 13/75
56 Ibid. 13/77
57 *Labour Leader* 26 April 1907
58 Ibid.
59 LP LPGC 13/78
60 BLPES Coll. Misc. vol. 2, p.45
61 *Justice* 27 April 1907
62 *Belfast Labour Chronicle* 23 September 1905

63 Ibid. 20 January 1906
64 Ibid. 7 October 1905
65 J.W. Boyle, 'Rise of the Irish Labour Movement', p. 308
66 *Belfast Labour Chronicle* January 1905
67 *Forward* 11 January 1908

CHAPTER 4

1 In the years following Catholic Emancipation in 1828 largely unsuccessful attempts were made to ban all processions (Hereward Senior, *Orangeism in Ireland and Britain*, pp.247 and 281). The ban lapsed by 1849 but the notorious affray at Dolly's Brae that year led to its re-imposition in 1850 (M.W. Dewar *et al. Orangeism*, p.137).
2 Liberals provided cash and Johnston's supporters helped elect Thomas McClure the Liberal to the second seat in the constituency (Thomas McKnight, *Ulster as it is*, vol. 1, pp.151–169).
3 *Orangeism: its History and Progress. A Plea for First Principles*, pp.28–29
4 PRONI Belfast Trades Council Minutes, 22 July 1902
5 McKnight, vol. 1, p.283
6 *Northern Whig* 27 March 1880. See this and other election meetings in favour of Dr Seeds, the new 'Independent' candidate.
7 'Magheramorne Manifesto', *Northern Whig* 14 July 1905
8 *Northern Whig* 14 July 1902
9 J.W. Boyle, 'The Belfast Protestant Association', pp.119–120
10 Ibid. p.122
11 *Northern Whig* 9 August 1902
12 *Belfast News-Letter* 18 August 1902
13 *Northern Whig* 9 August 1902. Sloan is also described as 'a sub-contractor' in M. Stenton and S. Lees, *Who's Who of British Members of Parliament*, vol. 2, pp.219–220.
14 *Northern Whig* 8 August 1902. Two members of the Trades Council who spoke in Sloan's favour were Alex Boyd, a future labour leader who had left the Conservatives a week earlier, and John McKeown who was to play a consistently sectarian role in Belfast Labour politics.
15 J.W. Boyle, 'The Belfast Protestant Association', pp.124–125 states that only three lodges lost their warrants but *Orangeism: its History and Progress*, p.56, gives six.
16 Reginald Lucas, *Colonel Saunderson, MP*, p.345
17 *Orangeism: its History and Progress*, p.8
18 Ibid. p.61
19 Entry in *American Biography – A New Cyclopedia*
20 Independent Orange Order, *Imperial Grand Lodge Report for 1906*, proceedings of Grand Lodge meeting 3 June 1905
21 The four who signed the manifesto were T.H. Sloan MP, R. Lindsay Crawford, Richard Braithwaite (General Secretary) and the Rev. D.D. Boyle. John McKeown, a violent critic of the manifesto, was told by Richard Braithwaite that Crawford wrote the manifesto (*Northern Whig* 28 July 1905).
22 *Northern Whig* 14 July 1905
23 *Irish News* 14 July 1905
24 Sean Cronin, *The McGarrity Papers*, p.20
25 *Northern Whig* 24 July 1905
26 Ibid. 14 July 1905. The selection of Henry was a desperate attempt by Conservatives to stop T.W. Russell, elected as a Liberal Unionist in 1900 and now an independent with increasing sympathy for the Liberals. The Unionists hoped to offset Russell's Protestant tenant farmer votes with those of conservative Catholics.
27 Independent Orange Order, *Imperial Grand Lodge Report for 1906*
28 Ibid. and see also *Northern Whig* 1 August 1905
29 Patterson, *Class Conflict and Sectarianism*, p.64

30 Thomas Carnduff, 'The Orange Society', pp.28–29
31 *Northern Whig* 1 January 1906. Just how far this conspiracy went is revealed in a letter dated 15 January 1906 from Edward Bradshaw, of York Lodge LOL 145, to James Davidson, Assistant Deputy Grand Secretary of the Old Order. At Bradshaw's lodge meeting 'Br Leathem gave a long report of the negotiations between the Liberal Unionists and the Conservative Association and Mr Sloan and Mr Glendinning. It was agreed after a good deal of talk that there would be no contest in South Belfast or West Belfast and a written declaration to that effect was drawn up, one of the conditions also being that Mr Lindsay Crawford was to be no more Grand Master of the Independents' (McClelland Collection).
32 *Northern Whig* 3 January 1906. Edward Bradshaw told James Davidson that 'it was far worse than reported in the papers' (McClelland Collection).
33 *Northern Whig* 9 January 1906
34 For this see J.R.B. McMinn, 'Liberalism in North Antrim, 1900–1914', which while noting the significant role of the Independents in the election, also pinpoints the political limitations of North Antrim Liberalism.
35 *Northern Whig* 13 July 1906
36 J.W. Boyle, 'The Belfast Protestant Association', p.144
37 Ibid. pp.137–138. In 1905, R. Braithwaite contested a Belfast Council election against the Lord Mayor under Belfast Protestant Association auspices.
38 J.W. Boyle, 'Rise of the Irish Labour Movement', p.366
39 *Ulster Guardian* 18 May 1907. This reference, in Crawford's own paper, seems to prove conclusively that the BPA and the IOO split. There is, however, strong evidence that radicals within the IOO took over the BPA. By 1906 Arthur Trew had left the BPA and formed the Belfast Constitutional Protestant Association, the imprint on his leaflet *Orangemen on Guard, or beware of Traitors in the Camp*. By early 1908 the Secretary of the BPA was Thomas Braithwaite, already a socialist. When later in the year this now unlikely organisation left its rooms in Royal Avenue, Edward Bradshaw noted what came out and proved the BPA's direct connection with the IOO, as IOO publications and regalia were taken away, along with BPA furniture (McClelland Collection, Edward Bradshaw to James Davidson, 1 May 1905, 10 February 1908, 16 November 1908).
40 Postcard with extracts from IOO Annual Reports for 1906 and 1907 listing lodge numbers in various districts (McClelland Collection). See also Morgan, 'Politics, the Labour Movement and the Working Class', pp.506–507, who reaches broadly similar conclusions.
41 For the politics of the Catholic community see Morgan, ibid., pp.406–466, and F.J. Whitford, 'Joseph Devlin', M.A. thesis, University of London, 1959.
42 The chairman of a pro-Devlin meeting held in the National Club, Berry Street, on 14 January 1906 said that 'they had a shamrock with the name of Devlin on it, and he trusted that next Friday morning it would bear three names – Devlin, Walker, Sloan'. The basis of this allusion appears to have been a shamrock badge with a photograph of Devlin in the centre produced by John Jamison. See J.W. Boyle, 'The Belfast Protestant Association', pp.142–143, and *Northern Star* 20 January 1906.
43 J.W. Boyle, 'The Belfast Protestant Association', p.142
44 Devlin himself claimed that 'he received over 200 Protestant votes in order to win the election' (*Irish People* 17 February 1906), a quotation used by Arthur Trew's Constitutional Protestant

Association in *Orangemen on Guard, or Traitors Within the Camp*. Edward Bradshaw, assisted Trew with the leaflet, providing him with the song, 'Lines on South and West Belfast Elections', which exaggerated the collaboration in Devlin's 'clover leaf' in order to damage Sloan. The first verse ran thus:

> Would you like to leave Kilkenny?
> Says Tommy Sloan to Joe;
> Of course I would, says Devlin,
> Captain Smiley to overthrow.
> Says Tommy I'll mention now a plan,
> I think it is the best,
> If you'll stand by me in the South,
> I'll back you in the West.

For Sloan 'the trump card of the pack' is described as Alexander Carlisle, and Devlin's reward to Sloan is to get the 'clargy' to work on his behalf with their 'blackthorn sticks':

> And here's my solemn oath Tom,
> Low market you'll have this toime, [sic]
> And Walker will get the Nationalist vote
> In Marrowbone and round Ardoyne

(McClelland Collection).

45 *Northern Star* 31 August 1907
46 Ibid 6 July 1907
47 Bulmer Hobson, *Ireland, Yesterday, Today and Tomorrow*, pp.1–12

CHAPTER 5

1 PRONI D3358/1
2 *Forward* 16 February 1907
3 Ibid. 9 March 1907
4 Ibid. 13 April 1907
5 C. Desmond Greaves, *The Irish Transport and General Workers Union* pp.12–13. Cross-channel dockers had their office at 11 Victoria Street, deep sea dockers at 41 Bridge End.
6 PRONI Belfast Trades Council Minutes, 4 April 1907
7 *Belfast News-Letter* 30 April 1907
8 SPO CSORP 1908 20333, Clayton Report, par.8. Morgan, 'Politics, the Labour Movement and the Working Class', p.70, doubts the completeness of recruitment particularly of deep-sea dockers. McMullen typescript, Ch.2, p.3, remembered that even amongst cross-channel dockers 'never was complete organisation secured during this whole period'. What is not in doubt is the volatility of the situation in Larkin's favour.
9 *Belfast News-Letter* 13 August 1907
10 Ibid. 17 April 1907
11 McMullen typescript, Ch.4, pp.1–2. Charges were eventually dropped.
12 Morgan, 'Politics, the Labour Movement and the Working Class', p.100
13 *Northern Whig* 3 June 1907
14 PRONI Belfast Trades Council Minutes, 20 April and 2 May 1907. On the latter occasion Mr Spence argued that 'Mr Boyd was not now in the Labour movement and was merely using the Council so far as he could.'
15 *Irish News* 29 April 1907
16 Information re Sirocco is to be found in the Thomas Johnston Papers NLI MS 17, 109
17 *Irish News* 30 April 1907
18 *Belfast News-Letter* 30 April 1907
19 Ibid. and *Belfast Evening Telegraph* 30 April 1907
20 *Belfast News-Letter* 1 May 1907
21 NLI MS 17, 109. This is marked 1906, probably in error for 1907, a mistake, if it was one, compounded by Johnston in a controversy in 1914 over a similar poster aimed at the ITGWU and also in this file. At the ITUC in 1914 Connolly attacked Davidson and was supported by Johnston who said 'this circular was no new thing with this firm... he held in his hand a copy of a similar form dated 29 April 1906' (James Connolly in *Forward*, 20 June 1914).
22 *Belfast News-Letter* 29 April 1907
23 Ibid. 30 April 1907, see also SPO CSORP 1908 20333 Clayton Report pars.9–10
24 *Irish News* 9 May 1907

25 'Free Labour' was a major issue in Labour circles at the time and was raised by James Sexton at a joint meeting of the Parliamentary Committee of the TUC, the GFTU and the Labour Party on 26 November 1907 (BLPES, GFTU Management Committee Minutes).
26 *Irish News* 9 May 1907
27 Ibid. 12 August 1907
28 McMullen typescript, Ch. 4, pp.1–2
29 He was a governor of the Royal Victoria Hospital (Gallaher's Limited information sheet September 1982).
30 He chaired a Conservative meeting during the North Belfast by-election campaign of 1905.
31 *Belfast News-Letter* 11 May 1907
32 *Irish News* 9 May 1907
33 SPO CSORP 1908 20333 Clayton Report, par.12
34 All papers and the Clayton Report cover these events. Only the *Belfast Evening Telegraph* attempted to argue that the men from Liverpool 'were labourers brought over on board the *Caloric* for special work at York Dock', rather than blacklegs.
35 *Irish News* 9 May 1907
36 *Northern Whig* 10 May 1907
37 *Belfast Evening Telegraph* 9 May 1907 – a cutting sent with a furious letter of complaint to the Chief Secretary by the Shipping Federation (SPO CSORP 20333). One of the ships stormed was the *Balmarino*, later to achieve fame as a decoy ship in the Larne gun-running of 1912. Sam Kelly, as one of the organisers of the gun-running, also arranged the purchase of the *Clyde Valley*.
38 *Northern Whig* 10 May 1907
39 *Irish News* 10 May 1907
40 Ibid. 11 May 1907
41 Ibid. 14 May 1907
42 *Northern Whig* 18 May 1907
43 Ibid. 20 May 1907
44 SPO CSORP 1908 20333, Clayton Report, par.22
45 McMullen typescript, Ch.3, p.3
46 Ibid. Ch.3, p.4
47 *Belfast News-Letter* 16 May; SPO CSORP 1908 20333 Clayton Report, par.17
48 *Belfast News-Letter* 17 May 1907
49 SPO CSORP 1908 20333, Clayton Report, par.18
50 McMullen typescript, Ch. 3, p.6
51 SPO CSORP 1908 20333, Clayton Report, pars.17 and 18. See also evidence of Sir A. MacDonnell in *Report of the Select Committee on Employment of Military in Cases of Disturbance*, (1908, 236, vii), par.513, where he states that the troops were requisitioned 'for the purpose of preventing an apprehended attack on one of the Belfast quays – the Donegall Quay' and that 'no attack took place'.
52 *Irish News* 17 May 1907
53 SPO CSORP 1908 20333 General Dawson to Sir A. MacDonnell, 17 May 1907
54 *Belfast News-Letter* 18 May 1907
55 Ibid. 20 May 1907
56 *Irish News* 4 June 1907
57 Ibid. 6 June. Doran received the courtesy of a reply from the dockers; none was forthcoming from the employers (*Irish News* 11 July 1907).
58 PRONI D3358/1
59 See newspapers of 1 June 1907 for extensive accounts of the fracas. See also McMullen typescript, Ch.4, pp.2–4; and SPO CSORP 1908 20333 Clayton Report, pars.15 and 20.
60 *Belfast News-Letter* 24 July 1907
61 *Northern Whig* 13 May 1907
62 *Belfast News-Letter* 13 May 1907. SPO CSORP 1908 20333, Clayton Report, par.15 suggests the fire was malicious.
63 *Belfast News-Letter* 16 May 1907
64 SPO CSORP 1908 20333, District Inspector Clayton to Inspector General Chamberlain, 17 May 1907, and Commissioner Hill to Chamberlain, 13 June 1907
65 *Belfast Evening Telegraph* 17 June 1907
66 *Northern Whig* 15 June 1907

67 *Belfast Evening Telegraph* 19 June 1907
68 *Irish News* 31 May 1907
69 PRONI, Belfast Trades Council Minutes, 6 June 1907
70 *Irish News* 17 June 1907
71 Ibid. 19 June 1907
72 *Belfast Evening Telegraph* 3 June 1907
73 Ibid. 7, 8, 14, 22, and 27 June 1907

CHAPTER 6

1 *Belfast News-Letter* 21 June 1907
2 *Northern Whig* 29 June 1907
3 Ibid. 27 June 1907
4 Ibid. 22 June 1907
5 *Irish News* 26 June 1907
6 *Northern Whig* 27 June 1907; SPO CSORP 1908 20333 Clayton Report, pars. 24 and 26
7 *Belfast News-Letter* 29 June 1907
8 *Belfast Evening Telegraph* 28 June 1907
9 *Northern Whig* 28 June 1907
10 Ibid.
11 *Belfast Evening Telegraph* 29 June 1907
12 *Northern Whig* 27 June 1907
13 *Labour Leader* 12 July 1907; Hugh Stockman noted, 'These trade union blacklegs urged in their own defence that, being old men, they had to choose between blacklegging and forfeiting their claims to superannuation.'
14 *Northern Whig* 27 June 1907
15 SPO CSORP 1908 20333. A strikers' poster was sent from Derry to Dublin Castle on 25 June while the opposing posters of the employers were left unscathed – 'there are other notices posted up by Mr Woodney, shipping agent, Derry, offering good wages to labourers.'
16 Ibid. Report by Constable Edward Mulrooney dated 10 July 1907. At least four posters were produced by the NUDL in this period. In addition to those illustrated on p.64 and p.77 the others were: (a) A placard carried behind Gallaher's carts as they travelled through the city, reading: ' This cart is owned by the Belfast Steamship Co. Chairman, T. Gallaher, Tobaccoman and is assisting the imported Blacklegs to Smash the Belfast Men's Union.'
(b) A poster warning labourers to 'keep away' from the quays and to 'remember how the English blacklegs were treated'. Poster (a) was referred to Dublin Castle for possible prosecution. The Solicitor General agreed that this was technically possible but advised against, noting: 'Obviously a proceeding in respect of them [the posters] had to be considered in the light of prevailing conditions in Belfast.' According to Clayton, the poster was 'without doubt printed at the *Irish News* Office but it would not be judicious to make enquiry there as the paper would be certain to make capital out of it' (SPO CSORP 1908 20333).
17 McMullen typescript, Ch.4, pp.4–5
18 *Northern Whig* 28 June 1907
19 Ibid. 29 June 1907
20 SPO CSORP 1908 20333. Memo from District Inspector Clayton, 1 July 1907
21 Ibid. Marginal comment by Commissioner Hill on Clayton Report, dated 5 October 1907
22 *Belfast News-Letter* 29 June 1907
23 *Northern Whig* 1 July 1907
24 Ibid. 2 July 1907
25 Ibid.
26 McMullen typescript, Ch.6, p.3. and also Morgan, 'Politics, the Labour Movement and the Working Class', p.80
27 *Northern Whig* 27 June 1907
28 Ibid. 28 June 1907
29 SPO CSORP 1908 20333. Message in cypher from Dublin Castle to Hill, requesting protection for blacklegs travelling to Belfast from Dublin, and from England via Greenore, 26 June 1907
30 *Northern Whig* 28 June 1907
31 SPO CSORP 20333. Letter, 28 June 1907, from the Lancashire, Yorkshire, London and North Western Joint Railway Companies, and the Midland Railway Company to the Chief Secretary
32 *Northern Whig* 1 July 1907

33 Ibid.
34 McMullen typescript, Ch.7, p.4
35 *Northern Whig* 3 July 1907
36 Morgan, 'Politics, the Labour Movement and the Working Class', p.14
37 PRONI Belfast Trades Council Minutes, 1 May and 5 June 1902, when they were represented by Mr Harvey and were coping with cases of victimisation. By 1906 Alex Boyd was their main spokesman, see BTC Minutes, 1 and 17 February 1906.
38 SPO CSORP 1908 20333. Clayton Report, par.8
39 *Report from the Industrial Council on the methods of securing the due fulfilment of Industrial Agreements, and of enforcing Agreements throughout particular Trades or Districts. Minutes of Evidence* (1913, Cd. 6953, xxviii) p.406
40 *Belfast News-Letter* 2 July 1907
41 *Northern Whig* 2 July 1907
42 Ibid. 4 July 1907
43 *Irish News* 3 July 1907
44 *Northern Whig* 20 May 1907. Larkin remarked that 'now men were going about traducing him, saying his father had been hanged'. A leaflet was distributed on the Shankill during the Trades Council demonstration on 26 July, reading: 'Larkin the Fenian and the son of a Fenian is a liar when he says he can blend Orange and Green. He might as well say he can blend heaven and hell. Protestants awake. Remember the glorious deeds of your forefathers at Derry, Aughrim and the Boyne. If not, the reformation will have to be fought over again and the fires of Smithfield and of Bloody Mary will have once more to be endured.' (McMullen typescript, Ch.18, pp.4–6)
45 *Ulster Echo* 2 July 1907
46 *Northern Whig* 4 July 1907
47 See PRONI Belfast Trades Council Minutes, 4 July 1907, for membership of the committee to assist the dockers. The Trades Council nominees were Joseph Harris (Upholsterers), W.J. Murray (Boilermakers and Chairman of the Council), David Campbell (Insurance Agents), Alex Stewart (ASE), Green [?], John Murphy (Typeprinters), Joseph Mitchell (Bookbinders, and Assistant Secretary to the Council), D.J. McDevitt (Tailors) and Neal McAllister (NAUL).

CHAPTER 7

1 *Belfast Evening Telegraph* 4 July 1907
2 *Northern Whig* 5 July 1907. The absence of badges was important as the 'dockers button' had a key role in NUDL history. It was devised by Richard McGhee; and Sexton (*Sir James Sexton: Agitator*, p.102) noted that where men could not wear it membership collapsed. He described the badge thus: 'It bore on its face the figure denoting its date, with another which was the wearer's number on the branch roll, and a third figure – this on the back – indicated the branch to which he belonged. The shape and colour were changed each quarter.' See also *NUDL Rules*, xii, 3 and 4.
3 Ibid. 4 July 1907
4 SPO CSORP 1908 20333, 1 July 1907
5 Ibid. 7 July 1907
6 *Northern Whig* 28 June 1907
7 SPO CSORP 1908 20333, 28 June 1907
8 *Belfast Evening Telegraph* 1 July 1907
9 SPO CSORP 1908 20333, 2 and 3 July 1907
10 SPO CSORP 1908 20333, Clayton Report, par.35
11 *Northern Whig* 2 July 1907
12 SPO CSORP 1908 20333, 4 July 1907
13 *Belfast Evening Telegraph* 5 July 1907
14 *Northern Whig* 12 July 1907
15 Ibid. 17 July 1907
16 *Belfast News-Letter* 6 July 1907
17 *Belfast Evening Telegraph* 5 July 1907
18 *Belfast News-Letter* 4 and 5 July 1907
19 Ibid. 4 July 1907. As late as 8 August Harris still anticipated action from the Municipal Employees – 'The men in the tramway and gas department were just waiting for the word from their leaders

to come out' – but by then the Corporation Works Committee was in the process of laying off 150 men (*Irish News* 9 August 1907).

20 SPO CSORP 1908 20333, Commissioner Hill to Inspector General, 11 July 1907

21 *Belfast News-Letter* 9 and 12 July 1907. The employers' document was utterly uncompromising, stating, 'No person representing any union or combination will receive recognition, and they [the employers] will exercise the right to employ and dismiss any person they choose.'

22 *Northern Whig* and *Belfast News-Letter* 10 July 1907

23 *Belfast Evening Telegraph* 9 July 1907. SPO CSORP 1908 20333, Hill to Inspector General 9 July 1907: 'There was some trouble in the Falls District. Hughes, a firm of bakers in the Falls Road, started carting, and during the lunch hour the factory people assembled and some stones were thrown.' See also Clayton Report, pars. 37 and 41. Hughes Bread vans were again attacked in Divis Street and Durham Street on 18 July.

24 *Belfast News-Letter* 12 July 1907

25 *Northern Whig* 8 July 1907

26 *Ulster Guardian* 25 May 1907. 'The organising delegate, Mr Larkin, has been called a Fenian and all his men Fenians. Now a most peculiar circumstance is that. . . that 9/10ths of the Belfast Steamship Co's men are Old Order Orangemen and reside on the Shankill and Crumlin Roads.'

27 *Belfast News-Letter* 5 July 1907

28 *Irish News* 10 August 1907

29 See, for example, Desmond Ryan, *Ireland whose Ireland?*, p. 184

30 *Irish News* and *Northern Whig* 13 July 1907

31 *Belfast News-Letter* 15 July 1907

32 *Irish News* 16 July 1907

33 *Belfast News-Letter* 16 July 1907

34 Ibid. 17 July 1907

35 *Irish News* 18 July 1907

36 *Northern Whig* 19 July 1907

37 *Irish News* 20 July 1907

38 *Belfast News-Letter* 18 July 1907

39 *Belfast Evening Telegraph* 15 July 1907

40 Ibid. 16 July 1907. See also SPO CSORP 1908 20333, Acting Commissioner Morrell to Inspector General, 23 July 1907

41 *Belfast Evening Telegraph* 18 and 25 July 1907

42 *Irish News* 8 July 1907; SPO CSORP 1908 20333, Clayton Report par.45

43 *Irish News* 8 and 17 July 1907; SPO CSORP 1908 20333, Clayton Report, par.45

44 *Belfast Evening Telegraph* 18 July 1907

45 *Irish News* 10 and 11 July 1907

46 SPO CSORP 1908 20333. Morrell, in his message to the Inspector General on 15 July, did sound one note of caution: 'There is an element of danger in the fact of the coalmen coming out and the Harland and Wolff's men and the Clark's men [Workman and Clark's shipyard] being off for the week.' He had, however, spoken to the strikers, 'and they are all dead against any violence, and they say the Islandmen will not commit any depredations'.

47 Ibid. 17 July 1907. The agreement included the reservation that the use of cavalry would be seen as a provocation.

48 *Belfast News-Letter* 20 July 1907

49 PRONI D3358/1

50 *Irish News* 25 July 1907

51 PRONI D3358/1

52 Ibid. Joseph Cooper

CHAPTER 8

1 LP LPGC 17/28. Ramsay MacDonald in his reply did not even mention finance (17/29).

2 *Belfast News-Letter* 15 July 1907

3 Ibid. 24 July 1907

4 *Irish News* 1 January 1909

5 *Northern Whig* 24 July 1907

6 Ibid. 5 August 1907

7 *Irish News* 15 and 16 July 1907

8 Quoted in *Scottish Co-Operator* 16 August 1907. The Belfast Co-Op did not allow the strikes to disrupt its social activities. Members passed pickets at the Fleetwood steamer to go on their 12 July holiday to Blackpool (*Scottish Co-Operator* 12 July 1907).

9 *Belfast News-Letter* 19, 23 and 25 July 1907

10 Morgan, 'Politics, the Labour Movement and the Working Class', p.90; McMullen typescript, Ch.7, p.1

11 McMullen typescript, Ch.7, p.2

12 Ibid. See also *Irish News* 19 July 1907 for decision of Municipal Employees to raise a weekly levy on members of 6d.

13 *Irish News* 17 July 1907

14 Ibid. 23 July 1907

15 *Northern Whig* 26 July 1907

16 *Irish News* 20 July 1907. The *Belfast Evening Telegraph* 26 July 1907 revealed that although coal shortages had been the excuse for the lockout notice such shortages never existed.

17 *Belfast News-Letter* 23 July 1907

18 *Northern Whig* 20 July 1907

19 *Belfast News-Letter* 16 July 1907

20 Ibid. 22 July 1907

21 *Irish News* 20 July 1907

22 *Northern Whig* 20 July 1907

23 General Federation of Trades Unions, *The Recent Strikes: their Lessons and Dangers* (1905)

24 BLPES General Federation of Trades Unions Management Committee Minutes, 3 July 1907. These record an NUDL letter protesting at the GFTU decision to refuse benefit to the striking dockers. The minutes of 11 August record a sub-committee meeting on 30 July which took a more sympathetic view. Nonetheless, the September Quarterly Balance Sheet reveals that only £1,400 was paid to the NUDL during the dispute.

25 BLPES General Federation of Trades Unions, *Report of the Eighth Annual General Council Executive Meeting*, 4 and 5 July 1907

26 PRO 30/69 1151 Ramsay MacDonald Papers, Lansbury to MacDonald, 7 May 1907

27 *Belfast News-Letter* 22 July 1907

28 *Belfast News-Letter* and *Belfast Evening Telegraph* 26 July 1907

29 *Belfast News-Letter* 6 August 1907

30 Ibid.

31 *Belfast News-Letter* 26 July 1907

32 *Forward* 10 August 1907

33 *Report of the Select Committee on Employment of Military in Cases of Disturbance*, (1908, 236, vii), par.400

34 *Belfast News-Letter* 30 July 1907

35 *Belfast News-Letter* and *Northern Whig* 1 August 1907

36 Ibid. 2 August 1907. See also *Belfast News-Letter* 3 August 1907

37 *Belfast News-Letter* 6 August 1907

38 Ibid. 23 August 1907

39 Ibid. 27 July 1907, and *Northern Whig* 1 August 1907

40 *Northern Whig* 6 August 1907; *Belfast News-Letter* 7 August 1907

41 *Belfast News-Letter* 27 July 1907

42 *Irish News* 7 August 1907

43 Ibid. 17 August 1907

44 *Ulster Guardian* 3 August 1907

45 Richard Bell, Secretary of the ASRS, persuaded the men not to strike and to accept a system of Conciliation Boards. This proved unsatisfactory but in the event no strike action took place until 1911 (Pelling, *A History of British Trade Unionism*, pp.132–136).

46 PRONI Belfast Trades Council Minutes, 4 July 1907

47 *Labour Leader* 5 July 1907

48 Ibid. 12 July 1907

49 Ibid. 2 August 1907

50 *Belfast Evening Telegraph* 13 July 1907

51 Larkin quoted in *Irish News* 9 January 1909

CHAPTER 9

1 Quoted in *Belfast News-Letter* 18 July 1907. The *Constabulary Gazette*, despite its semi-official status, carried on a remarkably unfettered agitation on

behalf of the rank-and-file policemen. Sir Neville Chamberlain, Inspector General of the RIC, commented in a memorandum on the police troubles dated 14 September 1907, 'The *Constabulary Gazette* is a paper which I have already reported to the government and consider has been one of the main factors in fomenting indiscipline in the force for years past, and which is edited by a civil servant in the employment of the government' (SPO CSORP 1908 20333).

2 SPO CSORP 1907 5541. The report of the Belfast enquiry was scathing about promotions in Belfast. On 26 June 1906 the government announced its intention of publishing the report, but by 1 March 1907 Birrell changed his mind and announced that it was 'not necessary or desirable to publish it'. This about-turn stemmed from Chamberlain's protest dated 24 January 1907 in which he 'most strongly deprecate[d] the publication of any such explanation or return'.

3 *Belfast News-Letter* 29 July 1907
4 Ibid. 3 August 1907
5 PRONI D3358/1
6 *Northern Whig* 8 July 1907
7 *Irish News* 18 July 1907. Dermot Keogh, *The Rise of the Irish Working Class*, p.109, allocates an instrumental role to Larkin and, in effect, blames his assumed adventurism for the undoubted political difficulties raised by the police mutiny.
8 *Belfast Evening Telegraph* 31 July 1907
9 *Irish News* 2 August 1907. The Inspector General, in his memorandum of 14 September, suggested that until Barrett got involved the leading agitator had been Constable Fox.
10 Quoted *Belfast News-Letter* 3 August 1907
11 *Irish News* 25 July 1907
12 SPO CSORP 1908 20333, Morrell to Inspector General, 24 July 1907
13 Ibid.
14 *Northern Whig* 26 July 1907
15 Quoted *Belfast News-Letter* 3 August 1907
16 SPO CSORP 1908 20333. Sir A. MacDonnell in his 'Memorandum or History of Military and Police Arrangements in connection with Police Agitation in Belfast' stated, 'The earliest notice that this office had of any trouble in the police force in Belfast was from the notice in the newspapers of Thursday 25th July.'
17 *Irish News* 29 July 1907
18 SPO CSORP 1908 20333, Morrell to Chamberlain 25 July 1907. Morrell's statement confirms that the *Irish News* had acquired a basically accurate report of events, although he referred to 'personal discourtesy' rather than violence.
19 SPO CSORP 1908 20333, Sir A. MacDonnell 'Memorandum'
20 *Irish News* 26 July 1907
21 Ibid. 27 July 1907. Barrett was at pains to establish his credentials. He had been suspended (indeed arrested) twice but 'about a month ago I was the recipient of a first-class favourable record, and five pounds for efficient service. I have been a member of the force for over eleven years; and, whatever my demerits and shortcomings are – and I admit there are many – my record in the force is, in police parlance, unblemished.' Aged thirty-two, and from Ballyduff, Co. Kerry, he had joined the force in 1896. His brothers, Edmond and James, were in the London Metropolitan Police (Joan Boyd, 'Police Strike').

CHAPTER 10

1 *Irish News* 29 July 1907
2 The lowest estimate was that of the *Belfast News-Letter,* the highest that of the *Irish News*. Sir A. MacDonnell later gave evidence that 'out of a police force of 1,000, 600 struck' (*Report of the Select Committee on Employment of Military in Cases of Disturbance,* ((1908, 236, vii)), par.513). Keogh,

pp.108–9, is therefore incorrect when he says that 'less than 200 RIC men were directly involved in the action'.
3. *Irish News* 9 August 1907, evidence of Head Constable Gerity during disciplinary proceedings against Constable Fay.
4. Ibid. The disciplinary charge against Constable Reynolds was that he had refused to close the gates. District Inspector Gelston said Barrett had argued that 'the gates should not be shut as he wanted the public to see what took place inside'.
5. Ibid. 29 July 1907
6. Ibid.
7. Ibid. Assistant Inspector General Gambell appears to have taken this rumour seriously, and MacDonnell relayed it to Birrell on 30 July saying 'there are doubts about surrendering their arms and ammunition' (SPO CSORP 1908 20333).
8. *Irish News* 29 July 1907
9. SPO CSORP 1908 20333, Chamberlain to Morrell, 26 July 1907 – 'You are to say nothing at the meeting.'
10. Ibid. Morrell to Chamberlain, 27 July 1907
11. Ibid. Chamberlain 'Memorandum'
12. *Irish Independent* 29 July 1907
13. *Belfast Evening Telegraph* 29 July 1907
14. *Irish News* 30 July 1907
15. *Irish Independent* 29 July 1907
16. Ibid.
17. *Northern Whig* 29 July 1907
18. SPO CSORP 1908 20333, Gambell to Chamberlain, telephone message 29 July 1907
19. *Belfast Evening Telegraph* 30 July 1907
20. SPO CSORP 1908 20333, Gambell to Chamberlain 29 July 1907
21. Ibid. Undated note
22. Leon O'Broin, *The Chief Secretary*, p.11
23. SPO CSORP 1908 20333, MacDonnell to Chamberlain
24. Ibid. A marginal note to MacDonnell's statement of opinion.
25. *Report of the Select Committee on Employment of Military in Cases of Disturbance*, (1908, 236, vii), par.513
26. SPO CSORP 1908 20333, Gambell to Chamberlain, 29 July 1907
27. Ibid. Clayton Report par.62
28. *Belfast News-Letter* 2 August 1907
29. Ibid. 3 August 1907
30. SPO CSORP 1908 20333, MacDonnell to Birrell 12.12 a.m. 31 July 1907
31. *Northern Whig* 2 August 1907. This was a long-standing courtesy visit but its occurrence was, from the Government's point of view, timely.
32. *Belfast News-Letter* 2 August 1907. Barrett found work as warden at Dunville Park. Later he managed a pub at the junction of Grosvenor Road and Distillery Street. His photograph still hangs in the Hall of Martyrs in Moscow and he seems to have remained active in politics. He was a bodyguard for Winston Churchill on his stormy visit to the city in 1912. On his death in 1940, aged sixty-five, an obituary appeared in *Irish Workers Weekly* (February 1940). Constable Fay worked for the *Belfast Evening Telegraph*, while, more tragically, Constable Reynolds frequented the York Road district, where he had been stationed, 'often in a distraught state' (McMullen typescript, Ch.17, p.6; Joan Boyd, 'Police Strike').
33. SPO CSORP 1908 20333. Amongst those who were transferred were Sergeants Kerrigan and De Vere, both of whom had given evidence against their superiors to the Burke Commission of Enquiry in 1906. They both now complained of victimisation, despite immunity granted when giving evidence in 1906. It is little wonder that MacDonnell should have commented, 'I think it unfortunate that this particular moment should have been selected for the transfer.'
34. *Irish News* 3 August 1907
35. *Belfast News-Letter* 3 August 1907
36. Ibid.
37. *Irish News* 3 August 1907

38 SPO CSORP 1908 20333, Clayton Report, par.64. More than 100 of those transferred were from 'B' division.
39 Ibid. Hill to Chamberlain 20 November 1907
40 *Belfast Evening Telegraph* 29 July 1907
41 See SPO CSORP 1908 20333, Clayton Report, par. 64: 'The trouble had clearly been organised in "B" district which is the Nationalist or West Division of the city.' Morgan, 'Politics, the Labour Movement and the Working Class', p.98, and Patterson, *Class Conflict and Sectarianism*, p.69, both quote from official sources which may have originated with Clayton, and hence imply a greater degree of ethnic, i.e. Catholic, mobilisation than is justified by the additional evidence cited here.
42 MacDonnell blamed the labour unrest in Belfast, and so did Gambell, as on 29 July 1907 when he said, 'The spirit of the strikers has fomented the men thoroughly.'
43 *Belfast News-Letter* and *Irish News* 3 August 1907. See also SPO CSORP 1908 20333, memo from MacDonnell, 30 July 1907, noting that 'in the selection of constables for service in Belfast particular attention has of course to be paid to religious considerations'.
44 SPO CSORP 1908 20333, Clayton Report, par.64. Although more than 100 men were transferred from West Belfast, only thirty-seven replacements came from outside Belfast. Clayton made this point because in later disturbances the county replacements became a major issue. Some county men did immediately go on duty in the area because on 7 August Gambell reported to Chamberlain, with misplaced optimism, that 'in Mr Kelly's district the people are fraternising with them'.
45 Ibid. MacDonnell, in his 'Memorandum', recounted Hill's comments on Kelly: 'It is evident that this officer was either out of touch with his men or that he was so careless and apathetic in his discharge of his duty as not to know what was going on among them.' For Kelly's resignation see *Irish News* 6 August 1907.
46 *Northern Whig* 5 August 1907

CHAPTER 11

1 *Northern Whig* 30 July 1907
2 *Belfast News-Letter* 26 July 1907
3 *Irish News* 29 July 1907
4 PRONI D3358/1, James Clarke
5 SPO CSORP 1908 20333, Clayton Report
6 PRONI D3358/1, Joseph Cooper
7 *Irish News* 2 August 1907
8 Ibid. 17 August 1907
9 McMullen typescript, Ch.14, p.2
10 *Liverpool Weekly Courier* 20 July 1907
11 *Belfast Evening Telegraph* 2 August 1907
12 *Belfast News-Letter* 6 August 1907
13 Ibid. 3 August 1907
14 *Irish News* 2 August 1907
15 Ibid. 5 August 1907
16 *Ulster Guardian* 10 August 1907
17 *Belfast News-Letter* 6 August 1907
18 *Northern Whig* 6 August 1907
19 *Belfast News-Letter* 6 August 1907
20 Ibid. 2 August 1907
21 *Irish News* 30 July 1907. The Chamber later denied that their demands went as far as this (*Belfast News-Letter* 31 July 1907).
22 *Belfast News-Letter* 31 July 1907
23 *Northern Whig* 30 July 1907
24 *Belfast News-Letter* 2 August 1907
25 *Northern Whig* 6 August 1907 and *Irish News* 7 August 1907
26 *Irish News* 7 August 1907
27 SPO CSORP 1908 20333, Clayton Report
28 Ibid. Gambell to Chamberlain, 4 August 1907
29 *Belfast News-Letter* 7 August 1907
30 *Northern Whig* 8 August 1907
31 SPO CSORP 1908 20333, Gambell to MacDonnell 7 August 1907
32 Ibid. MacDonnell to Birrell, 7 August 1907

33 *Belfast News-Letter* 9 August 1907
34 SPO CSORP 1908 20333
35 *Belfast Evening Telegraph* 8 August 1907
36 *Belfast News-Letter* 9 August 1907
37 SPO CSORP 1908 20333
38 *Belfast Evening Telegraph* 8 August 1907
39 Ibid. 9 August 1907
40 Ibid. 5 August 1907
41 *Belfast News-Letter* 10 August 1907
42 *Belfast Evening Telegraph* 8 August 1907
43 *Northern Whig* 10 August 1907
44 *Belfast Evening Telegraph* 10 August 1907
45 PRONI D3358/1, Joseph Cooper, William Hughes
46 *Belfast News-Letter* 7 June 1898. Referring to riots on the Shankill, the paper saw 'the soldiers being everywhere cheered, while the police are execrated'.
47 PRONI Belfast Trades Council Minutes, 4 July 1907
48 *Belfast News-Letter* 8 August 1907
49 Ibid. 2 August 1907
50 *Nomad's Weekly* 12 August 1907
51 *Belfast Evening Telegraph* 13 August 1907
52 *Irish News* 9 August 1907; *Belfast News-Letter* 10 August 1907
53 *Irish News* 10 August 1907
54 *Labour Leader* 10 May 1907. H.R. Stockman was elected first secretary (Ibid. 24 May 1907).
55 Ibid. 16 August 1907. This reported sales of sixteen dozen but by the issue of 30 August this had risen to thirty dozen.
56 BLPES Coll. Misc. 464. National Administrative Council of the ILP Minutes, 15 August 1907
57 Ibid. 24 August 1907
58 *Justice* 29 June 1907
59 Ibid. 24 August 1907. See also Nan Milton, *John MacLean,* pp.35–36. MacLean and other British militants made no reference in Belfast to theoretical schemes then current in British left-wing circles for dealing with the military threat. *Forward,* 24 August, discussed this very matter: 'Some Socialists advise and advocate the formation of a Citizen Army, this Citizen Army is really a sort of universal "compulsory volunteering" proposal, and is granted by its projectors to be the only safeguard against capitalistic utilisation of the military forces.' It was not until November 1908 that Larkin first mentioned the idea in an Irish context (Emmet Larkin, p.58).
60 *Irish News* 8 August 1907
61 Ibid. 12 August 1907
62 At the meeting it was announced that 'Mr Sloan promised that if possible he would be with them that afternoon. He had wired since that it was impossible for him to attend owing to another engagement.' On 15 August a letter from Sloan appeared in the *Northern Whig* saying, 'I neither promised nor wired Mr Larkin anything of the kind, nor had I any communication with him.' On 19 August Larkin replied, quoting a letter from Sloan to Boyd in the latter's capacity as co-ordinator of the strike committee:
> Dear Boyd,
> I am sorry it is not possible for me to attend the meeting on Saturday. I have a long standing engagement for that date.
> Yours truly, Thomas H. Sloan.
63 *Irish News* 12 August 1907
64 *Northern Whig* 12 August 1907

CHAPTER 12

1 SPO CSORP 1908 20333, Gambell to Chamberlain 8 August 1907
2 Ibid. Clayton Report, pars. 68 and 73
3 *Belfast Evening Telegraph* 10 August 1907 and *Belfast News-Letter* 12 August 1907
4 SPO CSORP 1908 20333, Sir A. MacDonnell to Birrell, 12 August 1907. By the time he sent this, serious rioting had occurred, but he was reporting earlier fears.

5 SPO CSORP 1908 20333, Clayton Report, par. 78. All the Belfast papers give a full account of the events of 11 August on the following day.
6 *Belfast News-Letter* 12 August 1907
7 *Northern Whig* 12 August 1907
8 *Belfast News-Letter* 13 August 1907; *Irish News* 24 August 1907
9 *Belfast Evening Telegraph* 12 August 1907
10 *Northern Whig* 13 August 1907
11 *Irish News* 3 September 1907
12 McKeown, p.24
13 *Northern Whig* 13 August 1907
14 *Irish News* 3 September 1907
15 McKeown, p.24
16 Birrell said of Maggie Lennon's death that 'they all felt deeply distressed for the young woman who lost her life while seeking for a younger brother' (*Northern Whig* 16 August 1907).
17 SPO CSORP 1908 20333, Clayton Report, par. 75
18 *Northern Whig* 14 August 1907
19 *Labour Leader* 23 August 1907, partly corroborated by Clayton (par. 88): 'Definite information had been received, which has since been verified beyond all doubt, that the Nationalists had procured every available revolver or rifle which they could get.' Clayton also reported rumours that 'they had purchased a quantity of vitriol, in order to throw it on the military and police'. Clayton's verification may have come from Stockman's published account.
20 NLI MS 13,074, Roger Casement to Miss Bannister, 14 August 1907
21 *Belfast News-Letter* 14 August 1907
22 Ibid. 13 August 1907
23 *Northern Whig* 14 August 1907
24 *Irish News* 5 September 1907
25 Ibid.
26 *Report of the Select Committee on Employment of Military in Cases of Disturbance,* (1908, 236, vii), pars. 14 and 104
27 Ibid. par. 182
28 *Belfast News-Letter* 12 August 1907
29 *Northern Whig* 12 August 1907
30 *Belfast Evening Telegraph* 12 August 1907
31 Patrick Buckland, *Irish Unionism 1885–1923*, p.215
32 *Northern Whig* 16 August 1907
33 *Belfast News-Letter* 13 August 1907
34 Ibid.
35 *Irish News* 14 August 1907
36 *Belfast News-Letter* 14 and 15 August 1907
37 *Northern Whig* 19 August 1907
38 Ibid. 20 August 1907
39 Ibid. 14 August 1907
40 *Belfast News-Letter* 14 August 1907
41 *Northern Whig* 19 August 1907
42 SPO CSORP 1908 20333, Gambell to Chamberlain, August 1907
43 *Belfast News-Letter* 16 August 1907. There was other evidence of the close relations between the Catholic clergy and the RIC. A number of priests petitioned on behalf of transferred policemen (SPO CSORP 1908 20333).
44 *Belfast Evening Telegraph* 30 September 1907
45 *Labour Leader* 30 August 1907. As early as 1889 Lansbury visited Ireland on a deputation from East End Radical Clubs, 'to see what crimes are being committed in our name' (*Dictionary of Labour Biography,* vol.2, pp.214–226).
46 *Liverpool and Vicinity United Trades and Labour Council. Annual Report, 1907–1908*
47 SPO CSORP 1908 20333
48 *Justice* 24 August 1907
49 *Scottish Co-Operator* 23 August 1907
50 *Clarion* 16 August 1907. Blatchford was a former army sergeant, had supported the Boer War, and would support the war effort in 1914. Author of the classic *Merrie England,* which James Connolly gave as a present to friends, he was in the last years of his life to vote Conservative (*Dictionary of Labour Biography,* vol.4, pp.34–42).
51 *Northern Whig* 14 August 1907

CHAPTER 13

1. SPO CSORP 1908 20333
2. *Northern Whig* 14 August 1907
3. NLI Thomas Johnson Papers MS 17146
4. Askwith, p.109
5. Ibid. p.111
6. PRONI D3358/1, William Hughes
7. Ibid. William Hunter
8. Askwith, p.112
9. *Northern Whig* 17 August 1907
10. Askwith, p.110
11. Ibid. p.112
12. Sexton, *Sir James Sexton: Agitator*, p.206
13. *Northern Whig* 16 August 1907
14. Askwith, pp.112–3
15. McMullen typescript, Ch.15, p.2
16. *Belfast News-Letter* and *Northern Whig* 16 August 1907
17. *Belfast News-Letter* 16 August 1907
18. *Irish News* 14 August 1907
19. *Northern Whig* 15 August 1907
20. Ibid. 16 August 1907
21. *Irish News* 16 August 1907
22. SPO CSORP 1908 20333, MacDonnell to Birrell 22 August 1907
23. *Northern Whig* 15 August 1907
24. *Belfast News-Letter* 22 August 1907
25. *Irish News* 27 August 1907
26. SPO CSORP 1908 20333, MacDonnell to Birrell, 26 August 1907
27. *Irish News* 28 August 1907
28. SPO CSORP 1908 20333, Letters from McKeown to MacDonnell, 27 and 28 August 1907. He claimed that carters of fifteen years experience were being refused employment at £1 a week and that some carters had received only 9d. overtime for a seventy-seven-hour week. Alex McDowell denied the allegations in a letter to MacDonnell dated 29 August, and MacDonnell replied to McKeown on 31 August, simply repeating McDowell's denials.
29. *Northern Whig* 20 August 1907
30. *Irish News* 27 and 29 August 1907
31. SPO CSORP 1908 20333. McDowell wrote to MacDonnell on 2 September 1907 reporting that Gallaher had met with two men who had suggested that the strikers 'would not insist on. . . getting back' and had drawn up a memorandum on this basis which he presented to a meeting of the men on 2 September. When McDowell read the draft 'there were loud murmurs of discontent and instantly more than a third of the men left the room'. McDowell concluded that the workers remained 'exceedingly hostile and bitter'.
32. *Belfast Evening Telegraph* 6 September 1907
33. *Irish News* 31 August 1907
34. SPO CSORP 1908 20333, Clayton Report, pars. 100 and 101
35. PRONI Belfast Trades Council Minutes, 3 October 1907
36. Letter from James Wilson in the author's possession

CHAPTER 14

1. PRONI Belfast Trades Council Minutes, 5 September 1907
2. Ibid. 12 September 1907
3. *Irish News* 13 September 1907
4. Ibid. 23 September 1907
5. *Belfast Evening Telegraph* 7 September 1907
6. PRONI Belfast Trades Council Minutes, 3 October 1907
7. LPL Liverpool Labour Representation Committee Minutes, 4 September 1907. An unsigned telegram received by Ramsay MacDonald on 3 September may relate to the reversal of the Liverpool executive's recommendation. This read: 'Henderson writes from Bath – executive members there favour Hill – no reply from Liverpool yet – am writing again' (PRO Ramsay MacDonald Papers 30/69 1151).
8. *Scottish Co-Operator* 4 October 1907
9. *Labour Leader* 4 October 1907
10. *Labour Leader* 13 September 1907. For a wider discussion of the malign influence of sectarianism on Liverpool Labour politics see Joan Smith, 'Labour

Tradition in Liverpool and Glasgow'.
11 *Belfast News-Letter* 17 October 1907
12 *Belfast Evening Telegraph* 14 September 1907
13 Ibid. 14 September 1907
14 *Irish News* 16 November 1907
15 *Belfast Evening Telegraph* 18 November 1907
16 *Irish News* 21 November 1907
17 *Belfast Evening Telegraph* 16 November 1907
18 *Irish News* 18 November 1907
19 Ibid. 19 and 21 November 1907
20 Ibid. 21 November 1907
21 *Belfast Evening Telegraph* 22 November 1907
22 *Irish News* 21 and 22 November 1907
23 Ibid. 26 November 1907
24 Ibid. 27 November 1907
25 PRONI D3358/1, James Clarke
26 *Report from the Industrial Council on the methods of securing the due fulfilment of Industrial Agreements, and of enforcing Agreements throughout particular Trades or Districts. Minutes of Evidence*, (1913, Cd.6953, xxviii), p.406
27 Sexton, *Sir James Sexton: Agitator*, p.210
28 *Report from the Industrial Council on the methods of securing the due fulfilment of Industrial Agreements, and of enforcing Agreements throughout particular Trades or Districts. Minutes of Evidence*, (1913, Cd.6953, xxviii), p.406
29 *Irish News* 28 November 1907
30 *Northern Whig* 15 January 1907
31 *Irish News* 28 November 1907
32 *Labour Leader* 22 November 1907
33 Ibid. 6 December 1907
34 Ibid.
35 Robert McElborough, *Autobiography of a Belfast Working Man*, p.9
36 *Belfast News-Letter* 17 December 1907
37 *Irish News* 29 October 1907

CHAPTER 15
1 The fullest published account of the Newry dispute, although hostile to Larkin and Fearon, is Keogh, pp.113–117.
2 Emmett Larkin, pp.49–50
3 *Forward* 4 July 1908
4 Greaves, *The Irish Transport and General Workers Union*, p.24
5 Keogh, p.133
6 Greaves, *The Irish Transport and General Workers Union*, p.20, and Keogh, pp.134–137. See also *Forward* 25 July 1908, reporting the formation of an Irish National Union of Workers by P.T. Daly.
7 Keogh, p.134
8 Greaves, *The Irish Transport and General Workers Union*, p.135
9 *Sinn Fein* 28 November 1908
10 Greaves, *The Irish Transport and General Workers Union*, p.25
11 The first rule book appears to date from May 1909 (Greaves, ibid., p.34), nonetheless it reflects the 'pragmatic' change in Larkin's approach, evident from the union's formation.
12 Letter from Sexton to the Parliamentary Committee of the ITUC dated 19 July 1909 (E.W. Stewart, p.6)
13 *Forward* 15 August 1907
14 Ibid. 30 May 1907
15 *Northern Whig* 21 May 1908
16 Ibid. 10 and 11 June 1908
17 Carnduff, 'The Orange Society', p.29
18 *Northern Whig* 4 July 1908
19 Ibid. 20 June 1908
20 Ibid. 29 June 1908
21 Ibid. 2 June 1908
22 Greaves, *The Irish Transport ana General Workers Union*, p.25
23 *Irish News* 9 January 1909. Paddy Devlin, 'Michael McKeown – A Founding Father', p.15, suggests an instrumental role for McKeown who put the case for an Irish union 'the previous year in Belfast', and was 'to the fore in discussions' in late 1908. The developments on 28 December were

certainly less of a surprise to McKeown than he implied at the 8 January meeting, for he ended payments to NUDL headquarters on 12 December 1908 (*Northern Whig* 16 January 1909).

24 Greaves, *The Irish Transport and General Workers Union*, p.27
25 McMullen, 'Early Days in Belfast', p.10
26 Letter from Boyd in *Irish News* 11 January 1909
27 *Northern Whig* 9 January 1909
28 *Sinn Fein* 23 January 1909
29 McMullen, 'Early Days in Belfast', p.10
30 Ibid. p.11
31 *Irish News* 11 January 1909
32 Greaves, *The Irish Transport and General Workers Union*, p.29
33 McMullen, 'Early Days in Belfast', p.12
34 Ibid. p.11
35 *Irish News* 13 January 1909
36 *Northern Whig* 14 January 1909
37 Ibid. 15 January 1909
38 Ibid. 16 and 23 January 1909
39 McMullen, 'Early Days in Belfast', p.10
40 *Irish News* 18 January 1909
41 *Northern Whig* 15 January 1909
42 *Northern Whig* 13 January 1909 described it as being founded 'a few months ago on Donegall Quay' but on 10 February 1909 said that it had been operating 'since shortly after the last trouble at the quays'.
43 *Irish News* 18 January 1909
44 *Northern Whig* 9 January 1909
45 Ibid.
46 Ibid. 9, 10, 12 and 13 February 1909
47 Ibid. 10 February 1909
48 Greaves, *The Irish Transport and General Workers Union*, p.31
49 McMullen, 'Early Days in Belfast', p.13
50 Ibid. For James and John Flanagan see the reminiscences of Ellen Grimley (NLI MS 13096): 'The two Flanagans. . . were Protestants but were staunch upholders of our union which they had helped form and maintain'. Evidently James Flanagan backed the ITGWU in Connolly's time, however Grimley adds that he thought Connolly 'must have been mad' to get involved in 1916.
51 Greaves, *The Irish Transport and General Workers Union*, p.37
52 PRONI D3358/1

CHAPTER 16

1 NLI Thomas Johnston Papers MS 17146
2 The Irish Communist Organisation, later metamorphosed into the British and Irish Communist Organisation, has, in *The Two Irish Nations* (1971), rediscovered this analysis, commonplace in pre-First World War Unionist circles, see for example Thomas McKnight, *Ulster as it is* (1896), vol. 2, pp.380–1: 'The undeniable truth is that there are two antagonistic populations, two different nations on Irish soil – there is no community of feeling and therefore can be no common citizenship between the two sections of the Irish people.' In a Belfast context such arguments were and are readily adopted or re-interpreted to justify sectarian division rather than working-class unity.
3 The strikers' own figure for those seeking relief on 24 July. Morgan, 'Politics, the Labour Movement and the Working Class', p.72, gives 2,340 but this may exclude many casual dockers, especially at the deep-sea docks by then laid off.
4 Concentration on preceding organisations leads to underestimation of the significance of 1907. Patterson, in *Class Conflict and Sectarianism*, p.66, subsumes the episode within a general analysis of 'Labour's weakening position'.
5 The Industrial Workers of the World were founded in Chicago a mere two years earlier in 1905 (Pelling, p.134).
6 E.L. Taplin, *Liverpool Dockers and Seamen*, p.83
7 Greaves, *The Irish Transport and General Workers Union*, p.328
8 See references to all of these in A.T.Q. Stewart, *The Ulster Crisis*

9 The metaphor is not entirely original. Owen Dudley Edwards, in *Sins of our Fathers*, p.152, quotes E.P. Thompson's *The Making of the English Working Class* with approval where he speaks of 'a popular oscillation between politics and religion – negative and positive poles of the social process'. Morgan, 'Politics, the Labour Movement and the Working Class', p.215, speaks of 'the Protestant working class faced with the polar orientations of labourism or loyalism'. My objective here is to reveal more fully the devastating dynamics of the relationship.

10 Reprinted in *The Connolly Walker Controversy* (Cork 1974)

11 J.W. Boyle, 'William Walker', p.63

12 Ibid.

13 J.W. Boyle, 'Rise of the Irish Labour Movement', p.311. In the same year Robert Gageby also gave up politics, becoming manager of Belfast's first employment exchange (McMullen typescript, Ch.18, p.3).

14 Boyd may have left Belfast by 1912 – he disappears from the Street Directory – but he was later an ILP councillor for St Anne's in 1920, although not then associated with the Municipal Employees (McElborough, p.26). His Labour politics still had a distinctly loyalist hue, as when he alleged that, during the war, shipyard vacancies had been filled by men 'from the South and West' and argued that war veterans 'should have been re-instated no matter who was dismissed' (Patterson, *Class Conflict and Sectarianism*, p.134).

15 Morgan, 'Politics, the Labour Movement and the Working Class', p.124. The assault on Protestant Labour activists had been a matter of long-standing discussion in Orange and Unionist circles. In December 1909 Edward Bradshaw attended the Labour selection meeting for North Belfast as a Unionist spy. He reported back to the Executive Committee of the Unionist Association and asked, 'Whose fault was it that there were 2,000 socialists in North Belfast? I said it was the Protestant employers. . . and if the employers would start and weed them out, and give employment to the Protestants and Orangemen who are walking the streets at present, you would have these men to work and vote for you on the day of election.' Bradshaw was pleased with the response and afterwards 'Mr Clark [of Workman and Clark], Mr Thompson [later Unionist MP for North Belfast] and the Secretary spoke to me, and wanted to know if I could give more information.' Soon after he was at a Unionist bazaar in Ballymacarrett and was told 'that they in the East division had since the same question up' (McClelland Collection, Edward Bradshaw to James Davidson, Asst. Deputy Grand Secretary of the Orange Order, 20 December 1909).

16 Greaves, *The Irish Transport and General Workers Union*, p.57. McKeown had rejoined the ITGWU in August 1910 but recruitment made minimal headway until Connolly's arrival (pp.61–62).

17 Quoted in Ruth Dudley Edwards, *James Connolly*, p.101

18 *Northern Whig* 15 February 1909

19 William O'Brien and Desmond Ryan, *Devoy's Post Bag*, vol.2, pp.394–5

20 For Crawford's American career see J.W. Boyle, *A Fenian Protestant in Canada*, and entry in *American Biography – A New Cyclopedia*

21 Introduction by William McMullen to James Connolly, *The Workers' Republic*, pp.20–21

22 The poetic attack on Sloan appeared on a postcard (LHL). Arthur Trew also attacked him in verse in *Belfast Constitutional Protestant Association: Lines on etc.*

Did you hear that Tommy Rot
Was awarded a jam pot –
He claims to have been made a

> new J.P.
> And he still aspires higher,
> For he signs himself Esquire,
> Sure he's one of the high-born nobility.

At the time of the attack on his home, described in Morgan, 'Politics, the Labour Movement and the Working Class', p.139, he was suffering from a blood clot on the brain: he recovered although increasingly dependent on whisky, and in 1914 was last heard of in Winnipeg 'trying to get someone to take him up so that he may give lectures' (McClelland Collection, Bradshaw to Davidson, 28 June 1912 and 9 March 1914).

23 Budge and O'Leary, pp.161–2
24 See Frank Wright, 'Protestant Ideology and Politics in Ulster', pp.265–8 and E. Rumpf and A.C. Hepburn, *Nationalism and Socialism in Twentieth Century Ireland*, pp.206–7

BIBLIOGRAPHY

MANUSCRIPT MATERIAL

Material in public repositories

Bodleian Library, Oxford (B)
    Asquith Papers
    Birrell Papers
British Library of Political and Economic Science (BLPES)
    General Federation of Trades Unions Papers
    Labour Representation Committee Minutes
    National Administrative Council of the Independent Labour Party Minutes
    Ramsay MacDonald Papers
    Mrs MacDonald Papers
Central Library, Belfast (BPL)
    Scrapbook containing leaflets printed by Hugh Quinn
Irish Transport and General Workers Union (ITGWU)
    William McMullen, typescript history of the 1907 dock strike
Labour Party, London (LP)
    Labour Party Archives
Linen Hall Library (LHL)
    A.A. Campbell Collection, scrapbook relating to Belfast Police Mutiny
    Thomas Carnduff, incomplete typescript of autobiography
    Postcard Collection
Liverpool Public Library (LPL)
    Liverpool Labour Representation Committee Minutes
    Liverpool Trades and Labour Council Minutes
National Library of Ireland (NLI)
    Roger Casement correspondence with Miss Bannister
    Ellen Grimley (neé Gordon) recollections
    Bulmer Hobson papers
    Thomas Johnston Papers
    William O'Brien collection (This very extensive collection contains a variety of ephemeral material relevant to the Labour movement in Belfast)
Public Record Office, London (PRO)
    Ramsay MacDonald Papers
Public Record Office of Northern Ireland, Belfast (PRONI)
    Transcripts of interviews with 1907 veterans by David Bleakley and Sam Hanna Bell undertaken in 1957–8
    Belfast Trades Council Minutes
    William Walker documents
    Belfast Chamber of Commerce Minutes
State Paper Office, Dublin (SPO)
    CSORP 1908 20333. Contains almost all Dublin Castle material relating to the 1907 dispute including District Inspector Clayton's 59 pp report. See also CSORP 1907 5541 for additional police material.

Material in private hands

Edward Bradshaw correspondence with James Davidson, McClelland Collection (The collection of the late Aiken McClelland also includes a wide range of

Protestant and Orange ephemera of the period)
John McKeown, typescript autobiography (in the possession of Professor and Mrs Dawes, copy available at Linen Hall Library)
Alex Hogg, album of ninety-two photographs relating to the 1907 strike (Mr P. Fox)

Theses

Bleakley, D.W. 'Trade Union Beginnings in Belfast and District with Special Reference to the Period 1881–1900, and to the Work of the Belfast and District United Trades Council', M.A., Queen's University Belfast, 1955

Boyle, J.W. 'The Rise of the Irish Labour Movement, 1880–1907', Ph.D., Trinity College Dublin, 1961

Harbinson, J.F. 'A History of the Northern Ireland Labour Party, 1891–1949', M.Sc., Queen's University Belfast, 1966

Morgan, A. 'Politics, the Labour Movement and the Working Class in Belfast, 1905–1923', Ph.D., Queen's University Belfast, 1981

Rebbeck, D. 'The History of Iron Shipbuilding on the Queen's Island up till July 1874', Ph.D., Queen's University Belfast, 1950

Whitford, F.J. 'Joseph Devlin', M.A., University of London, 1959

PARLIAMENTARY PAPERS

Report of the Commissioners of Inquiry into the origin and character of the riots in Belfast in July and September 1857; with Minutes of Evidence and Appendix (1857–8, 2309, xxvi)

Report of the Commissioners of Inquiry, 1864, respecting the magisterial and police jurisdiction, arrangement and establishment of the borough of Belfast (1865, 3466, xxviii)

Report of the Belfast Riots Commission, with Evidence and Appendices (1887, C.4925, xviii)

Reports of the Inspector of Factories upon the conditions of Work in Flax Mills and Linen Factories, and upon the Mortality amongst Textile Operatives, &c., in the United Kingdom; with Appendices (1893–4, C.7287, xvii)

Report from the Select Committee on the Belfast Corporation Bill, and the Londonderry Improvement Bill; with the Proceedings, Evidence and Index (1896, 233, viii)

Census of Ireland, 1901, Vol. III, 'Province of Ulster, City of Belfast' (1902, 1123a, cxxvi)

Report upon the Conditions of Work in Flax and Linen Mills as affecting the Health of the Operatives employed therein (1904, Cd.1997, x)

Belfast Health Commission: Report to the Local Government Board for Ireland (1908, Cd.4128, xxxi)

Report of an enquiry by the Board of Trade into Working Class Rents, Housing, Retail Prices and Standard Rate of Wages in the United Kingdom (1908, Cd.3864, cvii)

Report of Departmental Committee on Checking of Piece-Work wages in Dock Labour (1908, Cd.4380, xxxiv)

— *Evidence* (1908, Cd.4381, xxxiv)

Report of the Select Committee on Employment of Military in Cases of Disturbance (1908, 236, vii)

Report of an Enquiry by the Board of Trade into the Earnings and Hours of Labour of Workpeople of the United Kingdom, Part I 'Textile Trades in 1906' (1909, Cd. 4545, lxxx)

Report of an Enquiry by the Board of Trade into the Earnings and Hours of Labour of Workpeople of the United Kingdom, Part VI, 'Metal Engineering and Shipbuilding Trades in 1906' (1911, Cd.5814, lxxxviii)

Report of the Committee on conditions of Employment in the Linen and other making-up trades of the North of Ireland, with Evidence (1912–3, Cd.6509, xxxiv)

Report from the Industrial Council on the methods of securing the due fulfilment of Industrial Agreements, and of enforcing Agreements throughout particular Trades or Districts. Evidence. (1913, Cd.6952, xxviii)

Report of the Departmental Committee on humidity and ventilation in Flax Mills and Linen Factories (mainly in Ireland) (1914, Cd.7433, xxxvi)

ANNUAL REPORTS (PARLIAMENTARY)

Abstract of Labour Statistics
Chief Registrar of Friendly Societies
Factory Inspectors
Strikes and Lockouts

ANNUAL REPORTS AND PUBLICATIONS (NON-PARLIAMENTARY)

Army List
Belfast and Province of Ulster Directory
Belfast Town Relief Fund, 1878–9
Belfast United Trades Council
City and County Borough of Belfast Handbook
General Federation of Trade Unions
Independent Labour Party, General Conference
[Independent Orange Order] Imperial Grand Lodge
Irish Trades Union Congress
Labour Party
Labour Representation Committee
Liverpool and Vicinity United Trades and Labour Council
National Union of Dock Labourers
[Orange Order] Grand Lodge of the Belfast Orange Order
Report on the Health of the County Borough of Belfast
Royal Irish Constabulary List and Directory
Trades Union Congress

CONTEMPORARY NEWSPAPERS AND PERIODICALS

Belfast Evening Telegraph
Belfast Labour Chronicle
Belfast Protestant Record
Belfast News-Letter
Belfast Wheatsheaf
Clarion
Commercial Motor
Constabulary Gazette

Forward
Illustrated London News
Irish Independent
Irish News
Justice
Labour Leader
Liverpool Weekly Echo
Nomad's Weekly
Northern Star
Northern Whig
Orange Independent
Scottish Co-Operator
Shan van Vocht
Sinn Fein
Ulster Echo

BOOKS, PAMPHLETS AND ARTICLES

The Acts of the Prophets. A Sketch of the Struggle for Supremacy at the Customs House Steps (Belfast n.d.)
Adams, Gerry. *Falls Memories* (Dingle 1982)
Alcock, G.W. *Fifty Years of Railway Trade Unions* (London 1922)
American Biography – A New Cyclopedia (American Historical Association 1928)
Armstrong, D.L. 'Social and Economic Conditions in the Belfast Linen Industry: 1850–1900', *Irish Historical Studies*, vol VII (1950–51)
Askwith, Sir George. *Industrial Problems and Disputes* (London 1920)

Bagwell, P.S. *Railwaymen: The History of the NUR* (London 1964)
Baker, Sybil E. 'Orange and Green', in J.H. Dyos and M. Wolff (eds.), *The Victorian City*, vol.2 (London 1973)
Baker, Sybil E. See also Gribbon, Sybil
Bardon, Jonathan. *Belfast: An Illustrated History* (Belfast 1982)
Barron, John. *The Air Borne Theory of Typhoid* (Belfast 1902)
Beckett, J.C. and R.E. Glasscock (eds.). *Belfast: The Origin and Growth of an Industrial City* (Belfast 1967)
Belfast and District Trades Council 1881–1951 (Belfast 1951)
Belfast Meeting of the Trades Union Congress (Belfast 1893)
Belfast Police Manual, 2nd edition (Belfast 1898)
Belfast Steamship Company – A Century of Service (Belfast 1924)
Belfast: The Making of the City (Belfast 1983)
Bell, Geoffrey. *The Protestants of Ulster* (London 1976)
Bell, Geoffrey. *Troublesome Business – The Labour Party and the Irish Question* (London 1982)
Bew, Paul. 'Politics and the Rise of the Skilled Working Man', in *Belfast: The Making of the City* (Belfast 1983)
Black, R.D.C. 'The Process of Industrialisation', in T.W. Moody and J.C. Beckett (eds.), *Ulster since 1800: A Political and Economic Survey* (Belfast 1955)
Black, R.D.C. 'William James Pirrie', *Threshold*, vol. 1, no.1 (February 1957)
Black, R.D.C. 'William James Pirrie', in Conor Cruise O'Brien (ed.), *The Shaping of Modern Ireland* (London 1970)

Black, W. 'Industrial Change in the Twentieth Century', in J.C. Beckett and R.E. Glasscock (eds.), *Belfast: The Origin and Growth of an Industrial City* (Belfast 1967)

Bleakley, D.W. 'Industrial Conditions in the Nineteenth Century', in T.W. Moody and J.C. Beckett (eds.), *Ulster Since 1800: A Political and Economic Survey* (Belfast 1955)

Bleakley, D.W. *The Northern Ireland Trade Union Movement* (1954) reprinted from *Journal of the Statistical and Social Enquiry Society of Ireland*, vol. XX (1953–54)

Boal, Frederick W. 'Segregating and Mixing: Space and Residence in Belfast', in F.W. Boal and J.N.H. Douglas (eds.), *Integration and Division* (London 1982)

Boyd, Andrew. *Holy War in Belfast* (Tralee 1969)

Boyd, Andrew. *The Rise and Fall of the Irish Trade Unions* (Tralee 1972)

Boyd, Joan. 'Police Strike', *Sunday News* 4 March 1979

Boyle, Emily. 'The Linen Strike of 1872', *Saothar*, no. 2 (1976)

Boyle, Emily. '"Linenopolis": The Rise of the Textile Industry', in *Belfast: The Making of the City* (Belfast 1983)

Boyle, J. W. 'The Belfast Protestant Association and the Independent Orange Order', *Irish Historical Studies*, vol.XIII, (1962–1963)

Boyle, J. W. *A Fenian Protestant in Canada: Robert Lindsay Crawford* (Toronto 1971) reprinted from *Canadian Historical Review*, vol. 52, no. 2 (June 1971)

Boyle, J. W. 'Industrial Conditions in the Twentieth Century', in T.W. Moody and J.C. Beckett (eds.), *Ulster since 1800: A Political and Economic Survey* (Belfast 1955)

Boyle, J. W. 'William Walker', in J.W. Boyle, (ed.), *Leaders and Workers* (Cork 1967)

Boyle, J. W. See also Theses

Breathnach, Seamus. *The Irish Police* (Tralee 1974)

Brett, C.E.B. *Buildings of Belfast* (London 1967)

British and Irish Communist Organisation. *Economics of Partition* (Belfast 1971)

British and Irish Communist Organisation. *Ulster as it is* (Belfast 1973)

British and Irish Communist Organisation. See also Irish Communist Organisation

Buckland, Patrick. *Irish Unionism 1885–1923: A Documentary History* (Belfast 1973)

Buckland, Patrick. *Irish Unionism*, vol. 2 *Ulster Unionism and the Origins of Northern Ireland, 1886–1922* (Dublin 1973)

Budge, Ian and Cornelius O'Leary. *Belfast: Approach to Crisis* (London 1973)

Burns, Gerry. 'Newry – the first town outside Belfast to fight for union rights', *Newry Reporter* 26 January 1978

Byers, John W. *Public Health Problems* (Belfast 1906)

Carnduff, Thomas. 'I Remember', *The Bell*, vol.V, no. 4 (January 1943)

Carnduff, Thomas. 'The Orange Society', *The Bell*, vol. XVII, no. 4 (July 1951)

Carr, Alan. *The Belfast Labour Movement*, part 1, *1885–1893* (Belfast 1974)

Chambers, George. *Faces of Change: The Belfast and Northern Ireland Chambers of Commerce and Industry 1783–1983* (Belfast 1984)

City of Belfast. *Minutes of Evidence taken before the Special Committee... to Consider and Report on the present high Death Rate of Belfast* (Belfast 1896)

Clarkson, J.D. *Labour and Nationalism in Ireland* (New York 1925, reprinted 1970)

Clarkson, L.A. 'Population Change and Urbanisation 1821–1911', in Liam Kennedy and Philip Ollerenshaw (eds.), *An Economic History of Ulster* (Manchester 1985)

Coe, W.E. *The Engineering Industry of the North of Ireland* (Newton Abbot 1969)
Collins, Brenda. 'The Edwardian City', in *Belfast: The Making of the City* (Belfast 1983)
Collison, W. *Apostle of Free Labour* (London 1913)
Commercial Year Book (Belfast Chamber of Commerce 1909)
Connelly, T.J. *The Woodworkers* (London 1960)
Connolly, James. *Labour in Ireland* (Dublin n.d.)
Connolly, James. *The Workers Republic* (Dublin n.d.)
[Connolly, James and William Walker]. *The Connolly Walker Controversy* (Belfast 1968 and Cork 1974)
Cronin, Sean (ed.). *The McGarrity Papers* (Tralee 1972)

Deasy, J. *Fiery Cross: The Story of Jim Larkin* (Dublin 1963)
Devine, Francis. 'Who dares to Wear the Red Hand Badge,' *Liberty* (June 1984)
Devine, Francis and Peter Rigney. 'National Free Labour Association', *Saothar*, 2 (1976)
Devlin, Paddy. 'Michael McKeown – A Founding Father', *Liberty* (June 1984)
Devlin, Paddy. *Yes We Have no Bananas – Outdoor Relief in Belfast 1920–1949* (Belfast 1981)
Dewar, Rev. M.W. et al. *Orangeism* (Belfast 1967)
Dictionary of Labour Biography (London 1972–)
Doyle, Mel. 'Belfast and Tolpuddle', *Saothar* 2 (1976)

Edwards, Owen Dudley. *Sins of our Fathers* (Dublin 1970)
Edwards, Ruth Dudley. *James Connolly* (Dublin 1981)
Ellis, P. Berrisford. *A History of the Irish Working Class* (London 1972)
Ervine, St. John. *Mixed Marriage* (Dublin 1911)

Farrell, Michael, 'The Great Belfast Strike of 1919', *Northern Star* (Feb/March 1971)
Farrell, Michael. *Northern Ireland: The Orange State* (London 1976)
Farrell, Michael. *The Poor Law and the Workhouse in Belfast 1838–1948* (Belfast 1978)
Fifty Years of Liberty Hall: The Golden Jubilee of the Irish Transport and General Workers Union (Dublin 1959)
Fisk, Robert. *The Point of no Return: The Strike which Broke the British in Ulster* (London 1975)
Flax Spinners Association – Memorandum and Articles (Belfast 1907)
The Forgotten Conference (Belfast 1982)
Fox, R.M. *Jim Larkin and the Rise of the Underman* (London 1957)
Froggatt, Peter. 'Industrialisation and Health in Belfast in the Early Nineteenth Century', *Historical Studies*, vol.XIII (Belfast 1981)

Galway, Mary. 'The Linen Industry in the North', in W. Fitzgerald (ed.), *The Voice of Ireland* (Dublin c. 1923)
Gaughan, J. Anthony. *Memoirs of Constable Jeremiah Mee, RIC* (Dublin 1975)
Gaughan, J. Anthony. *Thomas Johnson* (Dublin 1980)
General Federation of Trades Unions. *The Recent Strikes* (1905)
Gibbon, P. *The Origins of Ulster Unionism: The Formation of Popular Protestant Politics and Ideology in Nineteenth Century Ireland* (Manchester 1975)
Gill, C. *The Rise of the Irish Linen Industry* (Oxford 1925)
Goldstrom, J.M. 'The Industrialisation of the North-East', in L.M. Cullen (ed.), *The Formation of the Irish Economy* (Cork 1969)

Good, J.W. *Ulster and Ireland* (Dublin 1919)
Gray, John. 'Popular Entertainment', in *Belfast: The Making of the City* (Belfast 1983)
Gray, John. 'Thomas Carnduff, 1886–1956: Chapters from an Unpublished Autobiography', *Irish Booklore*, vol. 4, no. 1 (1978)
Gray, John. '1907: A Year of Strikes in Belfast', in West Belfast Historical Society *Outline Annual*, 2 (1976)
Greaves, C. Desmond. *The Irish Transport and General Workers Union* (Dublin 1982)
Greaves, C. Desmond. *The Irish Transport and General Workers Union* (Dublin 1982)
Gray, John. '1907: A Year of Strikes in Belfast', in West Belfast Historical Society *Outline Annual*, 2 (1976)
Greaves, C. Desmond. *The Life and Times of James Connolly* (London 1961)
Green, E.R.R. 'Industrial Decline in the Nineteenth Century', in T.W. Moody and J.C. Beckett (eds.), *Ulster since 1800: A Political and Economic Survey* (Belfast 1955)
Green, E.R.R. *The Lagan Valley, 1800–1850* (London 1949)
Gribbon, Sybil. *Edwardian Belfast* (Belfast 1982)
Gribbon, Sybil. 'An Irish City: Belfast 1911', *Historical Studies*, vol. XIII (Belfast 1981)
Gribbon, Sybil. See also Baker, Sybil E.
Groves, R. *The Strange Case of Victor Grayson* (London 1975)

Hamling, William. *A Short History of the Liverpool Trades Council* (Liverpool 1948)
Hardinge Street Belfast Trades Preparatory School: Prospectus (Belfast Christian Brothers, 1912)
Heatley, Fred. 'Community Relations and the Religious Geography 1800–86', in *Belfast: The Making of the City* (Belfast 1983)
Heatley, Fred. *St. Joseph's Centenary 1872–1972 – Story of a Dockside Parish* (Belfast 1972)
Heatley, Fred. *The Story of St Patrick's Belfast 1815–1977* (Belfast 1977)
Henderson, James. *A Record Year in My Existence as Lord Mayor of Belfast in 1898* (Belfast 1899)
Henry, T. *History of the Belfast Riots* (Belfast 1864)
Hepburn, A.C. 'Belfast 1871–1911: work, class and religion', *Irish Economic and Social History*, vol. X (1983)
Hepburn, A.C. 'Employment and Religion in Belfast, 1901–1951', in R.J. Cormack and R.D. Osborne (eds.), *Religion, Education and Employment: Aspects of Equal Opportunity in Northern Ireland* (Belfast 1983)
Hepburn, A.C. and B. Collins. 'Industrial Society: the Structure of Belfast, 1901', in Peter Roebuck (ed.), *Plantation to Partition* (Belfast 1981)
Hobsbawm, E.J. *Industry and Empire* (London 1968)
Hobsbawm, E.J. *Labouring Men*. 2nd ed. (London 1971)
Hobson, Bulmer. *Ireland, Yesterday, Today and Tomorrow* (Tralee 1968)
Holton, B. *British Syndicalism: 1900–1914* (London 1976)
Hume, Rev. A. *Results of the Irish Census of 1861* (London 1864)
[Independent Orange Order]. *Orangeism, its History and Progress: A Plea for First Principles* (Belfast 1904)
Industries of Ireland, Part 1, *Belfast and the Towns of the North* (London 1891)

Infantile Mortality. . . with Special Reference to the City of Belfast (Belfast 1906)
Irish Communist Organisation. *The Two Irish Nations* (Belfast 1971)
Irish Communist Organisation. See also British and Irish Communist Organisation.
Isles, K.S. and N. Cuthbert. *An Economic Survey of Northern Ireland* (Belfast 1957)

Jefferson, H. *Viscount Pirrie of Belfast* (Belfast n.d.)
John Kelly Limited (Belfast 1952)
Jones, Emrys. 'Late Victorian Belfast: 1850–1900', in J.C. Beckett and R.E. Glasscock (eds.), *Belfast: The Origin and Growth of an Industrial City* (Belfast 1967)
Jones, Emrys. *A Social Geography of Belfast* (London 1960)
'Jurist'. *The Iron Heel* (Belfast 1903)

Kennedy, Liam and Philip Ollerenshaw (eds.), *An Economic History of Ulster, 1820–1940* (Manchester 1985)
Keogh, Dermot. *The Rise of the Irish Working Class* (Belfast 1982)
Killen, John. *John Bull's Famous Circus: A Postcard Discovery of Ulster History 1906–1985* (Dublin 1985) forthcoming
Knox, W.M. *Belfast Co-operative Society, 1889–1910* (Belfast 1910)

Labour Conditions in Ireland (Belfast 1913)
Labour War in Ireland (Liverpool c. 1909)
Larkin, Emmet. *James Larkin* (London 1965)
'Larkin's Strike', *Belfast News Letter*, 19 August 1953
Levenson, S. *James Connolly: A Biography* (London 1973)
Loftus, Belinda. *Marching Workers* (Belfast 1978)
Lovell, J. *Stevedores and Dockers* (London 1969)
Lyall, Sir Alfred. *The Life of the Marquis of Dufferin and Ava*. 2 vols. (London 1905)
Lyons, F.S.L. 'The Irish Unionist Party and the Devolution Crisis of 1904–5', *Irish Historical Studies*, vol. VI (1949)
Lucas, Reginald. *Colonel Saunderson* (London 1908)

McCarthy, Charles. 'The Impact of Larkinism on the Irish Working Class', *Saothar* 4 (1978)
McCormac, Henry. *An Appeal on Behalf of the Poor* (Belfast 1830)
McCormac, S. 'Tom Johnson, 1872–1963', *Liberty* (June 1974)
MacDonald, J.R. *Labour and the Empire* (London 1907)
McElborough, Robert. *The Autobiography of a Belfast Working Man* (Belfast 1974)
McKeown, John. See Manuscript Material
McKnight, Thomas. *Ulster as it is*. 2 vols. (London 1896)
McMinn, Richard. 'Liberalism in North Antrim, 1900–1914', *Irish Historical Studies*, vol. XXIII (1984)
McMullen, William. 'Early Days in Belfast', *Liberty* (June 1984)
McMullen, William. See also Manuscript Material
McNeill, D.B. *Irish Passenger Steamship Services*. 2 vols. (Newton Abbot 1969)
McNeill, Ronald. *Ulster's Stand for Union* (London 1922)
Maguire, Edward G. *The Sirocco Story* (Belfast c. 1961)
Malcolm, A. *Sanitary State of Belfast* (Belfast 1852)
Mann, T. *Tom Mann's Memoirs* (London 1923)
Mansergh, N. *Ireland in the Age of Reform and Revolution* (London 1965)
Martin, F.X. 'McCullough, Hobson and Republican Ulster', in F.X. Martin (ed.), *Leaders and Men of the Easter Rising* (London 1967)

Martin, Patrick. 'Jim Larkin and the Constable', *Garda Review* (November 1974)
Messenger, Betty. *Picking up the Linen Threads* (Belfast 1980)
Milford, R. *The Shankill Road* (Belfast 1971)
Milton, Nan. *John MacLean* (London 1973)
Mitchell, Arthur. *Labour in Irish Politics* (Dublin 1974)
Monaghan, J.J. 'The Rise and Fall of the Belfast Cotton Industry', *Irish Historical Studies*, vol. III (1943)
Moneypenny, W.F. *The Two Irish Nations* (London 1913)
Moody, T.W. 'Michael Davitt and the British Labour Movement 1882–1906', *Transactions of the Royal Historical Society*, 5th. Series, vol. 3 (1953)
Moody, T.W. and J.C. Beckett (eds.). *Ulster Since 1800: A Political and Economic Survey* (Belfast 1955)
Moran, Bill. '1913, Jim Larkin and the British Labour Movement', *Saothar* 4 (1978)
Morgan, A. 'James Connolly in Belfast, 1910–14', *Bulletin of the Society for the Study of Labour History*, 35 (Autumn 1977)
Morgan A. See also Theses

National Union of Dock Labourers, Rules (1901)
Nevin, Donal. 'Larkin Bibliography', *Saothar* 4 (1978)
Nugent, Joseph. 'Pawnbroking in Belfast', in West Belfast Historical Society, *Outline Annual*, 2 (1976)

O'Brien, William and Desmond Ryan. *Devoy's Post Bag*. 2 vols. (Dublin 1979)
O'Broin, Leon. *The Chief Secretary* (London 1969)
O'Hanlon, Rev. W.M. *Walks among the Poor of Belfast* (Belfast 1853, reprinted Wakefield 1971)
O'Hare, Fergus. *The Divine Gospel of Discontent* (Belfast 1981)
Oldham, C.H. 'A History of Belfast Shipbuilding', *Journal of the Social and Statistical Inquiry Society of Ireland*, 1911
O'Leary, Cornelius. 'Belfast Urban Government in the Age of Reform', *Historical Studies*, vol. XIII (Belfast 1981)
Orangemen on Guard, or Beware of Traitors within the Camp (Belfast 1906)
Owen, D.J. *History of Belfast* (Belfast 1921)
Owen, D.J. *Short History of the Port of Belfast* (Belfast 1917)

Patterson, Henry. *Class Conflict and Sectarianism: The Protestant Working Class and the Belfast Labour Movement 1868–1920* (Belfast 1980)
Patterson, Henry. 'Conservative Politics and Class Conflict in Belfast', *Saothar* 2 (1976)
Patterson, Henry. 'Independent Orangeism and Class Conflict in Edwardian Belfast', *Proceedings of the Royal Irish Academy*, vol.80, section C, no. 4 (1980)
Patterson, Henry, 'Industrial Labour and the Labour Movement, 1820–1914', in Liam Kennedy and Philip Ollerenshaw (eds.), *An Economic History of Ulster, 1820–1940* (Manchester 1985)
Patterson, Henry. 'James Larkin and the Belfast Dockers and Carters Strike', *Saothar* 4 (1978)
Patterson, Henry. 'The New Unionism in Belfast', *Bulletin of the Society for the Study of Labour History*, 35 (Autumn 1977)
Paul-Dubois, L. *Contemporary Ireland* (Dublin 1908)
Pelling, Henry, *A History of British Trade Unionism*. 2nd edition (London 1972)

Pelling, Henry. *Origins of the Labour Party* (London 1965)
Pirrie, W.J. *Speeches* (Belfast 1902)
Plunkett, H. *Ireland in the New Century* (London 1904)
Problems of a Growing City: Belfast 1780–1870 (Belfast 1973)
Purdon, C.D. *The Sanitary State of the Belfast Factory District* (Belfast 1877)

Quigley, J.A. 'The Independent Orange Order', *Northern Star*, 2 (1970)

Redmond, Rev. J. *Church: State: Industry, 1827–1929, in East Belfast.* (Belfast 1960)
Reid, Alistair. 'Skilled Workers in the Shipbuilding Industry', in Austen Morgan and Bob Purdie (eds.), *Divided Nation Divided Class* (London 1980)
Roney, Frank. *Frank Roney, Irish Rebel and Californian Labor Leader* (Berkeley 1931)
Rowntree, Seebohm. *Poverty: a Study of Town Life* (London 1902)
Royal Irish Constabulary Manual. 6th edition (Dublin 1910)
Rumpf, E. and A.C. Hepburn. *Nationalism and Socialism in Twentieth Century Ireland* (Liverpool 1977)
Ryan, Desmond. *Ireland Whose Ireland?* (London 1940)
Ryan, W.P., *The Irish Labour Movement* (Dublin 1919)
Ryan, W.P. *The Labour Revolt and Larkinism* (London 1913)

Saville, J. 'Trade Unions and Free Labour', in A. Briggs and J. Saville (eds.), *Essays in Labour History* (London 1960)
Semmell, Bernard. *Imperialism and Social Reform* (London 1960)
Senior, Hereward. *Orangeism in Britain and Ireland, 1795–1836* (London 1966)
Sexton, James. 'My Life Story', in *Empire News*, 22 November 1925–21 February 1926 (Held in scrapbook form LPL)
Sexton, James. *The Riot Act: a Play in Three Acts* (London 1914)
Sexton, James. *Sir James Sexton: Agitator* (London 1936)
Sinclair Seamen's Presbyterian Church Souvenir (Belfast 1957)
Smiles, Samuel. *Men of Invention* (London 1884)
Smith, Joan. 'Labour Tradition in Glasgow and Liverpool', *History Workshop*, 17 (1984)
A Statement of the Municipal Grievances of the Roman Catholic Ratepayers and Inhabitants of Belfast (Belfast 1896)
Stenton, M. and S. Lees. *Who's Who of British Members of Parliament.* 2 vols. (Hassocks 1976)
Stewart, A.T.Q. *The Ulster Crisis* (London, 1967)
Stewart, E.W. *The History of Larkinism in Ireland* (1912)
Strauss, Eric. *Irish Nationalism and British Democracy* (London 1951)

Taplin, Eric. *The Dockers' Union: A study of the National Union of Dock Labourers 1889–1922* (Leicester 1986) forthcoming
Taplin, Eric. 'James Larkin, Liverpool and the National Union of Dock Labourers: The Apprenticeship of a Revolutionary', *Saothar* 4 (1978)
Taplin, Eric. *Liverpool Dockers and Seamen: 1870–1890* (Hull 1974)
Thompson, E.P. *The Making of the English Working Class* (London 1974)
Trew, Arthur. *Belfast Constitutional Protestant Association: Lines suggested by the Following Announcement... Harvest Thanking Services will be held in the Independent Orange Hall* (Belfast 1910)

Waller, P.J. *Democracy and Sectarianism: A Political and Social History of Liverpool 1868–1939* (Liverpool 1981)
Walker, Brian. *No Mean City* (Belfast 1983)
Whitford, F.J. 'Joseph Devlin', *Threshold*, vol.I, no. 2 (Summer 1957)
Wright, Arnold. *Disturbed Dublin* (London 1914)
Wright, Frank. 'Protestant Ideology and Politics in Ulster', *European Journal of Sociology*, XIV (1973)

INDEX

Aberdeen 192
Aberdeen, Lord (John Campbell Gordon, Earl of) 31
Agricultural labourers 5, 6
Amalgamated Coalmen and Carters' Union 183
Amalgamated Society of Engineers 30
Amalgamated Society of Joiners and Carpenters 29, 30, 99
Amalgamated unions 26, 193
Antrim Iron Ore Company 69, 108
Appleton, W.A. 108, 139, 141, 142
Apprentices 18, 19, 20
Arbitration 31, 107, 169–71, 173, 176, 187, 193, 199, 206
Army 65, 66, 71, 83, 84, 94, 95, 100, 121, 128, 129, 139, 142–6, 148–55, 171, 175, 185, 207, 208
Arrests 68, 95, 139, 202, 206
Askwith, G.R. 171–4
Aspdell, Mr 181
Ayr Steamship Company 185, 207, 208

Badges 83, 121, 188
Bakers 99
Balfour, Arthur, MP 45
Ballot Act 44
Bamber, Richard 67, 68
Bands 41, 62
Bannister, Gertrude 160
Barrett, Constable William 115–26, 129, 130, 132, 133, 144
Barrow steamer 70, 71, 76
Belfast Chamber of Commerce 31, 94, 185
Belfast Coalworkers and Carters Benefit Society 183, 184
Belfast Co-Operative Society 98–100, 150
Belfast Corporation 10, 11, 19, 64, 75, 189, 214
Belfast Evening Telegraph 25, 63, 114, 115, 125, 127, 137, 138, 163, 178–82, 207
Belfast Harbour Commissioners 86, 143, 184–6
Belfast News-Letter 63, 127, 138, 160, 163–5
Belfast Protestant Association 33, 36, 37, 46, 52, 213
Belfast Socialist Society 13, 112, 150, 188
Belfast Steamship Company 1, 50, 60–63, 67, 68, 72–6, 83, 84, 140, 141, 176
Belfast Trades Council 13, 26–32, 45, 46, 54, 57, 69, 78, 99, 104, 110, 148, 149, 176, 182, 183, 188, 198, 199, 203
Bell, Richard, MP 110
Benevolent societies 22

Birrell, Augustine, MP 12, 84, 119, 128, 129, 144–6, 149, 154, 167, 169–71, 175
Blacklegs 25, 61–4, 67, 72, 73, 76, 83, 96, 97, 110, 115, 135, 154, 175, 185, 186, 188, 201, 211
Blatchford, Robert 167
Board of Trade 175, 183, 187, 188
Boyd, Alex 57, 62, 75, 78–81, 90–92, 99, 100, 103, 106, 107, 126, 141, 149, 152, 164, 174, 182, 189, 192, 197–200, 203, 211, 212
Braithwaite, Richard 213
Brett, Michael 59
British United Engine and Crane Men's Trade Union 184

Calvin, Rev. J. 90
Campbell, Samuel 78
Cantrell and Cochrane Ltd. 21
Carlisle, A.M. 39, 54, 86, 169
Carnduff, Thomas 8, 13–15, 24, 50, 196
Carpenters 29, 30
Carters 7, 75–86, 88, 91–7, 102, 104, 106, 115, 140–42, 146, 147, 154, 171–6, 183–5, 206
Carters' Society 77, 78
Casement, Roger 159, 160
Catholic Defence Association 54
Catholic Representation Association 53
Chamberlain, Inspector General Sir Neville 111, 124, 126, 127
Chambers, W. 59
Cherry, Richard, MP 144, 145
Child labour 8
Citizens' Association 35
Clarion 167
Clark, G.S., MP 39, 40, 207
Clarke, Isaac 186
Clarke, James 203
Clayton, District Inspector Edward 74, 118, 147
Coal Merchants Association 143
Cochrane, 'Covey' 158
Combe Barbour Ltd. 93, 146
Connolly, James 55, 211–13
Conservative and Unionist Party (in Ulster) 32–6, 38–41, 44, 46, 49, 50–52, 181, 207, 208
see also Ulster Unionist Council
Conservatism, of the working class 20, 21
Considine, Deputy Inspector General Heffernan 128
Constabulary Gazette 115, 131
Convent laundries, inspection of 45, 47

251

Convery, Father P. 156, 165, 166, 214
Cooper, Joseph 56
Cork 25, 130, 173, 192
Corporation Square 91
Cotton industry 12
Court Ward 42
Cowan and Company 76, 83, 147
Cranemen 185, 186
Crawford, Fred 163, 207
Crawford, Lindsay 8, 47, 50, 52, 89, 91, 92, 108, 141, 151, 152, 189, 195–7, 213, 214
Cullen Allen and Company 147
Cupples, Thomas 60
Curran, Pete, MP 33, 38, 57, 144, 168
Custom House steps 17, 91

Davidson and Company 108
Davidson, John 56, 179
Davidson, Samuel 4, 21, 58
Davis, Murray 33
Davitt, Michael 25
Dawson, Brigadier General Vesey John 66, 85, 94, 144
Devlin, Joseph, MP 32, 52–5, 57, 151–5, 160, 163, 169, 190, 209, 214
Devoy, John 213
Disturbances 61, 62, 65, 67, 68, 83, 87, 88, 95, 101, 139, 143, 146, 149, 150, 153, 154, 185
see also Riots
Dixon, Sir Daniel, MP 36, 38, 39, 41
Dock area (Sailorstown) 17, 57, 66
Dockers 2, 3, 6, 7, 22, 24, 25, 28, 56, 59–75, 79–82, 87–94, 100–109, 114, 115, 137–41, 154, 171–88, 191, 199–203, 206
Docks, the
  casual labour at 6, 7, 23, 202
  coal quays 59, 61–3, 69, 87, 90, 94, 99, 102–9, 137, 139, 173–91
  cross-channel quays 1, 23, 60–140, 175–7, 201, 202, 206
  deep-sea 23, 93, 201, 202
Donnelly, Joseph 142
Doran, Alderman George 66, 67
Doyle, Father J. 166
Drogheda 25, 185, 203
Dublin 153, 188, 191, 192, 194, 195, 197, 205
Dublin Steamship Company 69
Dublin Trades Council 26, 99
Dufferin, Lord Frederick Temple, Marquess of Dufferin and Ava) 21
Dunbar-Buller, Charles William 46
Duncairn Ward 188
Dundalk 185, 194
Dungannon Clubs 41, 55, 131, 135

Education 11, 12
Elections
  Belfast Corporation (1893) 33; (1896) 31, 33; (1905) 41; (1907) 35, 57; (1908) 41, 189
  Westminster: Colne Valley (1907 b/e) 150; Jarrow (1907 b/e) 57; Kirkdale (1907 b/e) 182; Leith Burghs (1910) 211; North Antrim (1906) 51; North Armagh (1906 b/e) 52; North Belfast 34, 205, (1905 b/e) 36–8, (1906) 38, (1907 b/e) 38–41, 56–7
Engineering industry 5, 29
Ewart, William, MP 44, 46
Ewart's mill 93
Expulsions from work 18, 212

Falls Road area 15, 16, 42, 88, 91, 92, 96, 135, 144, 154–65, 169, 189
Fearon, James 191, 194
Fenian movement 44
Fines at work 7
Flanagan, James 198, 199
Flax Spinners' Association 175
Fleetwood steamer 70, 71, 73–5, 83, 176
Flour mills 175
Football 17
Foremen 5, 22
Forward 150

Gageby, Robert 33, 34, 71, 78–80, 102, 211
Gallaher, Thomas 4, 22, 50, 63, 65, 66, 68, 138, 176
Gallaher's Tobacco Factory 17, 22, 64–6
Gambell, Assistant Inspector General Alexander 124–8, 144, 145
Gang warfare 15
Gee, Alderman Allen 101–4, 107, 137, 139, 141, 142, 172, 175
Gelston, District Inspector John 121
General Federation of Trade Unions 101, 102, 106–10, 137–9, 172, 208
Getgood, Bob 112
Ghettos 16
Glasgow 25, 76
Glasier, Bruce 15, 33
Glendinning, R.W., MP 51
Grain and Flour Merchants Association 143, 147
Grain ships 93
Grand Opera House 17
Grayson, Victor, MP 150, 151, 168
Great Northern Railway 93
Greene, Major Edgar 158
Gregg, Messrs 147
Greig, Robert 57, 58
Griffith, Arthur 193, 198

Haldane, R.B., MP 162, 168
Hamill, Hughie 97
Hardie, Keir, MP 1, 34
Harland and Wolff 4, 21, 40, 46, 86
Harland, Sir Edward, MP 4, 33
Harris, Joseph 87, 88, 149
Harrison, Sir Richard 175
Hart, Harry 96
Haslett, Sir James, MP 11
Head Line 202
Health 8–11
Healey, Father J. 156, 166
Henderson, Arthur, MP 1
Henderson, Sir James 3, 7
Henry, Bishop Henry 53
Henry, Denis 50
Heysham steamer 70, 71, 73–5, 85, 115, 176
Hill, Commissioner Hugh O'Halloran 74, 83, 84, 87, 93, 135
Hill, John 182
Hobson, Bulmer 55, 169
Home Rule 15, 20, 36, 38–40, 166, 195, 196, 214
Housing 10, 16
Hughes Bakery 88
Hughes, Bernard 18
Hughes Dickson Ltd. 96, 154
Hughes, William 95, 96
Hume, Rev. A. 18
Hunter, William 95

Imperialism 21, 22, 36
Independent Labour Party
 (Belfast) 33, 150, 183, 188, 189, 191, 195, 206
 (British) 33
Independent Orange Order 44, 47–52, 89, 90, 189, 190, 195–7, 205, 213, 214
Ireland's Saturday Night 125
Irish Citizen Army 214
Irish Co-Op League 195
Irish Federated Trade and Labour League 26
Irish News 53, 113, 114, 122
Irish Parliamentary Party 26, 32, 53, 57, 162
Irish Self-Determination League (Canada) 213
Irish Trades Union Congress 3, 7, 26, 27, 31, 32, 110, 203, 211
Irish Transport and General Workers Union 193, 194, 197–200, 202, 203, 206, 210–12
Ironmoulders 69, 102, 103

Johnston, Councillor F.C. 33, 124–6, 134

Johnston, Thomas 13, 25, 37, 39, 58, 171, 204
Johnston, William, MP 44, 46
Jones, Mr (of Birmingham) 112
Justice 150

Keaveney, District Inspector Thomas 115
Kelly, District Inspector Michael 135
Kelly, Samuel 59, 62, 207
Kemp, Mr 115
Kennedy, Thomas 40
Keown, John 181
Kessack, James O'Connor 104
King, Alexander 179, 180

Labour Bureau 201–3
Labour Electoral Association (Belfast) 31
Labour Leader 110, 150
Labour Party
 (Belfast) 32–43
 (Britain) 1, 15, 38, 43, 90, 126, 144, 146, 149, 162, 167, 168, 170, 182, 191, 208
Labour Representation Committee
 (Belfast) 20, 31, 34, 205
 (Britain) 1, 33, 38
Lancashire and Yorkshire Railway 70, 175
Lansbury, George 101, 167
Larkin, James 1–3, 55–8, 60–68, 71, 74–92, 100–108, 113, 114, 125, 138, 140, 141, 149–54, 163, 169–76, 179–202, 205–11
Larne gun-running 163
Lennon, Maggie 159
Leo, P.J. 27
Liberal government 74, 146, 150, 162, 168, 170, 171, 207, 208
Liberal Party
 (British) 38
 (Ulster) 39, 46, 52, 196, 197
Licensed Vintners' Association 53
Linen industry 5, 7, 8, 92
Linen lappers 99
Linen workers 8, 9, 27, 28, 96, 154
Liverpool 2, 3, 24, 62, 100, 129, 167, 182, 191, 194, 204
Living standards 7, 8, 13
Logue, Cardinal Michael 166
London and North Western Railway Company 70, 175
Londonderry 25, 73, 107, 121, 166, 185, 192, 203
Long, William, MP 56
Loyal Order of Ancient Shepherds 22

McCammond, Mr 33
McCartan, Patrick 49
McCormac, Henry 13

MacDonald, Ramsay 1, 34, 36–9, 101
McDonald, William 55
MacDonnell, Sir Anthony 84, 119, 128, 129, 145, 146, 154, 169, 171, 175, 176
McDowell, Alex 60, 103, 142, 173, 176, 186, 187, 207
McElborough, Robert 189
McGarrity, Joseph 49
McGhee, Edward 199
McGhee, Richard 5, 25
McGrath, Constable 118
McHugh, Edward 25
McKeown, John 157–9
McKeown, Michael 24, 57, 60, 67, 70, 76, 78, 80, 90, 157, 176, 183, 197, 198, 200, 201
McKeown, Mr 73
MacLean, John 150, 167
McMullen, William 64, 174, 204
Maddison, Joseph 103
Magheramorne Manifesto 48–52
Magowan, 'Mug' 60
Martindale, Miss 9
Master Carriers Association 76, 77, 79, 80, 83, 143
Maunders, Mr 71
Mear, Mr 110
Mercier, Messrs 147
Midland Railway Company 70, 75, 93, 175, 177
Mill sawyers 30
Mitchell, Alderman Isaac 101–4, 107, 137, 139, 141, 171
Mitchell, Mr 181
Moore, R.J. 77
Moore, William, MP 51
More Pay Movement 112, 113, 117
Morrell, Commissioner Henry B. 94, 115, 117–19, 121, 124
Morrow, John 56
Municipal Employees Association 28, 57, 62, 189, 198, 212
Municipal socialism 34, 35
Munn, Sam 179
Munro, Samuel 27
Murphy, John 30, 31, 33, 34, 57, 58, 98, 105
Murphy, Joseph 164
Murray, W.J. 90, 98, 149, 174, 198, 199

Nannetti, J.P., MP 32
National Amalgamated Union of Labour 28, 57, 58
National Union of Dock Labourers 2, 3, 5, 24, 25, 60, 69, 70, 100–2, 172, 176, 178–88, 191–4, 198–203, 206
Nationalisation 40, 182

Nationalism 26, 32, 40, 41, 48, 138, 152, 160, 161, 163, 164, 190, 209–11, 213
Navy 129, 175
Newry 185, 191, 192, 194
Nolan, 'Sinn Fein' 159
Nomad's Weekly 137
Northern Ireland Labour Party 215
Northern Star 54, 152
Northern Whig 65, 80, 81, 163

Old age, provision for 9, 182
Orange Order 18, 20, 39, 40, 42, 45–7, 88, 89, 160, 181
Orr, John 96
Outworkers 9

Pawn shops 13
Picketing 74, 75, 83, 92, 96, 124, 125, 138, 139
Pirrie, William 21, 22, 29, 39, 46, 52
Plunkett, Horace 45
Police 62, 63, 68, 74, 83, 94, 95, 100, 111–137, 139, 140, 142, 143, 145, 146, 149, 152, 155, 164, 165, 171, 185, 200, 207, 208
Population, growth of 4
Printers 87
Protestant National Association 55
Protestants 15–22, 28, 32, 36–49, 79–81, 88–91, 134, 137, 144, 148, 151, 154, 160, 163, 169, 182, 184, 202, 209, 211–15

Quinn, John 56, 199

Railway companies 70–73, 76, 101, 140, 172, 175, 206
Redmond, John, MP 53
Reid, Hugh 202, 203
Religious discrimination 18, 19
Riots
  (Belfast to 1907) 15, 16, 18, 148,
  (1907) 95, 149, 155–67, 171, 207,
  (1912) 212, 214
  (Featherstone 1893) 167
  (Trafalgar Square 1887) 167
  (Winchester 1908) 162
  see also Disturbances
Roman Catholics 15–20, 23, 24, 37, 38, 40–42, 52–5, 79–81, 90, 91, 137, 144, 154, 159, 160, 161, 164–6, 169, 184, 202, 214, 215
Rowntree, Seebohm 8
Royal Irish Constabulary, see police
Russell, T.W., MP 51
Russia 82

Sabbatarianism 26, 215
Sailors 69, 175

St George's Ward 189
Sandy Row 9, 15, 16, 51, 92
Saunderson, Colonel Edward, MP 45, 47, 52
Savage, Walter 56, 88
Sectarianism 15–25, 36–41, 45, 47, 80, 89, 160, 163, 164, 178–84, 202, 207, 209, 211, 213
Sexton, James 3, 100–3, 105, 110, 125, 126, 132, 140, 141, 172, 173, 186–8, 192–4, 198–204, 210
Shaftesbury, Lord 63, 65, 66, 71, 72, 74, 75, 79, 80, 83, 84, 94, 102, 103, 107, 141, 144–6, 152, 159, 160
Shankill Road 16, 92, 104, 144, 157, 160, 181
Shipbuilding 5, 7, 9, 10, 19–20
Shipping Federation 59, 60, 143
Simms, Rev. S. 92
Sinn Fein 55, 193, 198, 213
Sirocco Engineering Works 4, 21, 58, 59, 61
Skilled workers 4, 12, 18–20, 22, 27, 29, 30, 42, 43, 66, 136, 205
Sloan, Thomas, MP 32, 46, 47, 50, 52, 54, 90, 151, 152, 163, 189, 195, 214
Smiles, Samuel 4
Snowden, Philip, MP 167, 168, 182
Social Democratic Federation 2, 150
Socialism 29, 33, 38, 87, 149–51, 159, 165
Stevedores 6
Stewart, Alex 91, 103, 125
Stewart, Mr (of Dublin) 106
Stewart, W. 150
Stockman, Hugh 38, 39, 103, 110, 159, 165, 183, 188, 189
Strike committee 81, 87, 90, 99, 108, 109, 153, 181
Strike funds 69, 90, 98, 99, 100, 110
Strike pay 67, 98, 100, 178, 181
Strikes and lockouts, attitudes to 27, 65, 87, 101
Strikes and lockouts, specific disputes
  Antwerp (1907 of dockers) 60
  Belfast (1892 of dockers) 25, (1892 of tobacco workers) 27, (1893 of shipyard labourers) 28, (1895–6 and 1897–8 of engineers) 29, (1899–1900 of joiners) 30, (1906 of linen workers) 31, (1907 of carters and dockers) 59–110, 137–54, 169–90, 200–15, (1907 of cranemen) 184, (1907 of engineering labourers) 58–61, (1907 of ironmoulders) 69, 102, 103, (1907 of sailors and firemen) 69, 175, (1907 of textile workers) 154, (1907 of tobacco workers) 65, 66, (1909 of dockers), 202, 203
  Cork (1891–2 of dockers) 25, (1908 of dockers) 173, 192
  Drogheda (1907 of dockers) 25
  Dublin (1908 of carters) 192, (1913–14) 205
  Dundalk (1907 of dockers) 185, 194
  Hamburg (1907 of dockers) 60
  Liverpool (1889 of dockers) 24, 100, 101, 204, 206, (1905 of dockers) 2, 3
  Londonderry (1891–2 of dockers) 25
  Lurgan (1892 of labourers) 5
  Montreal (1907 of dockers) 65
  Newry (1907–8 of dockers) 191
Suffolk Linen Company 93
Syndicalism 206

Textile Operatives Society 28
Thackeray, Major Martin, RM 157, 160
Tobacco workers' union 27
Traction engines 93, 95, 115
Trade, state of 3, 12, 13
Trades Disputes Act 74, 75
Trades Union Congress (British) 15, 26, 28, 101, 162
Trew, Arthur 33, 46, 135
Twelfth of July 45, 88–90, 94, 99

Ulster Echo 182, 207
Ulster Guardian 52, 196
Ulster Labourers' Union 5
Ulster Literary Theatre 55
Ulster Protestant 47
Ulster Steamship Company 175
Ulster Unionist Council 39, 49, 207
  see also Conservative and Unionist Party
Unemployment 29
Union Jack, the 41, 65
Union Jack Committee 22
United Ireland League 41, 53, 213
United Protestant Workingmen's Association of Ulster 44, 45
Unskilled workers 5, 6, 12, 13, 18, 19, 20, 22, 27–31, 42, 43, 58, 59, 207

Wages 4–9, 23, 28, 30, 63, 69–72, 76, 77, 103–5, 107, 111, 174, 176
Walker, William 27–43, 54, 56, 66, 106, 149, 151, 164, 165, 174, 182, 205, 206, 209–14
Walsh, Archbishop 53
Waters, Head Constable Fraser 115
Webb, Beatrice 4, 18
Women 8, 9, 24, 27, 28, 65, 96, 97, 99, 135, 155, 158, 173
Wordie and Company 76, 83, 96, 147
Workhouse, the 9, 13, 98
Workman Clark Ltd. 4, 39

York Street Mill 17, 96

214902-c.2